T0269526

SOCIAL MEDIA IN THE MARKETING CONTEXT

CHANDOS
SOCIAL MEDIA SERIES
Series Editors: Geoff Walton and Woody Evans
(emails: g.l.walton@staffs.ac.uk and kdevans@gmail.com)

This series of books is aimed at practitioners and academics involved in using social media in all its forms and in any context. This includes information professionals, academics, librarians and managers, and leaders in business. Social media can enhance services, build communication channels, and create competitive advantage. The impact of these new media and decisions that surround their use in business can no longer be ignored. The delivery of education, privacy issues, logistics, political activism and research rounds out the series' coverage. As a resource to complement the understanding of issues relating to other areas of information science, teaching and related areas, books in this series respond with practical applications. If you would like a full listing of current and forthcoming titles, please visit our website www.chandospublishing.com.

New authors: we are always pleased to receive ideas for new titles; if you would like to write a book for Chandos in the area of social media, please contact George Knott, Commissioning Editor, on g.knott@elsevier.com or telephone +44 (0) 1865843114.

SOCIAL MEDIA IN THE MARKETING CONTEXT

A State of the Art Analysis and Future Directions

CHERNIECE J. PLUME

YOGESH K. DWIVEDI

EMMA L. SLADE

AMSTERDAM • BOSTON • HEIDELBERG • LONDON
NEW YORK • OXFORD • PARIS • SAN DIEGO
SAN FRANCISCO • SINGAPORE • SYDNEY • TOKYO
Chandos Publishing is an imprint of Elsevier

Chandos Publishing is an imprint of Elsevier
50 Hampshire Street, 5th Floor, Cambridge, MA 02139, United States
The Boulevard, Langford Lane, Kidlington, OX5 1GB, United Kingdom

Notices

Knowledge and best practice in this field are constantly changing. As new research and experience broaden our
understanding, changes in research methods, professional practices, or medical treatment may become necessary.

Practitioners and researchers must always rely on their own experience and knowledge in evaluating and using any
information, methods, compounds, or experiments described herein. In using such information or methods they
should be mindful of their own safety and the safety of others, including parties for whom they have a professional
responsibility.

To the fullest extent of the law, neither the Publisher nor the authors, contributors, or editors, assume any liability
for any injury and/or damage to persons or property as a matter of products liability, negligence or otherwise,
or from any use or operation of any methods, products, instructions, or ideas contained in the material herein.

British Library Cataloguing-in-Publication Data
A catalogue record for this book is available from the British Library

Library of Congress Cataloging-in-Publication Data
A catalog record for this book is available from the Library of Congress

ISBN: 978-0-08-101754-8 (print)
ISBN: 978-0-08-101757-9 (online)

For information on all Chandos Publishing
visit our website at https://www.elsevier.com

Working together
to grow libraries in
developing countries

www.elsevier.com • www.bookaid.org

Publisher: Jonathan Simpson
Acquisition Editor: Glyn Jones
Editorial Project Manager: Lindsay Lawrence
Production Project Manager: Omer Mukthar
Cover Designer: Greg Harris

Typeset by MPS Limited, Chennai, India

DEDICATIONS

To my mum Andrea for her continuous support and guidance. I can never thank you enough.

Cherniece J. Plume

To Vaishnavi Dwivedi and Krishna Tiwari.

Yogesh K. Dwivedi

To my parents for their boundless time and love.

Emma L. Slade

CONTENTS

AUTHORS' BIOGRAPHY

Cherniece J. Plume is a PhD researcher in Business Management at Swansea University School of Management. She has an MSc in Marketing and BA (Hons) in Event Management from The University of South Wales. She has a background in the marketing and events sector, collaborating on a variety of projects with a number of organizations. In addition to work in industry Cherniece has also lectured in Business Research and Marketing Communications at the University of South Wales. Cherniece was an editor for the *International Journal of Leadership, Workplace Innovation and Engagement* and Chair of the University of South Wales Marketing Chapter. Her research interests include consumer behavior, consumer psychology, construction of self-concept, and social media marketing.

Yogesh K. Dwivedi is a professor of Digital and Social Media and director of Research in the School of Management at Swansea University, Wales, UK. His research interests are in the area of Information Systems (IS) including the adoption and diffusion of emerging ICTs and digital and social media marketing. He has published more than 100 articles in a range of leading academic journals and conferences. He has coedited more than 15 books on technology adoption, e-government, and IS theory, and had them published by international publishers such as Springer, Routledge, and Emerald. He acted as coeditor of 14 special issues; organized tracks, mini-tracks, and panels in leading conferences; and served as programme cochair of IFIP WG 8.6 Conference. He is associate editor of *European Journal of Marketing and Government Information Quarterly*, assistant editor of *Journal of Enterprise Information Management* and Senior Editor of *Journal of Electronic Commerce Research*.

Emma L. Slade is deputy director of Postgraduate Research in the School of Management, Swansea University. She has a PhD and MSc with Distinction in Business Management. Emma is working on a variety of research topics across marketing and information systems, including engagement with political parties on social media, consumer forgiveness, adoption of mobile payments, innovation through big open linked data, and diffusion of green IT/IS. Emma has published articles in a number of highly regarded journals including *Computers and Human Behaviour, Psychology & Marketing, Journal of Strategic Marketing,* and *Journal of Computer Information systems.*

FOREWORD

Social Media in the Marketing Context: A State of the Art Analysis and Future Directions is a major contribution to the rapidly growing field of social media marketing. Social media is having a major impact on the practice and theory of marketing in many industries. With nearly one-third of the world's population now estimated to be active users of social media, research into its role in marketing, beyond the process of gaining website traffic or attention through social media sites has grown significantly. Social media has dramatically changed the marketing landscape empowering consumers and other stakeholders to influence brands through digital word-of-mouth. Trying to make sense of this area researchers have focused on understanding the scope, nature, and use of social media, and have inevitably tried to examine the factors that influence usage and the ultimate consequences of its use, both for organizations and for customers. Given the multitude of platforms, user types, cultures, and research methods used, research could still be regarded as fragmented. Therefore given proliferation in social media usage (and consequently research endeavors), it seems pertinent to carefully take stock of our knowledge in this area, assessing what we know and where future research should take us.

This collection of essays provides a comprehensive account of the important research literature in the area paying particular attention to how social media influences the marketing environment (see chapter: The New Marketing Environment), the antecedents and consequences of participation in online brand communities (see chapter: Online Brand Communities), and the role of culture (see chapter: Culture) and self-construal (see chapter: Self-Construals) in influencing the nature of social media usage. It then concludes by synthesizing research in the area and offering guidance on future research directions (see chapter: Synthesis and Discussion of Research).

The book is both timely and relevant—congratulations to the team on creating an enriching and useful resource to help scholars and practitioners make sense of this dynamic and fast moving research area. Insights gained from this book should help marketers and scholars to more effectively tackle the challenges that remain within the field.

I very much welcome this book to the extant literature on social media and know it will be well received by the research and practitioner marketing communities.

Professor Ben Lowe
Kent Business School, University of Kent,
Canterbury, Kent, United Kingdom

FOREWORD

I am delighted to provide a foreword for this book.

Our experiences of marketing where the Internet is concerned are rooted in the 1990s where it was envisioned as a space through which one might capture consumers. Consumers have also long played a part in assisting the Internet-based marketing efforts of organizations. Sites such as Yahoo!, AOL, and Geocities relied on users generating content in groups and forums, placing advertising alongside it in order to generate revenue. This all occurred prior to the announcement of Web 2.0 by Tim O'Reilly in 2005, and with that notions of the participatory turn as related to the Internet. Since then of course we have seen a significant proliferation of social media platforms and their deployment in our lives in many parts of the world. These changes are increasingly pushing the geographic boundaries of where the Internet might be engaged in marketing efforts due to changes in telecommunications infrastructure and the lowering of costs of modes of access and the devices needed—particularly mobile technology. At the same time, the prominence of algorithms, the Internet of things, the quantified self, and the politics of platforms are challenging considerations in this context. What new forms of marketing data can be generated? By who? How can organizations keep hold of their marketing message? Should they even try to?

Social media is shaping society with us. From a marketing perspective this not only involves commercial organizations, charities, and the not-for-profit sector, it involves those consuming the products and services such entities seek to engage. Crucially, it also involves an increasing range of technologies which can, and do, play roles, sometimes very unexpected, in affecting the marketing capacities of the organizations associated with them. In 2014, hostages were held at gunpoint in central Sydney, Australia, and price surging occurred on the Uber app as the public sought to get to safety as quickly as possible. Uber chose not to halt the algorithm, which regulates the pricing of cab rides immediately and had to quickly apologize, make refunds, and convert to a plan of offering free rides during the rest of the seige. The marketing point of variable pricing based on demand that Uber often capitalized on, the complex algorithm associated with it, and the human decision to not intervene immediately all worked against them in this case.

Cases such as that of Uber are not isolated and demonstrate the significant need for a text such as this. The authors have done an excellent job here of bringing together key insights into social media marketing in an engaging and accessible way.

My research concerns people's everyday experiences of digital society. I am interested in questions of digital society concerned with digital (non)consumption practices, gender and sexuality, and digital methods. My last book, *Disconnection With Social Networking Sites*, was published by Palgrave MacMillan in 2014.

Professor Ben Light
Directorate of Social Sciences,
University of Salford, Salford, United Kingdom

PREFACE

Social media use by organizations has seen an undeniable rise, fundamentally changing the way in which they communicate with their stakeholders and engage in marketing activities. With growing numbers of individuals utilizing social media as part of their everyday lives, it has become a powerful and influential environment that has the ability to affect the success of the organization. However, many organizations are still finding it incredibly difficult to fully understand how to utilize social media for marketing purposes. This has inevitably led to many failed attempts at social media campaigns and use within many organizations.

The reason that organization and researchers are failing to effectively comprehend the social media environment is that it is multifaceted and therefore a lot of varying elements can affect it. The term itself brings with it many connotations depending on who is utilizing it, for instance, consumers see it as a socializing mechanism, whereas organizations see its strategic ability. Yet the undeniable association that springs to mind is *communication*. Nevertheless many organizations have failed to comprehend this most basic understanding, attempting to utilize the variety of social media platforms while simultaneously trying to gain a better understanding of the best way to do so. Research within this area has tried to develop frameworks and analysis techniques as a means of trying to develop effective strategies that organizations can use to help them develop their social media presence. It is simply impossible to craft one overarching social media strategy that is applicable to all organizations when so many platforms exist, each serving different needs. It would perhaps be more beneficial if organizations were able to effectively code and categorize the different social media, yet attempts at this have also been unsuccessful. The problem is that organizations are relying on research that has focused heavily on the disposition, use, and capacity of social media, which is limited given the changing preferences of consumers, cultures, and their motivations. Managers and marketers are constantly asking the same questions—*what is the most effective social media channel to use? What is the most effective social media strategy? How can we connect with consumers using this medium?*—with research suggesting a variety of differing answers that provide even more confusion. Managers and marketers are forgetting that they need to use social media as a way to *communicate* with their consumers, yet they are trying to develop strategies without understanding the value of social media for the organization itself and the individuals that use it.

Marketers need to recognize that developing an effective social media strategy should be individual and unique to the organization, specifically crafted to suit their needs and objectives. There needs to be an understanding of the social media environment itself and why it is beneficial to the organization, surrounding, and changing culture, and the consumers before this can be done—which is covered in subsequent chapters. Addressing these components and understanding how social media has changed the marketing environment will allow them to address strategy development in a more effective manner, leading to a more successful outcome.

Organizations are more than capable of using social media in an effective way, gathering data about their consumers, and interacting with them in a way that builds a valuable relationship for both parties. Extant literature and research has been more than forthcoming in identifying the myriad of benefits of social media for marketing purposes, identifying the core characteristics of social media that make it an effective marketing communication tool. Yet the gaps that remain in the literature mean that many organizations are falling into the trap of attempting to mimic others strategies, rather than identifying how and why social media will be beneficial for them.

There has been an undeniable focus on using social media to provide value to consumers, yet many organizations and marketers do not understand the underlying mechanisms of their consumers that initiate their engagement on social media platforms. It seems that organizations are concerned with the surface issues, attempting to utilize the platforms based on a limited amount of knowledge. The literature has pointed to many suggestions regarding how marketers should be using the platform, yet outlining these in a purely marketing perspective seems to be somewhat lacking. This book aims to bridge that gap by providing a comprehensive overview of social media from a marketing perspective. The questions that organizations should be asking is—*how are my consumers using social media? What makes some consumers engage with organizations while others do not? Are their differences between my consumers that can be used as a means of providing more value to them?*—which this book attempts to address.

It seems relevant that this book addresses social media in a marketing context, given the heavy focus that many industry professionals are placing on the medium. With new articles being posted everyday on how best to utilize a particular platform, and what to do or rather not do when trying to engage with consumers, organizations are becoming subject to a barrage of information that they do not understand. Providing an understanding of the social media environment itself and the consumers that use these platforms, this book aims to give researchers and practitioners knowledge and guidance into understanding the environment in a marketing context.

Social Media in the Marketing Context: A State of the Art Analysis and Future Directions is a book that provides the reader with a comprehensive overview of the current literature surrounding social media and the marketing discipline, highlighting future development opportunities in both knowledge and practice. The reader is guided through the main topics, pointing out the relevance of social media to the future of marketing. The continued study of this topic, with direction to both researchers and especially practitioners is vital in the effort to improve marketing strategies for all organizations. This book advances the topic, hoping to pave the way for many more outputs that shed light on the area.

ACRONYMS

CCLV   connected customer lifetime value
CLV   customer lifetime value
eWOM   electronic word of mouth
GOSIP   general online social interaction propensity
OBC   online brand community
ROI   return on investment
sWOM   social word of mouth
UGC   user-generated content
WOM   word of mouth

CHAPTER 1

Introduction

The undeniable growth of social media has affected both marketing practices (Bernoff & Li, 2008; Constantinides and Fountain, 2008), and the behavior of the consumers who utilize this medium (Berthon, Pitt, Plangger, & Shapiro, 2012; Deighton & Kornfeld, 2008). Enabling the facilitation of interactive communication amongst its users, the social media environment provides value to consumers on a level they have not encountered before (Baird & Parasnis, 2011). Engaging and inspiring the individuals who utilize this medium, social media provides a mechanism for information dissemination and sharing that empowers today's consumers (Hwang & Kim, 2015).

Organizations are finding it difficult to cope with the lack of control they now have in defining their own image, finding themselves at the mercy of consumers who are presenting their own perspectives, gathering information from one another as opposed to the organization or brand itself (Bernoff & Li, 2008). Despite attempts to gather adequate information from these social media sites, the vast amount of data that are produced pose problems for managers and marketers alike (Bello-Orgaz, Jung, & Camacho, 2016). The collaborative mechanisms consumers now have on these social media platforms make users more active participants in producing and disseminating content, adding to this data growth (Bouadjenek, Hacid, & Bouzeghoub, 2016). Collecting these data and understanding their meaning give brands and organizations the opportunity to personalize their product or service (Rust & Huang, 2014), allowing consumers' needs to be more effectively met and thus providing value (Chung, Wedel, & Rust, 2016). A recent report by Stelzner (2015) found that marketers want more information in the areas of "tactics, engagement, measurement, audience, and tools" (Stelzner, 2015, p. 6), with 87% unable to provide answers to questions in these areas. Yet despite this finding, the same report also found that 92% of marketers place high importance on social media for their businesses, which is questionable given the evidence that they do not fully understand this environment. The challenge for marketers is to provide value to consumers in a new

Social Media in the Marketing Context.

competitive marketplace that forces organizations and brands to adopt different approaches as a way of gaining an advantage and exposure (Baird & Parasnis, 2011).

The vast amounts of people who are now utilizing social media platforms have forced brands and organizations to develop complex strategies that allow them to engage with the public in a marketplace where they have been forced to communicate differently with a multitude of stakeholders (Appleford, Bottum, & Thatcher, 2014; Gruber, 2008). Enabling two-way communication, sharing, empowerment and coordination (Boyd & Ellison, 2008), the marketing discipline has undoubtedly felt the effects of this new and constantly changing environment. However, there is an undeniable problem of utilizing social media effectively for marketing purposes, with organizations and researchers alike failing to have a clear understanding of the medium (Appleford et al., 2014). The popularity of social media has meant that many organizations have been pressured into adapting to the various platforms without an effective strategy (Larson & Watson, 2011), with many organizations finding the task difficult (Bottles & Sherlock, 2011). Studies have highlighted the problem by trying to develop effective ways to analyze (e.g., Effing & Spil, 2016) and categorize (e.g., Winer, 2009) the social media environment. It is evident that developing any comprehensive understanding is difficult when critical metrics that are important for aiding understanding (Peters, Chen, Kaplan, Ognibeni, & Pauwels, 2013) are not available.

Social media has transformed the consumer decision-making process (Fulgoni, 2014), meaning understanding their behavior on this medium is critical for marketing success (Donthu & Garcia, 1999), as consumers are continuously utilizing the online realm to gain information to inform their purchasing decisions. However, the Internet and subsequent social media platforms mean that segmenting consumers and developing an effective typology is increasingly difficult (Barnes, Bauer, Neumann, & Huber, 2007), especially in an environment with increasingly heterogeneous consumers (Thomas, Price, & Schau, 2013). Individuals from varying parts of the world are now able to culminate together, sharing information and personal knowledge with others to affect decision making. Yet it can be argued that this poses many problems for marketers (Walters, 1997), with both culture and consumer behaviors playing important roles (Hofstede, 1994; Yavas & Green, 1992). The increasingly individualistic nature of consumers (Weijo, Hietanen, & Mattila, 2014) is making it difficult for managers and marketers to comprehend how they are going to both act and react to their marketing efforts within the social media environment. One way to understand the individual differences is by looking at how individuals typically regard themselves in relation to others and how they tend to interact with brands depending on its congruence with their "self" (Johnson & Eagly, 1989; Schembri, Merrilees, & Kristiansen, 2010; Schouten, 1991). The focus on how brands are used as extensions of the self (Belk, 1988), especially within the online environment (Belk, 2013), is readily understood within the traditional marketing context. However, extending the focus on individual utilization of these platforms may provide a beneficial way to identify behavioral patterns and thus effectively target consumers in a more effective way. With research into the social media environment relatively new to academia (Ngai, Tao, & Moon, 2015), the failure of many organizations and brands to fully understand and utilize the social media environment still needs to be addressed.

The main purpose of this book is to provide a comprehensive overview of social media from a marketing perspective by a thorough examination of the current literature and the identifications of future development opportunities in both knowledge and practice. This book will be of value to students, particularly postgraduate and PhD researchers, and university academics who have an interest in marketing, information systems, and business management. In addition, anyone with an interest in social media and marketing, practitioners, and academics from psychology and cross-cultural disciplines may also find this book useful.

The remaining sections of this book will be as follows:

Chapter 2—Discusses the social media environment and how this has affected marketers, with a focus on the development of research in this area in relation to the marketing discipline.

Chapter 3—Examines the concept of online brand communities and culminations of consumers, identifying how these are being utilized with the development of social media.

Chapter 4—Outlines the development of culture and how this has impacted the social media environment.

Chapter 5—Introduces the importance of self-construal theory when examining consumer's involvement in the social media environment.

Chapter 6—Identifies current, developing, and future research, elaborating on methodological and sampling choice of researchers of social media and suggestions for further development.

Chapter 7—Provides closing remarks with a summary of the main points.

REFERENCES

Appleford, S. J., Bottum, J. R., & Thatcher, J. B. (2014). Understanding the social web: Towards an interdisciplinary research agenda for information systems. *The DATABASE for Advances in Information Systems, 45*(1), 29–37.

Baird, C. H., & Parasnis, G. (2011). From social media to social customer relationship management. *Strategy & Leadership, 39*(5), 30–37.

Barnes, S. J., Bauer, H. H., Neumann, M. N., & Huber, F. (2007). Segmenting cyberspace: A customer typology for the internet. *European Journal of Marketing, 41*(1/2), 71–93.

Belk, R. W. (1988). Possessions and the extended self. *Journal of Consumer Research, 15*, 139–168.

Belk, R. W. (2013). Extended self in a digital world. *Journal of Consumer Research, 40* (October), 477–500.

Bello-Orgaz, G., Jung, J. J., & Camacho, D. (2016). Social big data: recent achievements and new challenges. *Information Fusion, 28*, 45–59.

Bernoff, J., & Li, C. (2008). Harnessing the power of the oh-so-social web. *MIT Sloan Management Review, 49*(3), 35–42.

Berthon, P. R., Pitt, L. F., Plangger, K., & Shapiro, D. (2012). Marketing meets web 2.0, social media, and creative consumers: Implications for international marketing strategy. *Business Horizons, 55*(3), 261–271.

Bottles, K., & Sherlock, T. (2011). Who should manage your social media strategy? *Physician Executive, 37*(2), 68–72.

Bouadjenek, M. R., Hacid, H., & Bouzeghoub, M. (2016). Social networks and information retrieval, how are they converging? A survey, a taxonomy and ananalysis of social information retrieval approaches and platforms. *Information Systems, 56*, 1–18.

Boyd, D. M., & Ellison, N. B. (2008). Social network sites: Definition, history, and scholarship. *Journal of Computer-Mediated Communication, 12*, 210–230.

Chung, T. S., Wedel, M., & Rust, R. T. (2016). Adaptive personalization using social networks. *Journal of the Academy of Marketing Science, 4*, 66–87.

Constantinides, E., & Fountain, S. (2008). Web 2.0: Conceptual foundations and marketing issues. *Journal of Direct, Data and Digital Marketing Practice, 9*(3), 231–244.

Deighton, J., & Kornfeld, L. (2008). *Digital interactivity: Unanticipated consequences for markets, marketing, and consumers.* Boston, MA: Harvard Business School.

Donthu, N., & Garcia, A. (1999). The internet shopper. *Journal of Advertising Research, 39* (3), 52–58.

Effing, R., & Spil, T. A. M. (2016). The social strategy cone: Towards a framework for evaluating social media strategies. *International Journal of Information Management, 36*, 1–8.

Fulgoni, G. M. (2014). "Omni-Channel" Retail Insights and The Consumer's Path-to-Purchase: How Digital Has Transformed the Way People Make Purchasing Decisions. *Journal of Advertising Research*, 377–380, December.

Gruber, T. (2008). Collective knowledge systems: Where the social web meets the semantic web. *Web Semantics: Science, Services and Agents on the World Wide Web, 6*(1), 4–13.

Hofstede, G. (1994). Management scientists are human. *Management Science, 40*(1), 4–13.

Hwang, H., & Kim, K.-O. (2015). Social media as a tool for social movements: The effect of social media use and social capital on intention to participate in social movements. *International Journal of Consumer Studies, 39*, 478–488.

Johnson, B. T., & Eagly, A. (1989). Effects of involvement on persuasion: A meta-analysis. *Psychological Bulletin, 106*(2), 290–314.

Larson, K. & Watson, R. (2011). The value of social media: Toward measuring social media strategies. In *Thirty Second International Conference on Information Systems* (pp. 1–18). Shanghai.

Ngai, E. W. T., Tao, S. S. C., & Moon, K. K. L. (2015). Social media research: Theories, constructs, and conceptual frameworks. *International Journal of Information Management*, *35*, 33−44.

Peters, K., Chen, Y., Kaplan, A. M., Ognibeni, B., & Pauwels, K. (2013). Social media metrics—A framework and guidelines for managing social media. *Journal of Interactive Marketing*, *27*(4), 281−298.

Rust, R. T., & Huang, M. H. (2014). The service revolution and the transformation of marketing science. *Marketing Science*, *33*(2), 206−221.

Schembri, S., Merrilees, B., & Kristiansen, S. (2010). Brand consumption and narrative of self. *Psychology and Marketing*, *27*(6), 623−638.

Schouten, J. W. (1991). Selves in transition: Symbolic consumption in personal rites of passage and identity reconstruction. *Journal of Consumer Research*, *17*(4), 412−425.

Stelzner, M. (2015). Social media marketing industry report: How marketers are using social media to grow their business. *Social Media Examiner*. June 6, 2015 from: <http://www.socialmediaexaminer.com/SocialMediaMarketingIndustryReport2015.pdf>.

Thomas, T., Price, L. L., & Schau, H. J. (2013). When differences unite: Resource dependence in heterogeneous consumption communities. *Journal of Consumer Research*, *39*, 1010−1033.

Walters, P. G. P. (1997). Global market segmentation: methodologies and challenges. *Journal of Marketing Management*, *13*(3), 165−177.

Weijo, H., Hietanen, J., & Mattila, P. (2014). New insights into online consumption communities and netnography. *Journal of Business Research*, *67*, 2072−2078.

Winer, R. S. (2009). New communications approaches in marketing: Issues and research directions. *Journal of Interactive Marketing*, *23*, 108−117.

Yavas, V. B., & Green, R. (1992). Global consumer segmentation versus local market orientation: Empirical findings. *Management International Review*, *32*(3), 265−272.

CHAPTER 2

The New Marketing Environment

The evolution of social media has had an undeniable impact on the way both consumers and organizations communicate. With a variety of disciplines taking an interest in the medium there is a huge amount of research that is continuing to emerge, providing insight into this new online environment, especially with regard to marketing. Social media is of a particular benefit to marketers due to the incredible access it allows to consumers, as well as the potential for relationship development as a way of creating value for both consumers and organizations. Yet the incredible power that consumers now hold is not unnoticed, with many exercising power through their user-generated content (UGC) as a way to communicate their feelings about a brand in addition to organizations adopting co-creation opportunities. However the majority of research is yet to fully uncover the potential of social media and thus leaves many opportunities open for investigation.

This section will start by highlighting the impact social media has had on the traditional marketing mix and how this has affected organizations and brands as well as defining the term itself. Subsequent sections will outline how organizations are trying to utilize social media based on strategy development, followed by highlighting the key characteristics of social media that make it such a powerful tool: structure and networks, relationships, co-creation, power and electronic word of mouth (eWOM), and social commerce. Next the topic of multiple platform research is covered, finally ending with a discussion of the key points, recommendations for future research, and marketing practitioners.

2.1 STIRRING UP THE MARKETING MIX

The traditional marketing mix used by organizations to help establish their brand offering to consumers was originally depicted by McCarthy (1960) of price, product, place, and promotion. The price element is crucial as it affects both the amount of sales and the consumer demand for a product, and can greatly affect the marketing strategy. Organizations must also take into account the differential and reference value of the product from the consumers' point of view, whereby the attributes (differential value) and price (reference value) are compared to other products by the consumer (Kotler & Keller, 2012). The product element must be considered in terms of consumer demands, wants, and needs with particular attention paid to the life–cycle of the offering—whether that be product or service. This element can also incorporate the product mix whereby the variety or amount of products can be altered. Careful consideration should be paid to the target market, positioning strategy, and available resources to enable an organization to create an effective plan. The place element refers to the actual distribution of the product to consumers, including point of sale, which needs to incorporate any supplier deals such as exclusivity. Finally the promotion element includes all elements of marketing communications such as advertising, public relations, sponsorship, exhibitions, and packaging (Pickton & Broderick, 2004), which is where social media has commonly been incorporated. The explosion of social media alongside technological advances have meant that the marketing environment is becoming progressively more complicated than originally conceptualized. Some have considered social media as an additional tool to the marketing mix (e.g., Atkinson, 2013; Mangold & Faulds, 2009), as they consider it to be an additional tool to strengthen their already established marketing communications mix (Killian & McManus, 2015), providing organizations with a new way to project influence and gain attention (Fulgoni, 2014; Hanna, Rohm, & Crittenden, 2011). Yet many have suggested that the rise of social media has led to somewhat of an imperviousness toward more traditional communication channels such as TV or radio (Bagozzi & Dholakia, 2006), thus their effectiveness is doubted (Edgecliffe-Johnson, 2008). Some researchers have questioned whether the concept of the original marketing mix is relevant for today's marketing environment, developing a new online marketing mix to address this (e.g., Talpau, 2014), focusing on the value consumers seek through these online platforms. However some argue that there is simply no evidence that traditional marketing methods are decreasing (Fulgoni, 2014; Winer, 2009). Although, it is evident that organizational budgets are shifting (Winer, 2009), with 96% participating in some form of social media marketing campaign (Stelzner, 2015).

The 4P's model was extended to the 7P's as a way of incorporating services more thoroughly in the mix. This incorporated People (in relation to organizational employees), Processes (any process that affects the product or service in anyway), and Physical Evidence (any reminder that the consumer engaged in a particular service) (Booms & Bitner, 1981). However due to the apparent lack of consumer focus, two theories developed versions of the 4C's concept as a way of addressing this. Trying to incorporate the growing niche groups of consumers, Lauterborn (1990) suggested Consumer (focusing on their needs and wants), Cost (not only the price, but other the costs relating to the time, conscience, and competitors), Communication (realizing the importance of two-way communication between an organization and its consumers), and finally Convenience (preference of consumers, ease of purchasing because of the Internet and new technologies). The second development of the 4C's concept was from Shimizu in 1973 (Shimizu, 1989), which proposed Commodity, Cost, Communication, and Channel, which was expanded to the 7C's Compass Model to incorporate Corporation, Consumer, and Circumstances. The model refers more to how an organization can ensure success and avoid failure, from more of an economic perspective. The 4C's concepts recognize that organizations now need to pay even more attention to the media messages, and objectives they set to address the changing dimensions of the marketing process (Hennig-Thurau et al., 2010; Little, 2012; Weinberg & Pehlivan, 2011). Traditional marketing focused on consumers who were merely the recipients of a message, in need of information that would inform, persuade, or engage (Berthon, Pitt, & Campbell, 2008). The marketing environment has changed to a place where consumers are not merely recipients of a message but instigators, who contribute to the marketing message (Hennig-Thurau et al., 2010; Hennig-Thurau, Hofacker, & Bloching, 2013), gain knowledge, and experience the whole consumption process (Hamill, Tagg, & Vescovi, 2010), centering on the experience rather than static mediums and websites.

It is evident that the process of communication has changed, allowing fragmentation of consumers, two-way communication, empowerment, co-creation, interaction, and relationship development (Hennig-Thurau et al., 2010), in what some have termed the "Pinball environment" (Hennig-Thurau et al., 2013). This has inspired researchers to delve deeper into the workings of this new environment to find out what it is that draws consumers' attention to this medium and how it can be used as a tool for marketing purposes (Hennig-Thurau et al., 2010, 2013). The notion that marketers are in need of the insights into the behavior of the consumer is not a new concept; however the need to gain these insights has been intensified by the digital age (Fulgoni, 2014).

2.2 DEFINING SOCIAL MEDIA

Social media has attracted a variety of different disciplines including marketing, management, information systems, and social sciences and psychology. This has caused problems when trying to concisely define the term (Chaffey & Smith, 2013), as each discipline focuses on different aspects when characterizing it. Heavily utilized in Marketing literature, this discipline has a strong inclination toward UGC and sharing, e.g., in the definitions by Constantinides (2014), Strokes (2009), and Weinberg and Berger (2011) shown in Table 2.1. These definitions acknowledge the variety of delivery mechanisms the social media environment embodies such as channels, platforms, and applications (such as the definitions by Strauss and Frost

Table 2.1 Definitions of Social Media From Marketing Discipline

Definition	Citation
Web 2.0 applications enabling the creation, editing, and dissemination of user-generated content	Constantinides (2014, p. 42)
Consists of a set of applications (e.g., Facebook, Twitter, Flickr) that are built to run on a "Web 2.0" platform. This Web-based platform inherently enables the creation and distribution/sharing of information created by users/consumers, namely, user-generated content	Weinberg and Barger (2011, p. 329)
The media that is published, created, and shared by individuals on the Internet, such as blogs, images, video, and more	Strokes (2009, p. 181)
Online tools and platforms that allow users to collaborate online content, share insights and experiences, and connect to business or pleasure	Strauss and Frost (2009, p. 326)
Channels in which active consumers engage in behaviors that can be consumed by others both in real time and long afterwards regardless of their spatial location	Hennig-Thurau et al. (2010, p. 312)
Dynamic, interconnected, egalitarian, and interactive organisms beyond the control of any organization	Peters, Chen, Kaplan, Ognibeni, and Pauwels (2013, p. 281)
Give marketers a means for direct interaction, which constitutes an ideal environment for creation of brand communities, establishing and reinforcing relationships, and gaining a better understanding of consumers through netnographical research	Scarpi (2010) and Kozimets (2002) as cited in Labrecque (2014, p. 134)

(2009) as shown in Table 2.1). There is an underlying reference to organization utilization, hinting at consumption activities, although it is evident that each definition fails to incorporate each of the elements previously mentioned, meaning an all-encompassing definition is lacking. The Information Systems discipline focuses on information dissemination rather than UGC and also recognizes the delivery mechanisms as well as noting the online nature, such as Effing and Spil (2016, p. 2) who describe social media as "specific part of strategic decision-making based on digital resources, more specifically a group of Internet-based information systems." However unlike the Marketing discipline, there is a tendency to refer to the strategic use of social media, as shown by Effing and Spil (2016). The Management discipline is similar to both Information Systems and Marketing disciplines as it outlines a focus on UGC, although focusing more on the functionality of social media than defining it precisely. For example, Mangold and Faulds (2009, p. 358) define it as a "wide range of online, word-of-mouth forums including blogs, company sponsored discussion boards and chat rooms, consumer-to-consumer e-mail, consumer product or service ratings websites and forums, Internet discussion boards and forums, moblogs (sites containing digital audio, images, movies, or photographs), and social networking websites." The social and psychological disciplines tend to adopt definitions from the Marketing, Information Systems, and Management disciples. However more often than not they tend to focus on one aspect of social media such as social networking sites that have their own definition.

It is suggested that the aspects of the definitions from each discipline should be combined to provide a more all-encompassing characterization of social media, such as:

An environment that provides a set of tools available to both individuals and organizations, enabling information dissemination, sharing and content creation to facilitate conversation guided toward completion of both strategic and social goals that may eventually lead to consumption.

However it must be noted that this definition needs more refinement and would benefit from a more thorough investigation to incorporate aspects of other disciplines that may have tried to define the term.

2.3 FRAMEWORKS, METRICS, AND MEASUREMENT OF SOCIAL MEDIA

The recognition of social media as integral for marketing means that it has inevitably gained attention within the literature. The sheer amount of research on social media denotes that a unified consensus on many aspects has not been possible, causing problems on utilizing it for marketing purposes. Categorizing social media is just one of these problematic areas as many have tried to outline its components. For example, interactivity and digital (Winer, 2009), and intrusive, nonintrusive, and UGC (Shankar & Hollinger, 2007), focus more on the characteristics of social media rather than on the content. Whereas categories such as relationship management, news gathering, creativity, and entertainment (Killian & McManus, 2015) have also been used. Yet it should be questioned how relevant these classifications are from the perspective of the consumer as the majority of these types of studies focus on how managers classify the various social media and these can therefore not be generalized. Attempts have also been made at trying to identify the principles of social media, with Hsieh (2016) finding multiple device accessibility, content reality, individualization, keyword-search engine, and identity feature functions as the most significant. Yet this is again somewhere that needs clarification in terms of the exact aspects.

The adoption of social media by consumers has put extensive pressure on organizations, forcing them to adapt to this new environment without effective strategies in place (Larson & Watson, 2011). It is evident that many organizations are finding this difficult (Bottles & Sherlock, 2011), with Dwivedi, Kapoor, and Chen (2015) emphasizing the need for effective tactics when trying to uphold a sufficient social media presence. Progress of organizations on developing effective strategies is impeded by the fact that there are very few frameworks available to effectively analyze the social media environment and thus they have no foundations to build upon (Effing & Spil, 2016). Attempts have been made to address this, such as Kietzmann, Hermkens, McCarthy, and Silvestre (2011) Honeycomb Framework. This framework tries to present a framework for helping an organization to understand their consumers through social media, identifying seven functionalities: relationships, reputation, conversations, sharing, groups, identity, and presence. Although, as noted by Effing and Spil (2016), this framework focused more on how to operationalize social media. They instead proposed the social strategy cone, developing a more intensive framework through three stages of maturity, representing the stages of an organization's social media strategy. The first stage, initiation, reflects identification and knowledge of the target audience and channel choice. The second stage reflects the diffusion of goals, resources, and policies, and finally the third stage (maturity) refers to content, activities, and monitoring.

However the social strategy cone was developed based on qualitative organizational case studies and thus could benefit from being validated through a more quantitative approach. Focusing on organizations, researchers have also attempted at trying to craft a universally applicable social media strategy, identifying visualization, virtualization, and interactive collaboration approaches by many organizations (Go & You, 2016), whilst others focus on the information that can be gleaned from social media to enhance organizational knowledge (He, Wu, Yan, Akula, & Shen, 2015). The quality of the social aspect in the brand offering can be improved by learning and paying attention to how consumers use social media, e.g., their sharing tendencies (Chen, Xu, & Whinston, 2011).

Another key determinant for organizations is the return on investment (ROI) they get from employing particular marketing strategies and this does not stop with social media. Recent studies have looked at e-commerce adoption utilizing social media such as Abed, Dwivedi, and Williams (2015a) who emphasize the issues small and medium-sized enterprises (SME's) have with finding the value from utilizing the platform. Many are confused as to whether social media is associated with financial gain, with arguments both for (e.g., Galeotti & Goyal, 2009) and against (e.g., Ng & Wang, 2013) its revenue-generating potential. Thus researchers have suggested that identifying which metrics to gather information, as well as particular measurement approaches, would be beneficial in helping organizations to establish the financial benefits of utilizing the social media environment. However the value of social media is still very difficult to quantify, yet are crucial when trying to give marketers the much needed influence amongst consumers (Bendle & Bagga, 2016). The composition of what metrics needs to be gathered has caused friction within the literature, with some suggesting functional metrics such as leads generated, ROI and volume (Barger & Labrecque, 2013), value of "like," customer lifetime value, and ROI (Bendle & Bagga, 2016). Whilst others focus more on content, e.g., UGC, engagement motivations, and interactions, network structure, and social roles (Peters et al., 2013). What is clear is that defining these metrics is crucial for marketer success (Bendle & Bagga, 2016).

Social media research as a whole sees a variety of theories, constructs, and conceptual frameworks used. Commonly used theories include uses and gratifications theory (e.g., Hollenbaugh & Ferris, 2014; Raacke & Bonds-Raacke, 2008), personality traits like the five factor model (e.g., Lonnqvist & Itkonen, 2016; Ryan & Xenos, 2011), social capital theory (e.g., Ellison, Steinfield, & Lampe, 2007), theory of planned behavior (e.g., Casaló, Flavián, & Guinalíu, 2010), technology acceptance model (e.g., Steyn, Salehi-Sangari, Pitt, Parent, & Berthon, 2010), social capital theory (e.g., Chai & Kim, 2010), social identity theory (e.g., Dholakia, Bagozzi, & Pearo, 2004), amongst others. Ngai, Tao, and Moon (2015) group the theories used in social media research under three themes: personal behavior theories, social behavior theories, and mass communication theories. Surprisingly many social media studies do not identify a dominant theory (e.g., Lonnqvist & Deters, 2016; Smith, Fischer, & Yongjian, 2012; Vigil & Wu, 2015), drawing on aspects of a variety of theories to ground their research. Ngai et al. (2015) identified platform attributes, user attributes, and social factors as common mediators, as well as user characteristics and social factors as common moderators within social media research as a whole. In addition, the same study highlighted common antecedents as social factors, user attributes, and organizational attributes, as well as personal and organizational context as common outcomes. It is clear that although a variety of theories have been utilized, understanding of social media as a whole is still incredibly fragmented.

2.4 STRUCTURE AND NETWORKS

The social media environment is characterized by consumer empowerment (Labrecque, Esche, Mathwick, Novak, & Hofacker, 2013), participation, and connection (Hennig-Thurau et al., 2013). Consumers now have the capacity to influence and communicate with other consumers, providing information and sharing experiences that can ultimately have an effect on their purchase intent (Hill, Provost, & Volinsky, 2006). Influencing brand management, customer relationships, and selling, Hennig-Thurau et al. (2013) characterizes this new environment in terms of the Pinball game whereby the marketing messages sent out by the organization are the balls and the various obstacles are consumers, some helping and some hindering the progression of the message to the intended consumer. For instance, Marder, Slade, Houghton, and Archer-Brown (2016) demonstrated the impact an audience or network can have on a consumer's behavior, finding that individuals restrict their behavior in terms of affiliating with political parties as a way to manage their impressions on others.

The characteristics of social media allow individuals to culminate in groups and subgroups (Fieseler & Fleck, 2013), all of which have varying degrees of connections between the individuals. As noted by Belk (2013), social media can be used as an extension of the self and thus the groups that an individual joins are a reflection of this. Thus it may be wise for organizations to remember the more intimate reasons consumers join groups, creating these intense networks, as a means of developing more sensitive strategies.

The connections between consumers are one of the key components of this new environment with consumers utilizing these networks to share their experiences and knowledge about a brand with each other. Often referred to as an audience (Lampe, Ellison, & Steinfield, 2008), these connections are normally severely underestimated by both consumers and organizations (Bernstein, Bakshy, Burke, & Karrer, 2013). Although not physically observable, these imagined audiences or visualizations can be extremely influential (Litt, 2012; Wolf, Gao, Berendt, & Pierson, 2015). It has been demonstrated that a consumers' network will influence how much value they place on information gained through these connections (Sohn, 2014), yet there is discrepancy in the literature on the benefits of the strength of these connections. For example, it has been shown that strong connections are better at influencing their networks (Nitzan & Libai, 2011), yet it has also been demonstrated that weak ties can also be beneficial in the transference of information (Granovetter, 1973). In addition, the similarity one shares with their network, or homophily, also plays an important role in determining the effectiveness of eWOM (Brown & Reingen, 1987). However Zafarani and Liu (2016) show that the distribution of an individual's friendship network changes as they join other social media platforms, finding that on average an individual has around 400 friends. Thus this may also play a part in the effectiveness of communications on social media.

2.5 RELATIONSHIPS

Rather than being the recipients of a message, consumers are now active participants in developing their relationships with companies (Malthouse, Haenlein, Skiera, Wege, & Zhang, 2013). Parise, Guinan, and Weinberg (2008) emphasize that consumers do not just want the product or service, they crave value from all of their relationships. They can now express themselves in ways that they were unable to before, embracing this newfound power, which can also affect reputations and thus the relationships that organizations have with all their other consumers (Gensler, Völckner, Liu-Thompkins, & Wiertz, 2013). Yet it is hard to maintain a relationship in a social media environment when so many other companies are trying to get the attention of the same consumers (Kietzmann et al., 2011). Organizations have adapted and started to manage their customer relationships in a more social manner, seeking out the needs and wants of consumers and collaborating with them in a more personal way to deliver the value that they crave (Baird & Parasnis, 2011). They can use the social media environment as a way to develop their existing relationships to establish a deeper connection with their consumers, as well as identifying new and potential customers (Sashi, 2012). Consumers crave value, which they get when they engage in a relationship (Canhoto & Clark, 2013), therefore organizations may want to focus on allowing consumers to develop a relationship based on choice and attraction to brand messages rather than trying to make them do something unwillingly (Diffley, Kearns, Bennett, & Kawalek, 2011).

Traditional approaches to relationships in the marketing discipline have focused on exchanges between sellers and buyers of a product or service (Gronroos, 1994). However the things that accompany this such as integrity (Kaufmann & Stern, 1988), commitment, and trust (Morgan & Hunt, 1994) are somewhat distorted by the social media environment and its characteristics of interactivity. Engaging consumers into relationships means that their lifetime value is improved (Malthouse et al., 2013), as well as ensuring that they remain loyal to the organization. Relationship loyalty is a great asset to an organization but it has to be asked whether this loyalty will sustain itself in a place where consumers are able to access multiple choices and perhaps cheaper prices—something that needs to be researched further (Hennig-Thurau et al., 2010).

The social media environment removes the constraints of face-to-face interaction, making it easier for individuals to communicate and express their needs and wants (Derks, Fischer, & Bos, 2008; Mathwick, 2002). The amount that consumers are willing to reveal is immense, with several studies examining this self-disclosure tendency (e.g., Hollenbaugh & Ferris, 2014; Loiacono, 2015), aiding brands in building connections with these consumers and forming strong relationships (Joinson, 2001). Li and Li (2014) argue that people utilize their offline relationship behavior to inform their online behavior with brands. They find that users of Twitter who do not use it heavily utilize a more exchange-based relationship rather than a communal relationship.

2.6 CO-CREATION

As consumers have become cocreators in their purchases this has given them even more power to create their own value (De Chernatony &

Christodoulides, 2004; Sanderson, 2007). Co-creation is linked to the increasing demand of consumers for personalization, meaning brands need to listen and engage in conversation (Hamilton & Hewer, 2010). This will enable consumers to gather more information that will allow them to make a more informed purchase decision, thus helping them financially (by reducing information searching costs) and on a more personal level (by making them feel more certain in their decision) (Brynjolfsson & Smith, 2000). In addition, the brand will benefit as co-creation provides a cost-effective way to both personalize and customize services and products to suit the growing needs of the consumer (Christodoulides, 2009). Rathore, Ilavarasan, and Dwivedi (2016) also highlight the importance of consumer co-creation for the benefit of the organization in product development. However the impact that this collaboration has on both the decision-making process and consumer's new found feelings of empowerment still needs to be further defined (Chung & Austria, 2010; Constantinides, 2014). Engaging with consumers on social media and observing what they say can help an organization to create and develop their brand offerings, providing a better chance of satisfying their needs and wants, as well as guiding them to develop a better opinion of the brand itself. UGC, which embodies all content created, shared, and disseminated by consumers through media such as pictures, videos, and eWOM, provides an expressive communication outlet for consumers (Boyd & Ellison, 2008; Smith et al., 2012). Created either individually or with the help of others, Smith et al. (2012) found that differing social media platforms produce and encourage different UGC. For example, they found that Twitter provides more of a utilitarian discussion and news sharing medium, whereas Facebook is more social in nature—a finding echoed by Hughes, Rowe, Batey, and Lee (2012). Gyrd-Jones and Kornum (2013) emphasize the value of stakeholders in both the online and offline realm in this co-creation process as this will maximize its value. In addition, Jurgens, Berthon, Edelman, and Pitt (2016) recognize the growing influence of secondary stakeholders, rather than focusing on just the primary ones.

Consumers have a preference for personalization, improving both their attitude to the product or service and their response (Franke, Keinz, & Steger, 2009; Howard & Kerin, 2004). Yet the topic of personalization is not straight forward, with no research confirming the most effective way to personalize a brand offering to consumers (Noar, Harrington, & Aldrich, 2009), and negative perceptions of attempted personalization proving troublesome compared to no message at all (Arora et al., 2008).

Although it may be that as long as a consumer perceives this personalization to be present, they become more satisfied and thus get more value (Li, 2016). It must also be noted that consumers may choose to use and abuse the co-creation opportunities that are available to them (Gebauer, Fuller, & Pezzei, 2013). The empowerment that consumers now have is fueling their perception of equality with the co-creation process (Fuchs, Prandelli, & Schreier, 2010).

2.7 POWER AND eWOM

Although it was first assumed that increased choice and access was the primary source of power consumers had in the new online environment (Bickart & Schindler, 2001), subsequent research have identified crowd-based, network, demand, and information as additional sources of power (Labrecque et al., 2013). Crowd-based power refers to the access consumers now have to resources on the Internet that allow them to group together a variety of information, combining the other three types of power together (Labrecque et al., 2013). Especially prevalent in groups of consumers (although can be utilized individually) such as that of online brand communities, this source of power allows consumers to combine group and individual resources for completion of community goals. This source of power is extremely beneficial for social commerce, creating value through networks, allowing better accessibility to offerings (Stephen & Toubia, 2010). Finally, there is an undeniable benefit from being involved in group- or community-based activity as it provides a sense of belonging for members (Muniz & O'Guinn, 2001), e.g., Grieve et al. (2013) found that Facebook was associated with connectedness and this was also associated with a greater satisfaction with life. Network-based power refers to the additional value that individuals can add to marketing content after its initial dissemination such as sharing, additional uses, comments (Labrecque et al., 2013). Strength of ties is important here as the connections an individual has on social media have the ability to significantly influence others. This two-way communication between many connections allows for a great deal of expression, although the virtual aspect of people being considered based on the information they share with these networks could become more prominently negative (Lanier, 2010). Reducing an individual to the fragment of what they share with their networks degrades their self and thus can begin to influence how they feel about themselves. Demand-based power refers to the use of social media for purchasing and consumption, with a reduction in barriers and increased ease of access (Day, 2011). Many organizations have had to face competitive pressure from the sheer amount of other brand offerings available to consumers through their use of social media, particularly in terms of price. Many have overcome this by adopting strategies that encourage consumers to engage in the creation process (Fuchs et al., 2010). Information-based power includes content production, which allows individuals to create their own content as a means of providing valuable insight into their opinion of a brand, and content consumption, which relates to how easily individuals can get information about a brand through their networks (Labrecque et al., 2013).

A key source of much of the power within social media is that of electronic word-of-mouth, although recent research has considered the type of communication that happens on social media to be social word of mouth rather than eWOM, which is any form of word-of-mouth that happens online (Labrecque et al., 2013). Consumers on social media are connected to a large variety of other consumers, thus anything they post allows the effect of eWOM to be more influential in this environment (Hennig-Thurau, Gwinner, Walsh, & Gremler, 2004). This earned media, between both brand and consumers and consumer to consumer, are not subject to traditional gatekeeping that accompanied the original marketing tools (Tilley & Cokley, 2008). All consumers can now be heard (Fieseler & Fleck, 2013), thus enabling them to seriously damage the reputation of any brand (Hennig-Thurau & Walsh, 2004). The efficiency, reach, and timeliness of social media allows it to be an excellent crisis management tool by providing quicker responses in real time, as well as being able to communicate with consumers on an individual basis (Hennig-Thurau et al., 2013). Not only this, but the networks that consumers create online and the information that is shared between them are found to be more trustworthy (by the consumer) than any message from a brand (Chung & Austria, 2010). Valence of eWOM also has an impact, with negative eWOM being much more influential to a brands well-being (Luo, 2009). However as found by Einwiller and Steilen (2015) organizations are not utilizing this interactive social media environment to successfully communicate with consumers and other stakeholders, deflecting complaints to other media.

The topic of eWOM has garnered great interest from researchers with many looking at issues such as customer acquisition (Trusov, Bucklin, & Pauwels, 2009), purchase intent (e.g., Baber et al., 2016; Bataineh, 2015; Luo & Zhang, 2013), message source (e.g., See-To & Ho, 2014), behavior (e.g., Kim, Sung, & Kang, 2014), and motivations for engaging in eWOM

(Hennig-Thurau et al., 2004). The majority of research focused on eWOM to date has concentrated on communication from unknown sources, where consumers have no pre-existing connection, such as e-commerce websites, forums, or review/rating sites. In addition, there has been an acknowledgment within the literature of the relevance of self to consumer perceptions, especially with regard to social media with Belk's (2013) notion of extended self. Consumers will therefore be more inclined to engage with organizations within this environment if marketers acknowledge the importance of self in their messages and communications, including eWOM (Berthon et al., 2008; Hennig-Thurau et al., 2004). The conversations online that are created through both brands and consumers generate a buzz that can be both negative and positive and can ultimately affect consumer purchase intention (Luo & Zhang, 2013). This can also potentially influence other types of social information—an area that could be further researched (Chung & Austria, 2010; Mangold & Faulds, 2009; Yadav, de Valck, Hennig-Thurau, Hoffman, & Spann, 2013).

2.8 SOCIAL COMMERCE

The speed at which marketers and managers have adopted the use of social media and its popularity amongst consumers leaves its capacity to generate revenue, which is one of the key concerns for organizations (Yadav et al., 2013). However recent attempts at utilizing this new form of commerce have been unsuccessful (Hennig-Thurau et al., 2013)—the reasons for which are unclear. Consumers' newfound empowerment, especially in relation to Labrecque et al. (2013) identification of demand-based power, as well as a focus on personalization, has enabled this new form of commerce to grow (Anderson, Knight, Pookulangara, & Josiam, 2014). Yet as noted by Yadav et al. (2013) very little research has been done on the topic and it is increasingly subject to confusion regarding it focus, involvement, and definition. Effectively it refers to how consumer decisions are influenced, in relation to commerce activities, by social media networks (Hajli & Sims, 2015; Yadav et al., 2013).

As a fairly new topic, so far studies have tended to focus on its role in value (e.g., Andrew and Toubia, 2010) and consumer behavior (e.g., Kim & Park, 2013). Research has also tried to define the stages of social commerce, such as that outlined by Harris and Dennis (2011) who identified creating consumer-centric experiences as the last stage in their four-step social commerce process. However it has been long established that if brands can provide an experience that appeals to emotions it will strengthen the relationships it has with its consumers (Fournier, 1998), and thus encourage their purchasing behavior. This emotional value can be developed through connections with a consumer's self-concept (Belk, 1988, 2013).

The newfound interest in social commerce has fueled the desire to learn more about it, yet many questions remain unanswered. Yadav et al. (2013) says that research needs to be conducted into how social media environments can be used as selling platforms for the creation of economic value. This includes measurement approaches not only toward sales but also across the consumer's decision-making process both within and separate from social networks. There is a great need to establish where information originates and how it is used as a way to measure how influential this information is to social commerce. Based on the characteristics of social media including empowerment, interactivity, relationships, and co-creation, it is evident that this new environment should be explored in more depth to examine how each platform is used by consumers, which will enable more insight into how to use it strategically for selling purposes. The four metrics identified by Peters et al. (2013) of UGC, engagement motivations, network structure, and social roles and interactions could be a good place to start.

2.9 MULTIPLE PLATFORMS

Social media encompasses various platforms that can be used as communicative tools and there are a variety of ways that these different social media platforms can be characterized. For example, Karapanos, Teixeira, & Gouveia, (2016, p. 888) refer to Facebook as an "online community," whereas Smith et al. (2012, p. 103) refers to the same site as a "social networking site." The sheer variety of terms used to categorize social media provides some problems in terms of synchronicity within the literature. To address this Kaplan and Haenlein (2010) and Agarwal (2009) as cited in Zafarani and Liu (2016, p. 84) categorize social media platforms into seven distinct categories: "(1) blogs and blogging, (2) media sharing (photo, audio, or video), (3) microblogging, (4) social bookmarking, (5) social friendship networks, (6) social news and search, and (7) location-based networks"— these distinctions are also observed by Gu and Widen-Wulff (2010) and Nicholas and Rowlands (2011). The differences between them can be distinguished by half-life of information (lifespan of information, how long it will stay in spotlight for) and depth of information (content) (Weinberg & Pehlivan, 2011). For example, Microblogs such as Twitter have a very short half-life and depth of information, whereas social networking sites (or social friendship networks) like Facebook have a relatively long half-life and depth of information. These differences are vital to take into account when choosing the best medium to communicate with consumers as different platforms can serve different objectives. For instance, Twitter can be used for bringing awareness to an already established brand whereas online communities can bring people together for deeper engagement (Weinberg & Pehlivan, 2011). The motivation behind social media use and the process behind the adoption of using certain social media are still not completely clear and needs to be researched further in order to fill this knowledge gap (Chung & Austria, 2010).

Not only are organizations being force to adapt to social media, they are having to contend with the multitude of online platforms, all of which serve different purposes. Researchers such as Ashley and Tuten (2015) highlight the importance of using a variety of social media platforms, yet few have utilized multiple channels for comparison (Smith et al., 2012). Each social media platform encourages its own environment including structure, norms, and cultural aspects, leading to variation in the reasons that they engage in that particular platform (Smith et al., 2012). There is an increase in social media users operating on more than one platform and transitioning between these platforms, although there is little evidence to show why they are doing this and what drives this particular behavior (Karapanos et al., 2016). It could be posited that the differing characteristics of the platforms, which provide unique environments, for the completion of different objectives (Smith et al., 2012) facilitates this movement.

Much of the research concerning social media platforms has focused on platforms in isolation rather than cross-comparison approaches. A few exceptions to this include Smith et al. (2012) who looked at brand-related UGC across Facebook, Twitter, and YouTube and found that Facebook and Twitter showed more of a negative brand sentiment than YouTube. They also found that Twitter is utilized for the spread of news and discussions and self-promotion is more pronounced on Facebook rather than the other two sites. This could be because of the reduced self-esteem that Facebook users feel from content fatigue, social surveillance and unfriending/untagging on the platform which gives users a negative experience, as found by Karapanos et al. (2016). Similarly, Tobina, Vanmana, Verreynnea, and Saeria (2015) found that lack of feedback from others reduced their self-esteem and sense of belongingness within Facebook. However this is inconsistent with findings from Ellison et al. (2007) who believe that Facebook could provide more benefits to users who exhibit low self-esteem because of its ability to create varying forms of social capital. Cross-platform research has also addressed the individual differences between the users who utilize them, with varying evidence found. For example, Hughes et al. (2012), who studied personality predictors of users on Twitter and Facebook, found that Facebook users tend to be more social whilst Twitter users are less so, seeking cognitive stimulation rather than a social experience. This affects behaviors such as how they seek information, e.g., Twitter users may get their information through more concrete cognitively based sources such as links within tweets whereas Facebook users may just ask their friends (Hughes et al., 2012). Other cross-platform research includes a study by Buccafurri, Lax, Nicolazzo, and Nocera (2015) that analyzed the privacy settings of Facebook and Twitter users, as well as Buccafurri, Lax, Nicolazzo, and Nocera (2016) who proposed a model to support design and development of multiple-social network applications primarily using Facebook and Twitter.

Much more research has focused on the individual platforms, e.g., Twitter, which provide evidence for the separate aspects that cross-platform research has found. For example, similarly to Hughes et al. (2012), Li and Li (2014) who looked at brand—consumer relationships on Twitter, concluded that users favored exchange relationship—based messages over communal relationship—based messages but only if they were not heavy Twitter users. Contradictory to this, Chen (2011), who also looked specifi-cally at Twitter, found that users who spend more time on the platform are able to satisfy their sense of connection with others. In addition, Yoo, Choi, Choi, and Rho (2014) positively attributed social conformity to frequent Twitter usage. It is pertinent that more narrow personality traits could be explored as this would provide more in-depth evidence to under-stand individual differences in online behavior (Hughes et al., 2012). However Lee and Kim (2014) suggest that the motivations and gratifica-tions that users seek dictate the way in which they use Twitter. The focus of research on Twitter is in a similar vein of research of other social media channels. There has been a focus on why people use the platform and how they use it (Jansen, Zhang, Sobel, & Chowdury, 2009; Naaman, Boase, & Lai, 2010); self-presentation (Marwick & Boyd, 2011); and behaviors (Boyd, Golder, & Lotan, 2010).

It is evident that the most common platform to be analyzed is Facebook. Using the uses and gratifications theory as a basis, Hollenbaugh and Ferris (2014) found relationship management and exhibitionism were the reasons behind Facebook users (who disclosed the most information) use of the platform, meaning more extraverted individuals will disclose more information in an effort to develop and maintain their relationships. Malik, Dhir, and Nieminen (2016) also used the uses and gratifications theory in the context of Facebook and found that users share photos in an effort to seek affection. Which, when looking at the findings of Hollenbaugh and Ferris (2014) coincides with maintenance of relationships as photo sharing is one way of getting attention from others and developing that relationship. Likewise, Grieve et al. (2013) found that Facebook is a prime environment to develop relationships and connectedness with others. In fact, several studies explore the use of Facebook for social support and relationship development and maintenance (e.g., Blight, Jageillo, & Ruppel, 2015; Tang, Chen, Yang, Chung, & Le, 2016). Facebook research has included satisfaction of a variety of needs including surveillance and social browsing (Dunne, Lawlor, & Rowley, 2010; Urista, Dong, & Day, 2009), ideal image portrayal (Dunne et al., 2010), identity maintenance and self-presentation (e.g., Brailovskaia & Bierhoff, 2016; Labrecque, Markos, & Milne, 2011; Zywica & Danowski, 2008), and building relationships (Ellison et al., 2007; Raacke & Bonds-Raacke, 2008). In addition, other research has focused on the uses and motivations behind Facebook use (Debatin, Lovejoy, Horn, & Hughes, 2009; Ellison et al., 2007) as well as functionality (Papacharissi, 2009), and addiction of use (Hong, Huang, Lin, & Chiu, 2014; Tang et al., 2016). There is also a great deal of research on Facebook that concentrates on personality traits of its users (e.g., Lee, Ahn, & Kim, 2014; Lonnqvist & Deters, 2016) particularly the Big Five personality traits (e.g., Lonnqvist & Itkonen, 2016; Ryan & Xenos, 2011; Seidman, 2013).

Other popular social media channels, such as Instagram, a media sharing social media platform, have received considerably less attention in the literature compared to social friendship networks such as Facebook and microblogs such as Twitter. Despite the growing popularity of media sharing as a means of communication online, very few have focused on these visually based social media sites (Bakhshi, Shamma, & Gilbert, 2014), even though the relationships on this platform can be comparable to those on Twitter (Golbeck, 2015).

A study by Hu, Manikonda, and Kambhampati (2014), which is one of the first to analyze the photos and users of Instagram, found eight different types of photos and five different types of users, who exhibit distinct characteristics. Another study by Bakhshi et al. (2014) found that Instagram photos that depict faces are the most likely to be popular on the platform. However as mentioned earlier, each platform will have its own culture, characteristics, and behaviors (Smith et al., 2012), but as research on this platform has only just started being done there is limited data to compare. The small amount of research that has been done mainly focused on cultural and social aspects of the images shared (e.g., Hochman & Manovich, 2013; Silva, Melo, Almeida, Salles, & Loureiro, 2013), although unique studies such as that by Hosseinmardi et al. (2014), which focuses on the use of Instagram and Ask.fm in cyberbullying, and Ferrara, Interdonato, and Tagarelli (2014), which look at the behavior and structure of the platform, have also been conducted.

With any communication from a brand it is the message and personality that is shown across all their communication channels that has to be the same and has to be consistent so consumers can decipher what it is the brand represents (Duncan & Moriarty, 1998; Erdem & Swait, 1998; Keller, 1999; Lange & Dahlen, 2003; Navarro-Bailon, 2012). This also has to be the same through every social media platform, which is why it is necessary to choose carefully what social media platform should be used and identify why it is being used in the first place. Tts structure, characteristics, and typical behaviors should be considered to determine the types of users more likely to engage in that particular platform (Smith et al., 2012). Multiple stimuli can generate interest in a brand as more attention is paid to a variety of stimuli rather than a standalone medium (Chang & Thorson, 2004; Edell & Keller, 1989; Putrevu & Lord, 2003). If there is an inconsistent brand message then this can be damaging for the company and confuse the consumer, giving them differing expectations and a diffuse brand image (Navarro-Bailon, 2012). Constantinides (2014) says that in order for a social media strategy to be successful other aspects must be in good standing. This is illustrated by the E-Pyramid marketing model (Constantinides, 2014), which says that the product/service must be good quality with a market/customer-oriented organization to deliver high value. In addition, the remnants of Web 1.0 must be credible and efficiently designed—only then can an organization think about engaging in social media marketing.

2.10 DISCUSSION AND CONCLUDING POINTS

The growth in social media and its popularity with both brands and consumers means that it has caught the eye of a variety of different disciplines, introducing different methods to try and comprehend the mechanisms of this new environment (Giglietto, Rossi, & Bennato, 2012). The sheer amount of data, as well as its availability, is challenging research practices and creating a multitude of research that is progressively growing (Karpf, 2012). The interactive "pinball" environment means that they can no longer send a message to consumers and hope it reaches them in the way it was intended (Hennig-Thurau et al., 2013). Organizations now need to manage the communication process and deliver value to consumers on a level that is far more personal than before (Cova & White, 2010). Based on the growing importance of social media for the majority of organizations, it may be beneficial that managers implement a social media culture within the organization to help develop employees who are adept at using these platforms (Hennig-Thurau et al., 2013). Organizations have to be flexible and cannot operate their social media in isolation, as it should be incorporated across the organization (Malthouse et al., 2013; Weinberg, de Ruyter, Dellarocas, Buck, & Keeling, 2013). This is echoed by Van Zoonen, Verhoeven, and Vliegenthart (2016), who highlights the need for organizational social media use. Social media should be utilized as a learning tool that has the ability to gain deeper insights into consumers and what they really want (Chen et al., 2011; Di Maria & Finotto, 2008; Mathwick, Wiertz, & De Ruyter, 2008; Stelzner, 2015. Although social media can provide great benefits to organizations and brands it is not without its problems. The time of the empowered consumer has arrived and they are becoming more and more demanding, fragmenting into ever more niche groups that make communication difficult on a large scale (Fieseler & Fleck, 2013). Consumers now want experiential meaning from the brands on a more personal level that delivers value, especially when the various platforms within the social media sphere are being exploited for economic gains in the growing popularity of social commerce (Yadav et al., 2013), thus future research needs to focus on how the brand can be better marketed by focusing on consumers' experiential meaning of the brand in question (Schembri, Merrilees, & Kristiansen, 2010).

Summary of Key Points
- Consumers are now cocreators of their own value, which they want brands to recognize and contribute to.
- Not all organizations are utilizing social media to their full potential; many underestimate its use and ability.
- Social media is an undeniable relationship building tool that provides organizations and brands the opportunity to engage with consumers and find out their needs and wants to develop product and service offerings.
- The development of multiple platforms means that organizations and brands are trying to accommodate them all, not paying attention to the specific uses and characteristics of each platform.
- Many are unsure on the specific measurement and metrics of social media and what it means for ROI.

Organizations, brands, and individuals have the opportunity to use social media as a way of engaging consumers and developing long-term relationships with them (Parise et al., 2008). Yet it is seemingly unclear what constitutes a successful strategy for surviving in this new found social environment, and organizations would benefit from conducting more research in this area (Hennig-Thurau et al., 2013; Yadav et al., 2013). The range of information now available to consumers can detract away from marketing messages and thus relationships can be harder to manage (Hennig-Thurau et al., 2010).

Integration is one of the crucial areas that marketers should focus on, as Navarro-Bailon (2012) proved that cross-tool campaigns are more effective at getting a message across. Organizations and brands can use social media as a way to reduce their costs of market research (Stelzner, 2015). Therefore consideration should be taken into the personalization strategies adopted by organizations as a personalized message that is not perceived in the right way may be more troublesome for a brand than no communication at all (Arora et al., 2008). Conversational messages could be one way of providing a more personalized communication; however this does not effectively measure ROI, again pointing out that considerations into metrics are important research areas (Kwok & Yu, 2013). It is also how consumers interact and what encourages them to become involved that poses the opportunity for future research that will be essential for marketers (Chung & Austria, 2010). The conversations online that are created through both brands and consumers generate a buzz that can be both negative and positive and can ultimately affect consumer purchase intention (Luo & Zhang, 2013). This can also potentially influence other types of social information—an area that could also be further researched (Chung & Austria, 2010; Mangold & Faulds, 2009; Yadav et al., 2013). Yadav et al. (2013) says that more research needs to be done into how the varying sources of information that consumers come into contact with impact the decision-making process when they are either consistent or deviated, outlining a desperate need to look at the valence of information such as eWOM (Kim & Johnson, 2016), including the valence of messages from organizations themselves (Li & Li, 2014) not just consumers. UGC, especially related to a brand, influences a variety of behavioral outcomes, e.g., purchase intention, engagement, and eWOM. Therefore it is important that brands are fully aware of what consumers are saying about them by putting in place a monitoring mechanism (Kim & Johnson, 2016). Not only will this allow brands to have an up-to-date view of what their consumers are saying, it will enable them to enhance and develop both new and existing products based on recognized opportunities highlighted by the consumers—again providing them with a way to gain value. It will also help them to respond and aide consumers with their brand experiences, thus enhancing their relationship and reputation. Colliander & Wien (2013) suggest that utilizing consumers who frequently respond to others' complaints could be approached as a way of replacing some of the monitoring mechanisms and thus saving the organization's money. Consumers are more likely to be influenced by other consumers, and therefore relying on these to communicate on behalf of the brand is a good way to try and build relationships with them.

Continuing research into how consumers are best approached through social media and what it is that differentiates their interactions on the variety of platforms is crucial to the development of organizational strategies (Hennig-Thurau et al., 2013; Yadav et al., 2013). There has been a clear focus on developing frameworks for the composition and analysis of social media, as well as its measurement and appropriate metrics. It is clear that existing communication frameworks need to be evaluated in order to gain insight into these consumers so that new strategies can be developed accordingly (Hennig-Thurau et al., 2013). It appears that in terms of methodology many studies are limited to one platform, with few using cross-platform analysis as a way of developing a more integrated marketing strategy. It would be beneficial to look at under researched platforms such as Instagram (Ferrara et al., 2014; Hu et al., 2014). Future research also needs to look into the global nature of social media use, perhaps starting at the differing motivations individuals from different culture have for utilizing these platforms (Yoo et al., 2014). In addition, it is suggested that the gap in literature regarding social media and e-commerce adoption could also be addressed cross-culturally (Abed, Dwivedi, & Williams, 2015b). The growing fragmentation of consumers means that this research needs to be based in more specialized domains such as specific online communities, which are dedicated platforms that allow like-minded consumers to share their thoughts and ideas and create content, becoming a plethora of information just awaiting the marketer's recognition. These domains will be a good area to research and gather metrics, such as Peters et al. (2013) recommendations as they thrive based on UGC, facilitate engagement, develop their own social roles, structures, and interaction preferences.

Key Points for Practitioners

- Focus on integrating social media into existing strategies rather than relying on it as the sole medium on which to communicate with consumers.
- Ensure that monitoring mechanisms are in place to keep track of what consumers are saying about your brand and identify potential ideas for new products or product development.
- Ensure that the entire organization incorporates some form of social media to help employees develop and become adept at utilizing the platforms in a professional way.
- Engage with consumers to find out exactly what it is they want from connecting with the brand on social media; this will highlight what type of value they want from the communication to ensure stronger relationships are built.
- Offer some form of benefit or redress when dealing with complaints or negative communications about the brand to help placate the customer and try and rebuild the relationship.
- Consider the creation of new applications or even platforms that help users express themselves and focus on a more emotional appeal.
- Ensure that you engage with consumers over a longer period of time to encourage positive eWOM/WOM, which can lead to deeper loyalty and a better relationship overall.

Brands should focus on creating new platforms for like-minded consumers, helping them to find others who wish to talk about their brand (Kim & Johnson, 2016). This may increase sales as it provides them with more access to information and thus they will take this into consideration when making a purchase. Many assume that connecting with a brand on social media will increase loyalty; however Baird and Parasnis (2011) found consumers who engage with a brand on these platforms already have a preference for it. Perhaps it will be beneficial to focus on creation of platforms based on an emotional level that encourages an individual to share with their network, due to the influence a network can have. In addition, Yoo et al. (2014) found that there is a need to create a functional aspect of social media that allows users to express themselves, due to their inherent nature to do this online. Users are predisposed to express themselves in a way that they feel will enhance their appearance to others (Belk, 2013). Thus they may manipulate information or brand messages to their advantage to enhance its social value, perhaps linking in with the underlying motivations of individuals to utilize social media platforms. Consideration should be made to the development of applications as well as established social media platforms such as Facebook (Yoo et al., 2014). Focusing on applications could provide a way to gain more intimate communicate, as shown by Karapanos et al. (2016), and thus attend to the aforementioned emotional value.

Brands and organizations need to take consumers' expectations of the relationship into account when designing their message strategies—What are consumers hoping to get from their online relationship? Are they merely looking for benefits or hoping to get more out of building that trust with the organization? Social media is not being fully utilized to its advantage, e.g., complaint handling, and thus consumers become increasingly frustrated with some of the strategies employed through social media platforms regarding this. Organizations should refrain from engaging in requesting more information or explaining situations when dealing with complaints, instead utilize a form of redress strategy that will give value to the customer (Einwiller & Steilen, 2015). External behaviors to the social media environment can also have an impact on how individuals react to brand messages (Li & Li, 2014), and therefore brands should ensure behavioral consistency. There has been much focus on how to analyze relationships online, with studies such as that by Hansen (2011) suggesting programs such as NodeXL to examine them. However suggestions like this are only effective if the data that are being analyzed are correct, suggesting more focus on data collection around relationships (Hansen, 2011).

Recommendations for Future Research

- Researchers should focus on developing cross-platform research to identify individual differences in interaction across the platforms.
- Valence of eWOM messages and UGC should be addressed in order to see the effect that this has on the consumer decision-making process.
- Gathering more information on metrics such as those mentioned by Peters et al. (2013) on UGC, engagement motivations, and interactions, network structure and social roles—which will provide more data to allow brands to make more informed decisions regarding their use of social media.
- The majority of social media research is based on platforms such as Facebook and Twitter; therefore it is suggested other platforms such as Instagram or Snapchat are more readily researched to gather a more rounded explanation of social media behavior.
- Social media has attracted the attention of a variety of disciplines; therefore it is advised that more mixed methods approaches are used to provide a holistic and in-depth look at social media behaviors.
- Motivations of consumers to use social media platforms should be investigated across cultures, as different cultures may emphasize different needs.

This chapter has explored the characteristics and research surrounding social media and its utilization as a marketing tool, highlighting its lack of coherent understanding by organizations, especially with regard to how they should use it. It presents recommendations for future research aimed at trying to develop a more rounded knowledge of social media for both managers and marketers. Chapter 3, Online Brand Communities, details the phenomenon of online brand communities, which is one such gathering of consumers that can develop on social media platforms, providing key opportunities for brands to gain a deeper insight into what consumers are saying about them.

REFERENCES

Abed, S. S., Dwivedi, Y. K., & Williams, M. D. (2015a). Social media as a bridge to e-commerce adoption in SMEs: A systematic literature review. *The Marketing Review, 15*(1), 39–57.

Abed, S. S., Dwivedi, Y. K., & Williams, M. D. (2015b). 'SMEs' adoption of e-commerce using social media in a Saudi Arabian context: A systematic literature review. *International Journal of Business Information Systems, 19*(2), 159–179.

Agarwal, N. (2009). *Social computing in blogosphere* (Ph.D. thesis). Retrieved from: ProQuest Dissertations and Theses http://search.proquest.com/docview/304846625/.

Anderson, K. C., Knight, D. K., Pookulangara, S., & Josiam, B. (2014). Influence of hedonic and utilitarian motivations on retailer loyalty and purchase intention: A Facebook perspective. *Journal of Retailing and Consumer Services*, *21*, 773–779.

Arora, N., Dreze, X., Ghose, A., Hess, J. D., Iyengar, R., Jing, B., et al. (2008). Putting one-to-one marketing to work: Personalization, customization, and choice. *Marketing Letters*, *19*(3-4), 305–321.

Ashley, C., & Tuten, T. (2015). Creative strategies in social media marketing: An exploratory study of branded social content and consumer engagement. *Psychology and Marketing*, *32*(1), 15–27.

Atkinson, W. (2013). Adding social media marketing to the mix. *New Equipment Digest*, *78*(6), D-E.

Baber, A., Thurasamy, R., Malik, M. I., Sadiq, B., Islam, S., & Sajjad, M. (2016). Online word-of-mouth antecedents, attitude and intention-to-purchase electronic products in Pakistan. *Telematics and Informatics*, *33*, 388–400.

Bagozzi, R. P., & Dholakia, U. M. (2006). Antecedents and purchase consequences of customer participation in small group brand communities. *International Journal of Research in Marketing*, *23*, 45–61.

Baird, C. H., & Parasnis, G. (2011). From social media to social customer relationship management. *Strategy & Leadership*, *39*(5), 30–37.

Bakhshi, S., Shamma, D.A., & Gilbert, E. (2014). Faces engage us: Photos with faces attract more likes and comments on Instagram. *CHI '14 Proceedings of the SIGCHI Conference on Human Factors in Computing Systems*, pp. 965–974. Available from: http://dx.doi.org/10.1145/2556288.2557403.

Barger, V. A., & Labrecque, L. I. (2013). An integrated marketing communications perspective on social media metrics. *International Journal of Integrated Marketing Communications*, *5*(1), 64–76.

Bataineh, A. Q. (2015). The impact of perceived e-WOM on purchase intention: The mediating role of corporate image. *International Journal of Marketing Studies*, *7*(1), 126–137.

Belk, R. W. (1988). Possessions and the extended self. *Journal of Consumer Research*, *15*, 139–168.

Belk, R. W. (2013). Extended self in a digital world. *Journal of Consumer Research*, *40* (October), 477–500.

Bendle, N. T., & Bagga, C. K. (2016). The metrics that marketers muddle. *MIT Sloan Management Review*, *57*(3), 73–82.

Bernstein, M.S., Bakshy, E., Burke, M., & Karrer, B. (2013). Quantifying the invisible audience in social networks. *Proceedings of the SIGCHI Conference on Human Factors in Computing Systems*, *ACM*, pp. 21–30. Available from: http://dx.doi.org/10.1145/2470654.2470658.

Berthon, P., Pitt, L., & Campbell, C. (2008). Ad lib: When customers create the ad. *California Management Review*, *50*(4), 6–30.

Bickart, B., & Schindler, R. M. (2001). Internet forums as influential sources of consumer information. *Journal of Interactive Marketing*, *15*(3), 31–40.

Blight, M. G., Jageillo, K., & Ruppel, E. K. (2015). Same stuff different day: A mixed method study of support seeking on Facebook. *Computers in Human Behavior*, *53*, 366–373.

Booms, B., & Bitner, M. J. (1981). Marketing strategies and organizational structures for service firms. In J. H. Donnelly, & W. R. George (Eds.), *Marketing of services* (pp. 47–51). Chicago, IL: American Marketing Association.

Bottles, K., & Sherlock, T. (2011). Who should manage your social media strategy? *Physician Executive*, *37*(2), 68–72.

Boyd, D., Golder, S., & Lotan, G. (2010). Tweet, tweet, retweet: Conversational aspects of retweeting on Twitter. *Proceedings of the 43rd Hawaii International Conference* on *System Sciences*, Kauai, IEEE Computer Society, pp. 1530—1605. Available from: http://dx.doi.org/10.1109/HICSS.2010.412.

Boyd, D. M., & Ellison, N. B. (2008). Social network sites: Definition, history, and scholarship. *Journal of Computer-Mediated Communication, 13*, 210—230.

Brailovskaia, J., & Bierhoff, H.-W. (2016). Cross-cultural narcissism on Facebook: Relationship between self-presentation, social interaction and the open and covert narcissism on a social networking site in Germany and Russia. *Computers in Human Behavior, 55*, 25—57.

Brown, J. J., & Reingen, P. H. (1987). Social ties and word-of-mouth referral behaviour. *Journal of Consumer Research, 14*(3), 350—362.

Brynjolfsson, E., & Smith, M. D. (2000). Frictionless commerce? A comparison of internet and conventional retailers. *Management Science, 46*(4), 563—585.

Buccafurri, F., Lax, G., Nicolazzo, S., & Nocera, A. (2015). Comparing Twitter and Facebook user behaviour: Privacy and other aspects. *Computers in Human Behavior, 52*, 87—95.

Buccafurri, F., Lax, G., Nicolazzo, S., & Nocera, A. (2016). A model to support design and development of multiple-social-network applications. *Information Sciences, 331*, 99—119.

Canhoto, I. A., & Clark, M. (2013). Customer service 140 characters at a time: The user's perspective. *Journal of Marketing Management, 29*(5—6), 522—544.

Casaló, L. V., Flavián, C., & Guinalíu, M. (2010). Determinants of the intention to participate in firm-hosted online travel communities and effects on consumer behavioral intentions. *Tourism Management, 31*(6), 898—911.

Chaffey, D., & Smith, P. R. (2013). *Emarketing Excellence: Planning and Optimizing Your Digital Marketing.* 4th Edition. Oxon: Routledge.

Chai, S., & Kim, M. (2010). What makes bloggers share knowledge? An investigation on the role of trust. *International Journal of Information Management, 30*(5), 408—415.

Chang, Y., & Thorson, E. (2004). TV and web advertising synergies. *Journal of Advertising, 33*(2), 75—84.

Chen, G. M. (2011). Tweet this: A uses and gratifications perspective on how active Twitter use gratifies a need to connect with others. *Computers in Human Behavior, 27*, 755—762.

Chen, J., Xu, H., & Whinston, A. B. (2011). Moderated online communities and quality of user-generated content. *Journal of Management Information Systems, 28*(2), 237—268.

Christodoulides, G. (2009). Branding in the post-internet era. *Marketing Theory, 9*(1), 141—144.

Chung, C., & Austria, K. (2010). *Social media gratification and attitude toward social media marketing messages: A study of the effect of social media marketing messages on online shopping value. Proceedings of the Northeast Business & Economics Association* (pp. 581—586). Academic Press.

Colliander, J., & Wien, A. H. (2013). Trash talk rebuffed: Consumers' defense of companies criticized in online communities. *European Journal of Marketing, 47*(10), 1733—1757.

Constantinides, E. (2014). Foundations of social media marketing. *Procedia-Social and Behavioral Sciences, 148*, 40—57.

Cova, B., & White, T. (2010). Counter-brand and alter-brand communities: The impact of Web 2.0 on tribal marketing approaches. *Journal of Marketing Management, 26*(3—4), 256—270.

Day, G. S. (2011). Closing the marketing capabilities gap. *Journal of Marketing, 75*(4), 183—195.

De Chernatony, L., & Christodoulides, G. (2004). Taking the brand promise online: Challenges and opportunities. *Interactive Marketing, 5*(3), 238—251.

Debatin, B., Lovejoy, J. P., Horn, A.-K., & Hughes, B. N. (2009). Facebook and online privacy: Attitudes, behaviors, and unintended consequences. *Journal of Computer-Mediated Communication, 15*, 83−108.

Derks, D., Fischer, A. H., & Bos, A. E. R. (2008). The role of emotion in computer-mediated communication: A review. *Computers in Human Behavior, 24*(3), 766−785.

Dholakia, U. M., Bagozzi, R. P., & Pearo, L. K. (2004). A social influence model of consumer participation in network- and small-group-based virtual communities. *International Journal of Research in Marketing, 21*(3), 241−263.

Di Maria, E., & Finotto, V. (2008). Communities of consumption and made in Italy. *Industry & Innovation, 15*(2), 179−197.

Diffley, S., Kearns, J., Bennett, W., & Kawalek, P. (2011). Consumer behaviour in social networking sites: Implications for marketers. *Irish Journal of Management, 30*(2), 47−65.

Duncan, T. R., & Moriarty, S. (1998). A communication-based marketing model for managing relationships. *Journal of Marketing, 62*(April), 1−13.

Dunne, A., Lawlor, M. A., & Rowley, J. (2010). Young people's use of online social networking sites—A uses and gratifications perspective. *Journal of Research in Interactive Marketing, 4*(1), 46−58.

Dwivedi, Y. K., Kapoor, K. K., & Chen, H. (2015). Social media marketing and advertising. *The Marketing Review, 15*(3), 289−309.

Edell, J., & Keller, K. L. (1989). The information processing of coordinated media campaigns. *Journal of Marketing Research, 26*(2), 149−163.

Edgecliffe-Johnson, A. (2008). Ad revenue slump rips through newspapers. *Financial Times.* Retrieved from: <http://www.ft.com/cms/s/0/749e9c0e-c61f-11dd-a741-000077b07658.html#axzz3j6wCAUm1>.

Effing, R., & Spil, T. A. M. (2016). The social strategy cone: Towards a framework for evaluating social media strategies. *International Journal of Information Management, 36*, 1−8.

Einwiller, S. A., & Steilen, S. (2015). Handling complaints on social network sites—An analysis of complaints and complaint responses on Facebook and Twitter pages of large US companies. *Public Relations Review, 41*, 195−204.

Ellison, N. B., Steinfield, C., & Lampe, C. (2007). The benefits of Facebook 'friends': Social capital and college students' use of online social network sites. *Journal of Computer-Mediated Communication, 12*, 1143−1168.

Erdem, T., & Swait, J. (1998). Brand equity as a signalling phenomenon. *Journal of Consumer Psychology, 7*(2), 131−157.

Ferrara, E., Interdonato, R., & Tagarelli, A. (2014). Online popularity and topical interests through the lens of Instagram. *HT '14 Proceedings of the 25th ACM conference on Hypertext and social media*, 24−34.

Fieseler, C., & Fleck, M. (2013). The pursuit of empowerment through social media: Structural social capital dynamics in CSR-blogging. *Journal of Business Ethics, 118*, 759−775.

Fournier, S. (1998). Consumers and their brands: Developing relationship theory in consumer research. *Journal of Consumer Research, 24*(4), 343−373.

Franke, N., Keinz, P., & Steger, C. J. (2009). Testing the value of customization: When do customers really prefer products tailored to their preferences? *Journal of Marketing, 73*(5), 103−121.

Fuchs, C., Prandelli, E., & Schreier, M. (2010). The psychological effects of empowerment strategies on consumers' product demand. *Journal of Marketing, 74*(1), 65−79.

Fulgoni, G. M. (2014). Omni-channel retail insights and the consumer's path-to-purchase: How digital has transformed the way people make purchasing decisions. *Journal of Advertising Research, 54*(4), 377−380.

Galeotti, A., & Goyal, S. (2009). Influencing the influencers: A theory of strategic diffusion. *Journal of Economics, 40*(3), 509−532.

Gebauer, J., Fuller, J., & Pezzei, R. (2013). The dark and the bright side of co-creation: Triggers of member behaviour in online innovation communities. *Journal of Business Research, 66*, 1516−1527.

Gensler, S., Völckner, F., Liu-Thompkins, Y., & Wiertz, C. (2013). Managing brands in the social media environment. *Journal of Interactive Marketing, 27*(4), 242−256.

Giglietto, F., Rossi, L., & Bennato, D. (2012). The open laboratory: Limits and possibilities of using Facebook, Twitter, and YouTube as a research data source. *Journal of Technology in Human Services, 30*(3−4), 145−159.

Go, E., & You, K. H. (2016). But not all social media are the same: Analyzing organizations' social media usage patterns. *Telematics and Informatics, 33*(1), 176−186.

Golbeck, J. (2015). *Introduction to social media investigation: A hands-on approach.* Atlanta, GA: Elsevier.

Granovetter, M. S. (1973). The strength of weak ties. *American Journal of Sociology, 78*, 1360−1380.

Grieve, R., Indian, M., Witteveen, K., Tolan, G. A., & Marrington, J. (2013). Face-to-face or Facebook: Can social connectedness be derived online? *Computers in Human Behavior, 29*, 604−609.

Gronroos, C. (1994). From marketing mix to relationship marketing: Towards a paradigm shift in marketing. *Management Decision, 29*(1), 7−13.

Gu, F., & Widen-Wulff, G. (2010). Scholarly communication and possible changes in the context of social media: A Finnish case study. *The Electronic Library, 29*(6), 762−776.

Gyrd-Jones, R. I., & Kornum, N. (2013). Managing the co-created brand: Value and cultural complementarity in online and offline multi-stakeholder ecosystems. *Journal of Business Research, 66*, 1484−1493.

Hajli, N., & Sims, J. (2015). Social commerce: The transfer of power from sellers to buyers. *Technological Forecasting & Social Change, 94*, 350−358.

Hamill, J., Tagg, S., & Vescovi, A. S. (2010). Editorial: Special edition—New developments in online marketing. *Journal of Marketing Management, 26*(3−4), 181−186.

Hamilton, K., & Hewer, P. (2010). Tribal mattering spaces: Social-networking sites, celebrity affiliations, and tribal innovations. *Journal of Marketing Management, 26*(3), 271−289.

Hanna, R., Rohm, A., & Crittenden, V. L. (2011). We're all connected: The power of the social media ecosystem. *Business Horizons, 54*(3), 265−273.

Hansen, D. L. (2011). Exploring social media relationships. *On the Horizon, 19*(1), 43−51.

Harris, L., & Dennis, C. (2011). Engaging customers on Facebook: Challenges for e-retailers. *Journal of Consumer Behaviour, 10*(6), 338−346.

He, W., Wu, H., Yan, G., Akula, V., & Shen, J. (2015). A novel social media competitive analytics framework with sentiment benchmarks. *Information & Management, 53*(7), 801−812.

Hennig-Thurau, T., Hofacker, C. F., & Bloching, B. (2013). Marketing the pinball way: Understanding how social media change the generation of value for consumers and companies. *Journal of Interactive Marketing, 27*, 237−241.

Hennig-Thurau, T., & Walsh, G. (2004). Electronic word-of-mouth: Consequences of and motives for reading customer articulations on the internet. *International Journal of Electronic Commerce, 8*(Winter), 51−74.

Hennig-Thurau, T., Gwinner, K. P., Walsh, G., & Gremler, D. D. (2004). Electronic word-of-mouth via consumer opinion platforms: What motivates consumers to articulate themselves on the internet? *Journal of Interactive Marketing, 18*(1), 38−52.

Hennig-Thurau, T., Malthouse, E. C., Friege, C., Gensler, S., Lobschat, L., Ranaswamy, A., et al. (2010). The impact of new media on customer relationships. *Journal of Service Research, 13*(3), 311−330.

Hill, S., Provost, F., & Volinsky, C. (2006). Network-based marketing: Identifying likely adopters of consumer networks. *Statistical Science, 21*(2), 256—276.

Hochman, N., & Manovich, L. (2013). Zooming into an Instagram city: Reading the local through social media. *First Monday, 18*(7), 1.

Hollenbaugh, E. E., & Ferris, A. L. (2014). Facebook self-disclosure: Examining the role of traits, social cohesion, and motives. *Computers in Human Behavior, 30*, 50—58.

Hong, F.-Y., Huang, D.-H., Lin, H.-Y., & Chiu, S.-L. (2014). Analysis of the psychological traits, Facebook usage, and Facebook addiction model of Taiwanese university students. *Telematics and Informatics, 31*, 591—606.

Hosseinmardi, H., Li, S., Yang, Z., Lv, Q., Rafiq, R.I., Han, R., et al. (2014). A comparison of common users across Instagram and Ask.fm to better understand cyberbullying. *BDCLOUD '14 Proceedings of the 2014 IEEE Fourth International Conference on Big Data and Cloud Computing*, pp. 355—362. Available from: http://dx.doi.org/10.1109/BDCloud.2014.87.

Howard, D. J., & Kerin, R. A. (2004). The effects of personalized product recommendations on advertising response rates: The "try this. It works!" technique. *Journal of Consumer Psychology, 14*(3), 271—279.

Hsieh, M.-Y. (2016). The most potential principles of social media. *Computers and Electrical Engineering*, 1—13, Article in Press.

Hu, Y., Manikonda, L., & Kambhampati, S. (2014). *What we Instagram: A first analysis of Instagram photo content and user types. Eighth International AAAI Conference on Weblogs and Social Media* (pp. 595—598). Ann Arbor, MI: The AAAI Press.

Hughes, D. J., Rowe, M., Batey, M., & Lee, A. (2012). A tale of two sites: Twitter vs. Facebook and the personality predictors of social media usage. *Computers in Human Behavior, 28*, 561—569.

Jansen, B. J., Zhang, M., Sobel, K., & Chowdury, A. (2009). Twitter power: Tweets as electronic word of mouth. *Journal of the American Society for Information Science and Technology, 60*(11), 2169—2188.

Joinson, A. N. (2001). Self-disclosure in computer-mediated communication: The role of self-awareness and visual anonymity. *European Journal of Social Psychology, 31*(2), 177—192.

Jurgens, M., Berthon, P., Edelman, L., & Pitt, L. (2016). Social media revolutions: The influence of secondary stakeholders. *Business Horizons, 59*, 129—136.

Kaplan, A. M., & Haenlein, M. (2010). Users of the world, unite! The challenges and opportunities of social media. *Business Horizons, 53*, 59—68.

Karapanos, E., Teixeira, P., & Gouveia, R. (2016). Need fulfillment and experiences on social media: A case on Facebook and WhatsApp. *Computers in Human Behavior, 55*, 888—897.

Karpf, D. (2012). Social science research methods in Internet time. *Information, Communication & Society, 15*(5), 639—661.

Kaufmann, P. J., & Stern, L. W. (1988). Relational exchange norms, perceptions of unfairness, and retained hostility in commercial litigation. *Journal of Conflict Resolution, 32*(September), 534—552.

Keller, K. L. (1999). Managing brands for the long run: Brand reinforcement and revitalization strategies. *California Management Review, 41*(3), 102—124.

Kietzmann, J. H., Hermkens, K., McCarthy, I. P., & Silvestre, B. S. (2011). Social media? Get serious! Understanding the functional building blocks of social media. *Business Horizons, 54*(3), 241—251.

Killian, G., & McManus, K. (2015). A marketing communications approach for the digital era: Managerial guidelines for social media integration. *Business Horizons, 58*, 539—549.

Kim, A. J., & Johnson, K. K. P. (2016). Power of consumers using social media: Examining the influences of brand-related user-generated content on Facebook. *Computers in Human Behavior, 58*, 98—108.

Kim, E., Sung, Y., & Kang, H. (2014). Brand followers' retweeting behaviour on Twitter: How brand relationships influence brand electronic word-of-mouth. *Computers in Human Behavior, 37*, 8−25.

Kim, S., & Park, H. (2013). Effects of various characteristics of social commerce (s-commerce) on consumers' trust and trust performance. *International Journal of Information Management, 33*(2), 318−322.

Kotler, P., & Keller, K. L. (2012). *Marketing management* (15th ed.). Upper Saddle River, NJ: Prentice Hall.

Kwok, L., & Yu, B. (2013). Spreading social media messages on Facebook: An analysis of restaurant business-to-consumer communications. *Cornell Hospitality Quarterly, 54*(1), 84−94.

Labrecque, L. I. (2014). Fostering consumer-brand relationships in social media environments: The role of parasocial interaction. *Journal of Interactive Marketing, 28*, 134−148.

Labrecque, L. I., Esche, J. V. D., Mathwick, C., Novak, T. P., & Hofacker, C. F. (2013). Consumer power: Evolution in the digital age. *Journal of Interactive Marketing, 27*(4), 257−269.

Labrecque, L. I., Markos, E., & Milne, G. R. (2011). Online personal branding: Processes, challenges, and implications. *Journal of Interactive Marketing, 25*(1), 37−50.

Lampe, C., Ellison, N. B., & Steinfield, C. (2008). *Changes in use and perception on Facebook. Proceedings of the 2008 ACM Conference on Computer Supported Cooperative Work* (pp. 721−730). New York, NY: ACM. Available from: http://dx.doi.org/ 10.1145/1460563.1460675.

Lange, F., & Dahlen, M. (2003). Let's be strange: Brand familiarity and Ad-brand incongruency. *Journal of Product and Brand Management, 12*(6/7), 449−461.

Lanier, J. (2010). *You are not a gadget: A manifesto.* New York, NY: Alfred A. Knopf.

Larson, K. & Watson, R. (2011). The value of social media: Toward measuring social media strategies. In *Thirty Second International Conference on Information Systems* (pp. 1−18). Shanghai.

Lauterborn, B. (1990). New marketing litany: Four Ps passé: C-words take over. *Advertising Age, 61*(41), 26.

Lee, E., Ahn, J., & Kim, Y. J. (2014). Personality traits and self-presentation at Facebook. *Personality and Individual Differences, 69*, 162−167.

Lee, E.-J., & Kim, Y. W. (2014). How social is Twitter use? Affiliative tendency and communication competence as predictors. *Computers in Human Behavior, 39*, 296−305.

Li, C. (2016). When does web-based personalization really work? The distinction between actual personalization and perceived personalization. *Computers in Human Behavior, 54*, 25−33.

Li, Z., & Li, C. (2014). Twitter as a social actor: How consumers evaluate brands differently on Twitter based on relationship norms. *Computers in Human Behavior, 39*, 187−196.

Litt, E. (2012). Knock, knock. Who's there? The imagined audience. *Journal of Broadcasting Electronic Media, 56*(3), 330−345.

Little, B. (2012). Identifying key trends in sales−from a training perspective. *Industrial and Commercial Training, 44*(2), 103−108.

Loiacono, E. T. (2015). Self-disclosure behavior on social networking web sites. *International Journal of Electronic Commerce, 19*(2), 66−94.

Lonnqvist, J.-E., & Deters, F.-G. (2016). Facebook friends, subjective well-being, social support, and personality. *Computers in Human Behavior, 55*, 113−120.

Lonnqvist, J.-E., & Itkonen, J. V. A. (2016). Homogeneity of personal values and personality traits in Facebook social networks. *Journal of Research in Personality, 60*, 24−35.

Luo, X., & Zhang, J. (2013). How do consumer buzz and traffic in social media marketing predict the value of the Firm? *Journal of Management and Information Systems, 30*(2), 213−238.

Luo, X. (2009). Quantifying the long-term impact of negative word of mouth on cash flows and stock prices. *Marketing Science, 28*(1), 148−165.

Malik, A., Dhir, A., & Nieminen, M. (2016). Uses and gratifications of digital photo sharing on Facebook. *Telematics and Informatics, 33*, 129−138.

Malthouse, E. C., Haenlein, M., Skiera, B., Wege, E., & Zhang, M. (2013). Managing customer relationships in the social media era: Introducing the social CRM house. *Journal of Interactive Marketing, 27*(4), 270−280.

Mangold, W. G., & Faulds, D. J. (2009). Social media: The new hybrid element of the promotion mix. *Business Horizons, 52*(4), 357−365.

Marder, B., Slade, E., Houghton, D., & Archer-Brown, C. (2016). "I like them, but won't 'like' them": An examination of impression management associated with visible political party affiliation on. *Computers in Human Behavior, 61*, 280−287.

Marwick, A. E., & Boyd, D. (2011). I tweet honestly, I tweet passionately: Twitter users, context collapse, and the imagined audience. *New Media & Society, 13*(1), 114−133.

Mathwick, C. (2002). Understanding the online consumer: A typology of online relational norms and behavior. *Journal of Interactive Marketing, 16*(1), 40−55.

Mathwick, C., Wiertz, C., & De Ruyter, K. (2008). Social capital production in a virtual P3 community. *Journal of Consumer Research, 34*(6), 832−849.

McCarthy, J. E. (1960). *Basic marketing. A managerial approach.* Homewood, IL: Richard D. Irwin.

Morgan, R. M., & Hunt, S. D. (1994). The commitment-trust theory of relationship marketing. *Journal of Marketing, 58*(July), 20−38.

Muniz, A. M., & O'Guinn, T. C. (2001). Brand community. *Journal of Consumer Research, 27*(4), 412−432.

Naaman, M., Boase, J., & Lai, C.-H. (2010). *Is it really about me? Message content in social awareness streams.* Proceedings of the 2010 ACM Conference on Computer Supported Cooperative Work (pp. 189−192). Savannah, GA: Association for Computing Machinery. Available from: http://dx.doi.org/10.1145/1718918.1718953.

Navarro-Bailon, M. A. (2012). Strategic consistent messages in cross-tool campaigns: Effects in brand image and brand attitude. *Journal of Marketing Communications, 18*(3), 189−202.

Ng, C. & Wang, C. (2013). Best practices in managing social media for business. In *Thirty Fourth International Conference on Information Systems* (pp. 1−11). Milan.

Ngai, E. W. T., Tao, S. S. C., & Moon, K. K. L. (2015). Social media research: Theories, constructs, and conceptual frameworks. *International Journal of Information Management, 35*, 33−44.

Nicholas, D., & Rowlands, I. (2011). Social media use in the research workflow. *Information Services and Use, 31*(1-2), 61−83.

Nitzan, I., & Libai, B. (2011). Social effects on customer retention. *Journal of Marketing, 75*(6), 24−38.

Noar, S. M., Harrington, N. G., & Aldrich, R. S. (2009). The role of message tailoring in the development of persuasive health communication messages. In C. S. Beck (Ed.), *Communication yearbook 33* (pp. 73−133). New York, NY: Routledge.

Papacharissi, Z. (2009). The virtual geographies of social networks: A comparative analysis of Facebook, LinkedIn and A Small World. *New Media & Society, 1*(1/2), 199−220.

Parise, S., Guinan, P.J., & Weinberg, B.D. (2008). The secrets of marketing in a web 2.0 world. *The Wall Street Journal.* 15 December. Retrieved from: <http://www.wsj.com/articles/SB122884677205091919>.

Peters, K., Chen, Y., Kaplan, A. M., Ognibeni, B., & Pauwels, K. (2013). Social media metrics—A framework and guidelines for managing social media. *Journal of Interactive Marketing, 27*(4), 281−298.

Pickton, D., & Broderick, A. (2004). *Integrated marketing communications*. Essex: Pearson Education Limited.

Putrevu, S., & Lord, K. R. (2003). Processing internet communications: A motivation, opportunity, and ability framework. *Journal of Current Issues and Research in Advertising, 25*(1), 45−59.

Raacke, J., & Bonds-Raacke, J. (2008). MySpace and Facebook: Applying the uses and gratifications theory to exploring friend-networking sites. *Cyberpsychology & Behavior, 11*(2), 169−174.

Rathore, A. K., Ilavarasan, P. V., & Dwivedi, Y. (2016). Social media content and product co-creation: An emerging paradigm. *Journal of Enterprise Information Management, 29*(1), 7−18.

Ryan, T., & Xenos, S. (2011). Who uses Facebook? An investigation into the relationship between the Big Five, shyness, narcissism, loneliness, and Facebook usage. *Computers in Human Behavior, 27*, 1658−1664.

Sanderson, R. (2007). YouTube, Wikipedia Storm into 2006 top brand ranking. *Reuters, 26*(January). Retrieved from: <http://www.reuters.com/article/2007/01/26/us-brands-global-winners-idUSL2430497120070126>.

Sashi, C. M. (2012). Customer engagement, buyer-seller relationships, and social media. *Management Decision, 50*(2), 253−272.

Schembri, S., Merrilees, B., & Kristiansen, S. (2010). Brand consumption and narrative of self. *Psychology and Marketing, 27*(6), 623−638.

See-To, E. W. K., & Ho, K. K. W. (2014). Value co-creation and purchase intention in social network sites: The role of electronic word-of-mouth and trust—A theoretical analysis. *Computers in Human Behavior, 31*, 182−189.

Seidman, G. (2013). Self-presentation and belonging on Facebook: How personality influences social media use and motivations. *Personality and Individual Differences, 54*, 402−407.

Shankar, V., & Hollinger, M. (2007). Online advertising: Current scenario and emerging trends. *Marketing Science Institute Report*, 07−206.

Shimizu, K. (1989). *Advertising theory and strategies. (Japanese)* (1st ed.). Tokyo: Souseisha.

Silva, T. H., Melo, P. O., Almeida, J. M., Salles, J., & Loureiro, A. A. (2013). A picture of instagram is worth more than a thousand words: Workload characterization and application. *Computing in Sensor Systems (DCOSS), IEEE International Conference.* May 20−23.

Smith, A. N., Fischer, E., & Yongjian, C. (2012). How does brand-related user-generated content differ across YouTube, Facebook, and Twitter? *Journal of Interactive Marketing, 26*, 102−113.

Sohn, D. (2014). Coping with information in social media: The effects of network structure and knowledge on perception of information value. *Computers in Human Behavior, 32*, 145−151.

Stelzner, M. (2015). Social media marketing industry report: How marketers are using social media to grow their business. *Social Media Examiner*. Retrieved June 6, 2015 from:<http://www.socialmediaexaminer.com/SocialMediaMarketingIndustryReport 2015.pdf>.

Stephen, A. T., & Toubia, O. (2010). Deriving value from social commerce networks. *Journal of Marketing Research, 47*(2), 215−228.

Steyn, P., Salehi-Sangari, E., Pitt, L., Parent, M., & Berthon, P. (2010). The social media release as a public relations tool: Intentions to use among B2B bloggers. *Public Relations Review, 36*(1), 87−89.

Strauss, J., & Frost, R. (2009). *E-Marketing*. 5th Edition. Upper Saddle River, NJ: Prentice Hall.

Strokes, R. (2009). *eMarketing: The Essential Guide to Online Marketing*. Cape Town, South Africa: Quirk eMarketing Ltd.

Talpau, A. (2014). The marketing mix in the online environment. *Bulletin of the Transilvania University of Brasov. Series V: Economic Sciences*, 7(2), 53−58.

Tang, J.-H., Chen, M.-C., Yang, C.-Y., Chung, T.-Y., & Le, Y.-A. (2016). Personality traits, interpersonal relationships, online social support, and Facebook addiction. *Telematics and Informatics*, 3, 102−108.

Tilley, E., & Cokley, J. (2008). Deconstructing the discourse of citizen journalism: Who says what and why it matters. *Pacific Journalism Review*, 14(1), 94−114.

Tobina, S. J., Vanmana, E. J., Verreynnea, M., & Saeria, A. K. (2015). Threats to belonging on Facebook: Lurking and ostracism. *Social Influence*, 10(1), 31−42.

Trusov, M., Bucklin, R. E., & Pauwels, K. (2009). Effects of word-of-mouth versus traditional marketing: Findings from an internet social networking site. *Journal of Marketing*, 73(September), 90−102.

Urista, M. A., Dong, Q., & Day, K. D. (2009). Explaining why young adults use MySpace and Facebook through uses and gratifications theory. *Human Communication*, 12(2), 215−229.

Van Zoonen, W., Verhoeven, J. W. M., & Vliegenthart, R. (2016). How employees use Twitter to talk about work: A typology of work-related tweets. *Computer in Human Behavior*, 55, 329−339.

Vigil, T. R., & Wu, D. (2015). Facebook users' engagement and perceived life satisfaction. *Media and Communication*, 3(1), 5−16.

Weinberg, B. D., & Berger, P. D. (2011). Connected Customer Lifetime Value: The impact of social media. *Journal of Direct, Data and Digital Marketing Practice*, 12(4), 328−344.

Weinberg, B. D., & Pehlivan, E. (2011). Social spending: Managing the social media mix. *Business Horizons*, 54, 275−282.

Weinberg, B. D., de Ruyter, K., Dellarocas, C., Buck, M., & Keeling, D. I. (2013). Destination social business: Exploring an organization's journey with social media, collaborative community and expressive individuality. *Journal of Interactive Marketing*, 27(4), 299−310.

Winer, R. S. (2009). New communications approaches in marketing: Issues and research directions. *Journal of Interactive Marketing*, 23, 108−117.

Wolf, R. D., Gao, B., Berendt, B., & Pierson, J. (2015). The promise of audience transparency. Exploring users' perceptions and behaviors towards visualizations of networked audiences on Facebook. *Telematics and Informatics*, 32, 890−908.

Yadav, M. S., de Valck, K., Hennig-Thurau, T., Hoffman, D. L., & Spann, M. (2013). Social commerce: A contingency framework assessing marketing potential. *Journal of Interactive Marketing*, 27, 311−323.

Yoo, J., Choi, S., Choi, M., & Rho, J. (2014). Why people use Twitter: Social conformity and social value perspectives. *Online Information Review*, 38(2), 265−283.

Zafarani, R., & Liu, H. (2016). Users joining multiple sites: Friendship and popularity variations across sites. *Information Fusion*, 28, 83−89.

Zywica, J., & Danowski, J. (2008). The faces of Facebookers: Investigating social enhancement and social compensation hypotheses; predicting Facebook and offline popularity from sociability and self-esteem, and mapping the meanings of popularity with semantic networks. *Journal of Computer-Mediated Communication*, 14(1), 1−34.

CHAPTER 3

Online Brand Communities

The social media environment has allowed the creation and recognition of niche groups, facilitated by the fragmentation and specialization of both consumers and brands that have been enabled by this new technological platform.

One such culmination of these fragmented consumers is within online communities, which allow consumers with similar interests to gather and discuss their opinions and thoughts and share information with each other. These brand communities provide the perfect opportunity for brands to monitor and engage with consumers to find out their needs and wants in order to create value for them.

This section will discuss online communities and their distinction from traditional offline brand communities, highlighting the varying definitions and terms used to describe these groups of consumers. Engagement and interaction are core components of social media communication that can be amplified in online brand community (OBC) environments, which is also discussed in detail. This is followed by an analysis of the new focus on heterogeneity, delocalization, and individualism within these communities, in addition to consumer's consumption values, characteristics, and motivations for using these online environments. Finally, the section ends with a discussion of the key points, recommendations for future research, and marketing practitioners.

3.1 THE IMPORTANCE OF OBCs

The shift to a relational many-to-many approach (Gummesson, 2002, 2006) of marketing means that its focus has drastically changed. Now concentrating on community aspects (Penaloza, Toulouse, & Visconti, 2012; Schau, Muñiz, & Arnould, 2009), this is clearly visible with the fast adaptation and utilization of social media by organizations and brands (Hennig-Thurau et al., 2010; Labrecque, Mathwick, Novak, & Hofacker, 2013). Culminating on various platforms around specific interests and brands (Weijo, Hietanen, & Mattila, 2014), they allow consumers to gain and express their identity (Belk, 1988, 2013). The focus on information and the development of consumer culture, aided by the Internet, helped facilitate the development of online entities that were previously only studied offline, such as that of communities (Brogi, 2014). The lack of geographical boundaries, speed, and reach of social media allow for individuals to group together based around specific brands or interests to share experiences and information. The two-way communication that social media facilitates means that essential resources can be shared in a way that is cost effective and insightful leading to a deeper understanding of what it is that consumers want (Muniz & O'Guinn, 2001). Consumers can now communicate with both brands and other consumers and it is this that makes it the perfect breeding ground for both learning and knowledge creation as a means of creating the best value for consumers (Chen, Xu, & Whinston, 2011; Di Maria & Finotto, 2008; Mathwick, Wiertz, & De Ruyter, 2008; Von Hippel, 2005). Created by both consumers and brands themselves, the unique aspects of social media make these communities the perfect environment for maintaining a brand and protecting its personality (Fournier & Avery, 2011). Branding strategies have been redirected toward ensuring engagement with consumers, and finding platforms that facilitate and nurture this engagement (Naylor, Lamberton, & West, 2012; Van Doorn et al., 2010; Verhoef, Reinartz, & Krafft, 2010). Online communities are adept at encouraging interaction between individuals that in turn will develop into engagement (Habibi, Laroche, & Richard, 2014), and thus provide a vital tool, enabling deeper insight into the consumers' logic.

As social media is heavily reliant on the connections made between consumers, these networks provide an environment for communication that enables these brand communities to thrive (Habibi et al., 2014). Groups and subgroups can be created that cater for the increasing fragmentation and niche bodies of consumers in the new digital world (Fieseler & Fleck, 2013; Kietzmann, Hermkens, McCarthy, & Silvestre, 2011), allowing brands to see the more individualized preferences of their consumers. Delving into these networks of consumers will provide both opportunities and threats for organizations and brands as consumers can gain access to and spread both positive and negative information quickly. This is made even more complicated by the fact that consumers are normally members of various communities, which again has been made easier by the social media environment. Understanding the mechanisms of these multiple memberships and utilizing them is crucial to marketing success. Habibi et al. (2014) say that these niche groups or subcommunities vary in their identities so providing support to them needs to be more strategic from a marketing perspective rather than just transferring old strategies onto these new more heterogeneous communities (Pan, Lu, & Gupta, 2014). According to Moran and Gossieaux (2010) there is a need to understand not only the aspects of these communities that make them distinct and unique, but also the characteristics of the consumers that use them. Online communities are a key tool for managing consumer relationships and establishing the new objectives that organizations are adopting as part of the transition into social media, such as engagement, sharing, collaboration, and conversation (Weinberg & Pehlivan, 2011).

These OBCs have changed the way that consumers interact, serving both business and social functions in an environment, which is relatively informal, fostering a sense of trust and relationship commitment—which are also two fundamental needs of successful e-commerce (Wu, Chen, & Chung, 2010). Not only does social media provide brands and organizations with opportunities to interact but it also gives them the opportunity to engage with consumers on a more personal level and get to know them outside of their consumer status. These online communities of consumption have forced managers to respond to the growing interaction and influence that consumers are subjected to (Thomas, Price, & Schau, 2013). Despite this, research around this has tended to focus on three areas: motivations of consumers to contribute (Bagozzi & Dholakia, 2002; Dholakia, Bagozzi, & Pearo, 2004; Hennig-Thurau, Gwinner, Walsh, & Gremler, 2004; Wiertz & De Ruyter, 2007), the use of these communities to monitor what consumers are saying and using this information for strategy creation (Sawhney, Verona, & Prandelli, 2005), and the nature of these communities, with particular emphasis on their ability to affect consumer behavior (Algesheimer, Dholakia, & Hermann, 2005; Kozinets, 1999, 2001; McAlexander, Schouten, & Koenig, 2002; Muniz & O'Guinn, 2001; Muniz & Schau, 2005). Providing both managers and marketers with crucial information on how these communities can be utilized as an insightful tool (Godes et al., 2005).

3.2 TRADITIONAL VERSUS OBCs

Traditionally brand communities have three markers, which were identified by Muniz and O'Guinn (2001): shared consciousness (connection and sense of belongingness, shared collective sense of oneness), shared rituals and traditions (processes that help the community maintain its sense of self, helping the meaning of the community be reinforced through its own culture, rituals, and celebrations that establish boundaries, roles, and objectives), and obligations to society (the sense that members of the community should help one another through their obligation and recognizing what is right or wrong within the community).

These three markers have been readily researched in the online community environment with many finding support for their existence in this setting (Habibi et al., 2014; Laroche, Habibi, Richard, & Sankaranarayanan, 2012). Liao, Hsu, and To (2013) believe that the first marker, shared consciousness, is an area that is ripe for new insights and research, which is consistent with Brogi's (2014) notion that it is the most important marker within communities. However, there are several dimensions that vary amongst these online communities of consumption, including dispersion, focus, appeal, duration, orientation within the marketplace, resource dependency structure, and heterogeneity, the latter three of which are areas that are under researched (Thomas et al., 2013). However, all OBCs provide consumers with the means and opportunity to create value (Schau et al., 2009). One type of this value is in the form of helping to cocreate with brands and organizations (Vargo & Lusch, 2004), which gives them and consumers a chance to grow and help develop new products that are more relevant. This will ultimately cater for the increase in consumers' desire for personalization and provide a way to satisfy it (Thomke & Von Hippel, 2002; Von Hippel, 2005), which will increase purchase intent. Another form of this value is through the help and information other consumers can provide—thus helping other consumers make more informed decisions. Although the three markers of traditional communities can be found within the OBC environment, it can be argued that they are largely imagined communities, whereby the continuous social interactions and membership acknowledgment define the community (Anderson, 1983; Muniz & O'Guinn, 2001), rather than set markers. The boundaries that define the OBC could be one of the reasons that consumers are becoming more individualized in their use, as they are not subject to the traditional entry and exit barriers of traditional offline communities. It could be argued that although OBCs are a valid form of communication amongst consumers with similar interests they do not substitute real race to face interactions (Peris et al., 2002). However, in an offline communication with other consumers it is unlikely that someone's passion for a brand will come through as strongly as it would in the OBC environment as the focus and reason for communicating may be different.

OBCs differ from traditional communities because they have a commercial orientation, whereby consumers discuss a specific focal brand and share information that is intended to influence the other members of the group (Brogi, 2014). Various definitions have been outlined to define an OBC to distinguish it from the traditional brand communities that appear offline. Mainly based in the Marketing, Business, or Information Systems disciplines, these definitions generally encompass characteristics of group behavior, sharing of knowledge and information, common interests, and an online medium such as social media. Muniz and O'Guinn (2001, p. 412) describe brand communities as "specialized nongeographically bound community, based on a structured set of social relations among admirers of a brand." OBCs are based on computer-mediated environments where consumers connect through shared interests and enthusiasm for the activities of the community that can be initiated by consumers or the company/brand in question (Bagozzi & Dholakia, 2002; Koh & Kim, 2003; Kozinets, 1999; McAlexander et al., 2002; Poyry, Parvinen, & Malmivaara, 2013; Schau et al., 2009; Seraj, 2012). Li, Clark, and Wheeler (2013, p. 138) say OBCs are "those who have the same preference toward a certain brand, and who discuss, participate in, and pass on information about it." This definition is perhaps slightly more fitting as it does not focus on the community as being specialized, which is something that is becoming less prevalent within OBCs (Weijo et al., 2014). The juncture at which social media and brands collide, resulting in the creation of groups and communities, is also sometimes referred to as social media-based brand communities (Laroche et al., 2012), virtual communities (Liao et al., 2013), and OBCs (Laroche, Habibi, & Richard, 2013; Laroche et al., 2012).

3.3 ENGAGEMENT AND INTERACTION

With the new emphasis on personalization and the individualized consumer, marketers are trying to find ways that emphasize the more human and relational element of their brands (Chu & Kim, 2011; Jansen, Zhang, Sobel, & Chowdury, 2009; Lin & Pena, 2011). The characteristics of the OBC lend itself to being used for this purpose, as they allow bonds to be created with consumers (Habibi et al., 2014). Social media platforms are used for the purpose of interaction (with both other consumers and brands), which is reinforced by their engagement (Blazevic, Wiertz, Cotte, de Ruyter, & Keeling, 2014). It is the process of interaction that is vital in the creation of value for consumers, and therefore it can be assumed that interaction and engagement are suitable to be studied together to explain one another and contribute to the ongoing battle of learning how best to create value for consumers (Muniz & O'Guinn, 2001; Schau et al., 2009). If consumers interact more, then they are more likely to hold favorable opinions of brands as less interaction means less sense of belonging—therefore they may not feel the need to remain faithful to the community as they have no ties (Kwon, Kim, Sung, & Yoo, 2014) if they are not interacting. Frameworks for engagement are subject of problematic definitions within the literature, with a variety trying to conceptualize it and develop effective measurement strategies (e.g., Baldus, Voorhees, & Calantone, 2015; Hodis, Sriramachandramurthy, & Sashittal, 2015; Hollebeek, Glynn, & Brodie, 2014).

Consumers differ in their tendencies to interact online (Liu & Shrum, 2002), which can be related to the individual trait differences that make someone more or less likely to interact—an area that has recently gained momentum within social media studies. Blazevic et al. (2014) developed a scale for general online social interaction propensity (GOSIP) through both quantitative and qualitative studies, finding that GOSIP is specific to individual trait differences. They found that extraverts are more likely to engage in communication offline whereas introverts are more likely to interact with consumers in an online environment, which could be due to the anonymity characteristics of the Internet (Amichai-Hamburger, Wainapel, & Fox, 2002). This is reminiscent of Arndt (1967) who found that those more likely to engage in WOM are the more sociable. In addition, Wiertz and De Ruyter (2007) find that consumers who most frequently contribute to the community are driven by this commitment to the community rather than any commitment to the firm, meaning their inclination to interact online (or interaction propensity) and the informational value they receive is subject to how committed they are to the community. However, a recent study by Shao and Ross (2015) found that contributions to communities at first relied on entertainment, but later relied on their need for information. The development of parasocial interaction theory by Labrecque (2014), which like Blazevic et al. (2014) also used a multimethod approach, suggests that the theory may be used as a way to develop social media strategies. It is how consumers interact and what encourages them to become involved that poses the opportunity for future research that will be essential for marketers (Chung & Austria, 2010). Phang, Zhang, and Sutanto (2013) showed that the higher the interaction and participation of a consumer the more likely their consumption intentions will be enacted. The study utilized a student sample and therefore generalizability is limited and not applicable to all social media users. Many studies that have investigated interaction within social media environments have tended to be confined to one country such as Lee, Ho, and Chou (2015) based in Taiwan, which means the findings may not be replicable in other countries. These interactions allow for an environment that provides value in the form of support and can be an effective way to increase recommendations, return on investment, customer acquisition, and traffic as well as exposure for the brand (Hajli & Hajli, 2013; Jacobs, 2009; Stelzner, 2015; Zabin, 2009).

Yet not all organizations are aware of these differences within consumer's tendency to interact online and could therefore be designing strategies that are inappropriate (Blazevic et al., 2014). Consumers may have a presence online but not contribute directly, which leads to them "lurking" rather than "posting" (Wiertz & De Ruyter, 2007). Consumers who post content generally have a high GOSIP whereas consumers who just observe, or lurk, are often considered to be low in this regard (Blazevic et al., 2014). The GOSIP scale may also be relevant at establishing the interaction between hedonic and utilitarian motivations of consumers (Blazevic et al., 2014). The development of scales such as GOSIP are crucial in determining consumers' willingness to interact and can help managers and marketers develop effective communication strategies that are designed to get more consumers interacting (Blazevic et al., 2014). If more consumers are interacting then they are getting involved with marketing practices thereby adding value for themselves and to the brand.

The majority of interaction research is focused on website interaction and the outcomes of this interaction (Van Noort, Voorveld, & Van Reijmersdal, 2012). The willingness to communicate model, although quite effective at determining likelihood of interacting in an offline setting, does not adequately interpret interactions within the online environment because of the geographical and temporal reach and differing levels of disclosure (Blazevic et al., 2014; McCroskey & Richmond, 1990; McKenna & Bargh, 2000; Mehrabian, 1980).

It can be postulated that combining the OBCs with interaction and transactional behaviors can also help in the segmentation process so that profits are maximized through effective use of information for strategy (Ryals, 2008; Storbacka, 1997). De Valck, van Bruggen, and Wierenga (2009) looked at these communities from a specific marketing perspective, using a multimethod approach of surveys and netnography, finding that information shared within these communities has influencing power. These communities can help users cocreate brand messages and products for themselves. Although Dong and Wu (2015) found that the idea creation capability of online user innovation communities do not impact the value of the company, the implementation that is enabled by these communities does. Yet the ability of social media and these communities to facilitate interactions and bring people together should not be underestimated, as demonstrated by Ho (2015). In this study it was demonstrated that consumer and company identifications were enhanced by the interaction within the community. This addressed issues in previous studies that had only considered company—community identifications (Bhattacharya & Sen, 2003) or consumer—community identifications (Algesheimer et al., 2005). The findings were also consistent with Laroche et al. (2013) and Fournier and Avery (2011) about the ability of communities to facilitate interactions. These online communities of consumption have forced managers to respond to the growing interaction and influence that consumers are subjected to (Thomas et al., 2013).

Engagement, which is a core component to brand communities, enhances profitability and growth of sales and performance, having become a core component to strategies for many businesses in the social media age (Brodie, Ilic, Biljana, & Hollebeek, 2013). However, deciphering the key aspects of engagement and the scope and nature of such a big concept have become problematic over the years, especially now that the new online dynamic has to be incorporated (Brodie et al., 2013). Definitions to date have incorporated physical, cognitive, behavioral, and emotional elements (Patterson, Yu, & De Ruyter, 2006), participation and connection (Vivek, Beatty, & Morgan, 2012), context dependency (Hollebeek, 2011), instrumental and experiential value (Mollen & Wilson, 2010), iterative processes (Bowden, 2009), and consequences of engagement itself, e.g., trust, empowerment, satisfaction, and many others (e.g., Bowden, 2009). Brodie et al. (2013, p. 107) culminated all of the past definitions of engagement to come up with a working definition of engagement within an online community that covered all of the previously defined aspects of engagement:

Consumer engagement in a virtual brand community involves specific interactive experiences between consumers and the brand, and/or other members of the community. Consumer engagement is a context-dependent, psychological state characterized by fluctuating intensity levels that occur within dynamic, iterative engagement processes. Consumer engagement is a multidimensional concept comprising cognitive, emotional, and/or behavioural dimensions, and plays a central role in the process of relational exchange where other relational concepts are engagement antecedents and/or consequences in iterative engagement processes within the brand community.

Engagement can be associated with an orientation to approach things rather than avoid them and has also been linked to individual traits of proactivity, conscientiousness, and those who are internally driven (Smith, Wagaman, & Handley, 2009). However, it must then be asked whether consumers who do not proactively seek out experiences and tend to stay in the background, or lurk, in the online environment are also engaged (Blazevic et al., 2014). Their lack of interaction may contribute to them being less engaged than more interactive consumers, yet it is unclear whether their engagement can be achieved through different means. Engagement is a "behavioral manifestation" (Verhoef et al., 2010, p. 247) and the behaviors that consumers now use as a way to communicate with the brand were unheard of just a few years ago (Gummerus, Liljander, Weman, & Pihlstrom, 2012). Therefore it is evident that there are still many avenues unexplored about how consumers engage with brands through these online communities and the nature of this phenomenon including measurement (Gummerus et al., 2012; Weinberg & Berger, 2011). Consumer's engagement is highly dependent on the context in which it is undertaken and therefore can be considered a subjective phenomenon depending on the stance of the consumer (Brodie, Hollebeek, Biljana, & Ilic, 2011). The user-generated content consumers share on social media is laced with emotion (Rathore, Ilavarasan, & Dwivedi, 2016), which is a key component of engagement within brand communities (Chu, 2011; Davis, Piven, & Breazeale, 2014).

According to Dellarocas, Gao, and Narayan (2010) engagement within communities is similar to the engagement that can be observed through word of mouth (WOM). Taking this approach, Dichter's (1966) 4 WOM involvement communicators—product, message, self, and other involvement—can be interpreted as being applicable to the community environment. Product and message involvement has been the subject of quite a few recent studies, however, self and other involvement has not received as much attention. This seems questionable considering it has been found that the self is directly linked to engagement (Blazevic et al., 2014). If engagement in brand communities is similar to engagement in WOM it can be assumed that the reasons behind this engagement are also similar, e.g., self-enhancement, innovativeness and opinion leadership, ability and self-efficacy, individuation, neuroticism, and altruism (Dellarocas et al., 2010; King, Racherla, & Bush, 2014). Failure to address engagement within strategy will result in brands lagging behind other competitors and neglecting the huge potential that could improve strategy (Grensing-Pophal, 2009). Raies, Muhlbacher, and Gavard-Perret (2015) found that engagement within a community does not necessarily facilitate loyalty toward the brand. They show that varying commitment levels combined with engagement can lead to loyalty. Most importantly they find that lack of commitment to the community does not necessarily mean disloyalty.

Much research around relationships has focused on engagement and how this can be facilitated by social media. Habibi et al. (2014) and Davis et al. (2014) both identified five aspects of brand communities including a relational or social aspect linking the importance of these settings to relationship development. However, the study by Davis et al. (2014) used a grounded theory approach with a focus group and interviews, whereas Habibi et al. (2014) utilized a netnographical approach over a period of 2 years, which would have provided a more unobtrusive and natural environment of which to study online behaviors (Kozinets, de Valck, Wojnicki, & Wilner, 2010). Gummerus et al. (2012) who also looked at engagement within the OBC setting utilized a survey method and found that engagement has a positive effect on social, economic, and entertainment relationship benefits. Sashi (2012) used the new interest in the interactive social media features to explore engagement even further, with the development of a seven-stage customer engagement cycle. By studying these OBCs researchers are able to observe their behaviors without intruding so as to single out the more engaged consumers and their behaviors (Libai, 2011). A stream of research has emerged in this area, considering the differences between marketer- and consumer-created communities and content (e.g., Ding, Phang, Lu, Tan, & Sutanto, 2014; Lee, Kim, & Kim, 2011).

3.4 HETEROGENEITY, DELOCALIZATION, AND INDIVIDUALIZED CONSUMERS IN OBCs

The merging of interests and online communities, facilitated by the characteristics of social media, makes the multiple membership factor a key player in trying to define the structure and processes within brand communities. They can no longer be considered single homogeneous entities but must be looked at as a culmination of people who use and interpret what they see as a way to facilitate their knowledge and use this in other communities, perhaps increasing their status (Weijo et al., 2014). This shift in power from brands to the consumer has not only affected engagement but also brand meaning due to the collaborative co-creation processes consumers are now involved in (Brodie et al., 2013). Another way to refer to these communities is something which Joseph, Lid, and Suthers (2007) refer to as transcendent communities, where consumers who span various communities are able to use the information that they gather and apply it to other situations to find things out, which is a great source of value for them (Joseph et al., 2007). Delving deeper into this diversified consumer can aid strategy development (Weijo et al., 2014) and thus continue the quest for effective communication in the age of social media. It would seem that these new individualistic consumers are not subject to the issues that affect traditional culture crossing such as emotional, symbolic, and pragmatic issues, but instead thrive at the chance to be able to flit from community to community (Davies & Fitchett, 2003; Weijo et al., 2014). This may be because acculturation can occur and thus they are adept to learning new cultures (Evans, Jamal, & Foxall, 2009). However, the post-modern consumer, according to Simmons (2008), although craves individualism does not get this through communities with multiple interests, which contradicts recent findings by Weijo et al. (2014). Future research needs to look at the differences between the newly forming heterogeneous communities and the original homogeneous community (Pan et al., 2014). Thomas et al. (2013) say that by assuming that brand communities can be categorized by one interest and basing a definition on this assumption can lead to research myopia, which could also point out the need for a newly recognized definition of an OBC. Although consumers may benefit from the collaboration and information sharing between communities, it is still difficult to give these communities a distinct identity whilst maintaining a collaborative environment (Joseph et al., 2007). This is especially true with the high rates of fragmentation into smaller communities created by the new needs of personalization from individualistic consumers (Bruckman & Jensen, 2002). Therefore in order for these communities to succeed, it is the consumers themselves that need to facilitate their successful continuation (Levina & Vaast, 2005). Joseph et al. (2007) are some of the first to highlight the need for a good technological platform to enable consumers to access the full potential of being able to span collective communities. Wenger (1998) used the term participation—reification duality to describe the value that is created from the participation in a technological environment. Thus, the social media environment is the perfect place where consumers are able to access the technology needed to be able to use various communities simultaneously without upsetting the collective of each one.

A recent study by Weijo et al. (2014) has found that online communities of consumption are becoming increasingly delocalized through individualistic tendencies, allowing for community members to use the communities in an overlapping manner. Delocalization can be described as that which "manifests itself in significant overlap between communities and consequently freer movement of participants between them" (Weijo et al., 2014, p. 2072). The notion of delocalization is in a similar stream to Thomas et al. (2013) who stressed the idea of the heterogeneous community. A heterogeneous community is a culmination of a set of diverse entities including, most importantly, consumers and producers, as well as both social and economic resources (Thomas et al., 2013). This type of community can be based on actor–network theory, which posits that any form of social unit is a "patterned network[s] of heterogeneous materials" (Law, 1992, p. 381). The differing types of community such as homogeneous and heterogeneous and how they link together or relate to one another presents a gap within the literature previously identified by Canniford (2011). The weak ties that are found amongst consumers who communicate through the Internet and within OBCs, although not as strong as real life face-to-face interactive ties, could be the facilitating factor in the delocalization of online communities. This is because it is these weak ties that are more effective at connecting people across groups aiding the transference of information across networks (Brown & Reingen, 1987; Frenzen & Nakamoto, 1993; Reingen & Kernan, 1986). However, some believe that it is stronger ties, which have a much more influential impact on consumer behavior, with scholars such as Sun, Youn, Wu, and Kuntaraporn (2006) emphasizing the importance of strong social ties in the eWOM communication process. In addition, the continued pressure of normative influence on consumers may have forced consumers to detach themselves from the group, which also alters brand–choice congruence (Hoyer, MacInnis, & Pieters, 2013).

The majority of consumption community research is focused on the homogeneous features that unite communities such as shared norms and values (Muniz & O'Guinn, 2001); however, these shared assets that are present amongst individuals do not take into account the complex networked nature of communities, which are influenced by both experiential and external factors (Thomas et al., 2013). The hedonic benefits that OBCs can provide, such as entertainment values, that are not directly linked to any actual marketing of a product or brand can make consumers become more interested in browsing the site on a more regular basis. This will increase the likelihood of them being introduced to relevant information or products (Gummerus et al., 2012)—thus indirectly influencing their purchase intent. Authors have suggested that if heterogeneity is present within communities it can be an unruly source of tension that forces the community into a destabilizing state (DeLanda, 2006; Latour, 2005). However, a recent study by Thomas et al. (2013) has found that heterogeneity can actually be a positive contributing factor to online community survival, because the benefits the individuals receive from the community (such as social and economic) motivate the consumers to coexist alongside each other. This avoids the fragmentation of the community and therefore encourages its continuity. Not only does research focus on the homogeneous aspects of communities, but it stresses commitment levels and the level of expertise an individual has in their identity, which posits a static view of the "ideal" community member (Fox, 1987; Schouten & McAlexander, 1995). Davis et al. (2014) says that it is important to match the brand with the identities of consumers rather than to the identity of the brand as this can help provide value in terms of acknowledging the multifaceted self (Belk, 2013).

Divakaran (2013) suggested that when consumers contribute ideas to an online community with regard to a product or service, a network builds up around each idea. However, this principle needs to be reconsidered given that they are becoming more heterogeneous in nature (Weijo et al., 2014). Idea generation is the key to progressing with new innovative products that can specifically cater for what the consumer wants, thus increasing their likelihood of engaging with the product or brand and subsequent purchases (Divakaran, 2013). In another paper by Divakaran (2012) he suggested that the variables observed in the online environment are a reflection of what is happening in the offline world, therefore more understanding is needed as to whether this idea network is also replicated offline.

The new era of postmodern consumers has seen the reemergence of tribal behavior whereby consumers identify with a particular group or style (Evans et al., 2009). This is especially important as Cova and Cova (2002) in their definition of a tribe, define the consumers who occupy them as heterogeneous, which imply a degree of independence. Therefore it can be asserted that the new delocalization of online communities is a result of the postmodern consumers and this reemergence of tribalism that has led consumers to be more individualistic in their tendencies to engage in online communities (Evans et al., 2009; Weijo et al., 2014). Fragmentation has occurred, leading to multiple memberships that are in a state of constant change, also dividing collective meanings (Evans et al., 2009; Firat & Shultz, 1997). A recent study by Pan et al. (2014) found that as well as a sense of belongingness, perceived uniqueness is important for newcomers entering new online communities, which could add further strength to the new individualized consumer in the postmodern era. In addition, the study also found that surface-level dissimilarity is more important for newcomers than deep-level dissimilarity, which again could provide evidence that consumers are moving between communities and thus not needing to fulfill deeper level needs (Pan et al., 2014). By delving into the use of OBCs brands can enhance value creating practices and encourage brand loyalty (Laroche et al., 2013), which will affect their purchase intentions. The development of culture within the social media environment is discussed in more detail in the Chapter 4, Culture.

A study by Wu et al. (2010) regarding trust within online community members found that there was no relationship between commitment and stickiness, which could indicate more evidence for delocalization as even though consumers are committed this does not mean they will remain loyal to the one community. With stickiness being a direct result of consumer trust toward a brand (Liu, Marchewka, Lu, & Yu, 2004) it could be construed that there is a lack of trust within online communities, which has facilitated the development of the individual consumer and heterogeneous communities. Consumers could be developing the view that these online communities are best for gaining information and communication rather than any deeper commitment (Wu et al., 2010). Liao et al. (2013) acknowledges this sharing culture, believing that it is the best way for consumers to develop a positive attitude to the brand.

One of the major problems with OBCs is the issue of gaining new consumers in the community and sustaining the current consumers who are already joined (Ding et al., 2014). One of the ways that brands are trying to diversify their online presence is by having both marketer- and consumer-generated content within brand communities. However, a recent study by Ding et al. (2014) has found that consumer-generated and social marketer-generated content is best for stimulating growth but product-related, marketer-generated content does not have the same effect. This could be due to consumers perceiving user-generated content as more trustworthy and reliable than content directly from the brand, and points to the need for a collaboration approach within OBCs (Chung & Austria, 2010; Ding et al., 2014; Foux, 2006). Consumer-created OBCs have participants based on the likeability of the brand and the utilities it can provide to the consumer, whereas the marketer-created OBC has participants through their incentive and convenience seeking benefits (Sung, Kim, Kwon, & Moon, 2010).

The plethora of digital platforms that we now have access to has allowed us to become connected on a much larger scale and interact with people that we would otherwise not have had the chance to, especially those who have the same consumption interests. Although we have become more individualized in our approaches to consumption and OBC use, this new networked society brings with it clear implications of a much more connected environment where we have developed a larger yet more distinct sense of community (Putnam, 2000). This is something that has been termed "network individualism" (Belk, 2013, p. 496; Wellman, 2001) as we are indeed becoming more individualized as a whole, rather than one by one (Turkle, 2011).

3.5 CONSUMPTION VALUES

The personalization and newfound empowerment of consumers now means that consumers have specific needs and wants that they assume brands should meet. The five sources model proposed by Davis et al. (2014) is based on these needs and the motivation consumers have for these specific needs to be met by brands. The model identifies five core consumption values within brand communities on social media: functional, emotional, self-oriented, social, and relational. The functional value relates to the communities' ability to provide information and address problems, often when a failure is experienced, through reduced effort and cost savings, gaining knowledge through the sharing of others experiences and allowing the brand to receive feedback that could result in the implementation of change (Aksoy et al., 2011; Davis et al., 2014; Dholakia et al., 2004). The emotional value relates to the satisfaction that is achieved through interaction with other consumers creating a valued experience and enjoyment that provides support for gaps in a consumers' life or aspirations they have (Davis et al., 2014; Rosenbaum, 2008). The self-oriented value reflects the communities' ability to help consumers craft their identities through self-presentation and self-branding, allowing them to express themselves, which enables value creation and aids self-worth; often consumers will engage with brands based on their ability to reflect their own sense of self; if a brand is congruent with this then the consumer will be more likely to engage (Berger & Iyengar, 2013; Davis et al., 2014; Ho & Dempsey, 2010; Nambisan & Baron, 2010; Schouten, 1991). The social value conveys the social nature of communities and the collective culture they are built around, facilitating exchange, interaction, networking, and experiences (Davis et al., 2014; Gwinner, Gremler, & Bitner, 1998). The relational value refers to the community's ability to provide a brand with a personality on a more human level that is within reach of consumers and allows them to help in the co-creation process by providing the brand with deep insight and knowledge (Aaker, 1997; Avis, 2012; Davis et al., 2014; Seimiene, 2012).

These communities seem to have two levels of functions for consumers—a collective shared community function and a bolstering individualistic self-enhancing function (Davis et al., 2014)—both of which contribute to developing a stronger brand—consumer relationship (Kwon et al., 2014). Communities based on social media will help consumers become a more unified group, developing a sense of shared feelings, which connect them and gratify their emotional and functional needs. It will also help individuals define what the brand actually is and therefore help them identify what it is that this will add to their self-identity in addition to what the collective identity of the community will add to them and vice versa (Bagozzi & Dholakia, 2002; Davis, Buchanan-Oliver, & Brodie, 2000; Friedman, Abeele, & DeVos, 1992; Murray, 1991).

3.6 CONSUMER CHARACTERISTICS

It is the younger generation that has been subject to the integration of social media into their everyday lives without having a chance to know what previous generations experienced (Hardey, 2011). They experience consumer socialization from a young age, which is "the processes by which young people acquire skills, knowledge, and attitudes relevant to their functioning as consumers in the marketplace" (Ward, 1974, p. 2). The postmodern environment and the rise of social media has aided these consumers in becoming more individualistic.

Consumers within a brand community are what some would call more devoted consumers as they have taken the time to join a community, which is dedicated to a particular brand in order to communicate with these consumers, whether that be actively or passively (Anderson, 2005). Consumers become integrated into the identity of the brand and are deemed more loyal customers, giving brands the opportunity to collaborate with and disseminate information to these highly engaged consumers (Brown, Kozinets, & Sherry, 2003; Franke & Shah, 2003; Jin, Cheung, Lee, & Chen, 2009; McAlexander et al., 2002), even utilizing self-branding amongst the more regular users of the brand (Davis et al., 2014).

Anderson, Knight, Pookulangara, and Josiam (2014) found that information access and experiential shopping were shown to have an impact on loyalty; these are quite similar concepts in that experiential shopping and being involved in the experience includes communicating with other consumers and interacting through online channels. This interaction will lead to a transfer of information between consumers as it builds their knowledge base and gives them a deeper understanding of that particular brand or company. Both information and experience are both benefits of maintaining relationships in OBCs (Dholakia et al., 2004; Gummerus et al., 2012; Mathwick, Malhotra, & Rigdon, 2001). Loyalty will have a direct impact on the customer lifetime value (CLV) of consumers and therefore the development of a relationship, and the online nature of social media means that CLV is now more about connected CLV (CCLV) and the influence consumers have over other consumers (Weinberg & Berger, 2011). The relationship between information access and experiential shopping needs to be maintained in order to keep trust and loyalty in the company and so these consumers should not be neglected or their value to the company will be lost. Consumers who have a relationship with the company or brand are more likely to pass on their experiences and information to other consumers (aiding their information access) and this will therefore have a cyclic effect (De Vries, Gensler, & Leeflang, 2012; Naylor et al., 2012).

Some consumers will actively participate in the community by sharing thoughts and experiences whereas others will just read the content without contributing, which it is theorized could lead to higher engagement (Shang, Chen, & Liao, 2006). Gummerus et al. (2012) found that most of the consumers in OBCs were in fact passive rather than the active ones that create change and are noticed. Liao et al. (2013) agreed with this and called for more research into passive consumers who do not contribute, but also into consumers who used to contribute but do not anymore, i.e., ex-contributors. The more active users can be used as vehicles to create conversations online with other consumers, being utilized as influencers of a more social nature (Chu & Kim, 2011), which will help more consumers connect with one another. Marketers should thus leverage these highly involved consumers through group eWOM (Chang, Hsieh, & Tseng, 2013).

Although there are believed to be weaker ties in online communities due to the geographic dispersion of the community members, this seems to act as a way of bringing the consumers together on a deeper level (Constant, Sproull, & Kiesler, 1996; Granovetter, 1973; Tardini & Cantoni, 2005; Wellman, 2001). Marketers are able to take any message directly to their consumers rather than having to use an intermediary (Weinberg & Pehlivan, 2011). It can be argued that this deeper connection is one of the reasons that consumers engage in OBCs in the first place. Structural holes, whereby an individual acts as a bridge between others (weak ties), have been found to actually be beneficial as they are able to gather more information from multiple sources and thus elicit a certain degree of control (Burt, 1992, 1997). These communities provide a way for brands to maintain relationships, one of the fundamental implications from the revolution of social media, and this is done through the sharing of information and support, which help to fulfill emotional and psychological needs (Hennig-Thurau, Hofacker, & Bloching, 2013; Hennig-Thurau et al., 2010; Laroche et al., 2012; McAlexander et al., 2002), which Park, Kee, and Valenzuela (2009) identifies as socializing, entertainment, information seeking, and status seeking.

Consumers will join a brand community to help supplement their multiple selves and associate the symbols and meaning within the community to be congruent with their self (Schembri, Merrilees, & Kristiansen, 2010). It is the freedom that OBCs provide with its multitude of expressive outlets such as videos, writing, and pictures that can all be expressed through one platform that helps consumers in expressing and utilizing the benefits of the community. This content creation is not only a way for consumers to express themselves but also a way for brands to gain deep insightful knowledge about the users of their brand and thus priceless information that can help them to develop their strategies and improve the quality and value of their product or service (Arnone, Colot, Croquet, Geerts, & Pozniak, 2010), which will make consumers more inclined to purchase. Sensitive information can be revealed that is ordinarily inaccessible, thus allowing the marketer an in-depth look at the true selves of their consumers (De Valck et al., 2009). Customers are now cocreators and they help to produce and deliver their own value (Franke & Piller, 2004; Schau et al., 2009). Schau et al. (2009) identified four categories in which consumers help cocreate value: social networking, impressions management, community engagement, and brand use. All of these ways in which consumer's cocreate value for themselves are based on OBCs, and can create more loyal and trusting customers (Zhou, Zhang, Su, & Zhou, 2011). There is evidently a lack of focus on the economic benefits of utilizing OBCs, which is justified according to Gummerus et al. (2012), as it may be more productive to focus on the less tangible benefits, e.g., value creation, as a means of facilitating purchases in the long term rather than immediate future.

3.7 MOTIVATION

Motivations to join an OBC depend on the goal of the consumer (Ouwersloot & Odekerken-Schroder, 2008). In the case of brand communities on social media the consumer uses it for purposes of self-expression and identity creation (Veloutsou & Moutinho, 2009), with recent findings indicating the importance of understanding the role networks play in impression management (e.g., Marder, Slade, Houghton, & Archer-Brown, 2016). Consumers who are motivated to undertake something in the hopes of achieving a goal will put more time and energy into the process, resulting in greater effort to process information and make decisions (Hoyer et al., 2013). The greater the effort put in, the more consumers are likely to engage in deeper thought processes, which lead them to evaluate their decisions, causing them to have a greater understanding and comprehension and hence remember the overall process. However, motivation to achieve a goal is not a straight forward process and may be subject to biased perceptions by the consumer so that the information they gain is processed in a way that makes it possible to reach the conclusion they want to (Agrawal & Maheswaran, 2005; Jain & Maheswaran, 2000). This could be attributed to confirmation bias, whereby consumers focus only on the information that confirms what they already believe themselves (Hoyer et al., 2013). Cognitive dissonance, similar to balance theory, could play a role in altering motivational attitude, whereby if consumers hold two attitudes that are not the same about a particular thing then they will alter their attitude in a bid to try and gain homeostasis or equilibrium

(Evans et al., 2009; Festinger, 1957; Heider, 1958). Perception is also a crucial part of motivation where consumers can act with vigilance or defence in response to marketing messages (Evans et al., 2009). Gestalt theory is perhaps the best to describe the turbulent relationship between motivational and attitudinal aspects of consumer behavior as this theory proposes that nothing is seen in isolation, as other variables inevitably have an effect, no matter how big or small (Humphrey, 1924). This culmination of factors could explain why some consumers are becoming more individualistic in their tendencies to use online communities as they could be using them in a way in which they gain the information they want and then move onto another community to transfer the information or use the information as a way to help others and provide support (Weijo et al., 2014). This sort of behavior may be more visible when there is some threat to their self-esteem or when a particular goal is sought (DeMello, MacInnis, & Stewart, 2007; MacInnis & DeMello, 2005).

When a consumer becomes motivated and aroused or interested in a particular product or service then they are said to experience felt involvement (Celsi & Olson, 1988; Hoyer et al., 2013). However, this can be affected by the personal relevance and the degree to which something is congruent with the consumers' self-concept, values, and needs including utilitarian, hedonic, and social, as outlined by Yen (2013) as elements of perceived value as well as nonsocial, symbolic, and cognitive needs (Hoyer et al., 2013). Perceived risk can also play a part in determining the motivations of consumers, yet this varies between cultures. However, when placing this within the online community culture context, the new global dynamic, which allows communities to be based around loosely connected interests as speculated by Weijo et al. (2014), could mean that perceived risk is also becoming homogenized, with consumers perceiving the same risks regardless of context but based on a collective consensus.

The uses and gratifications theory proposed by Katz (1959) is often used to explain the motivations for social media use. Emphasizing "an object is best defined by its use" (Rubin, 2002, p. 527), the uses and gratifications theory looks at how individuals use particular media to gratify their needs, paying attention to both social and psychological aspects surrounding these. Originally heavily criticized for not distinguished between the gratifications an individual seeks and the gratifications an individual actually receives from their media use (Raacke & Bonds-Raacke, 2008), the theory was subsequently developed to identify gratifications sought and obtained as a way to address this weakness. One of the earliest categorizations of the motivations was by Katz, Gurevitch, and Haas (1973) who used five categories of needs—tension release, affective, cognitive, personal integrative, and social integrative. A more commonly used distinction that is readily adapted by researchers is McQuail's four categories of integration and social interaction, entertainment, information, and personal identity. Although developed specifically for traditional media, the theory has been adopted and applied to social media with many studies utilizing it as a basis to identify the motivations for using specific social media platforms. However, the classification of the motivations differ between studies with many forging their own categories based on the particular focus of the research. For example, Karnik, Oakley, Venkatanathan, Spiliotopoulos, and Nisi (2013) identified four main uses and gratifications of Facebook Groups—contribution, discovery, social interaction, and entertainment—whereas Johnson and Yang (2009) classified only two motives of social and informational use of Twitter. Whiting and Williams (2013) who looked at general social media use identified 10 uses and gratifications using a qualitative exploratory study: social interaction, information seeking, pass time, entertainment, relaxation, communicatory utility, convenience utility, expression of opinion, information sharing, and surveillance/knowledge about others. The majority of uses and gratifications studies focus on qualitative methods such as selfadministered questionnaires (e.g., Johnson & Yang, 2009; Karnik et al., 2013), which simply tell the researcher the motivations rather than any elaboration on this.

Consumers are active seekers of both advice and information, considering the opinions of others as important contributors to their decisionmaking abilities (De Valck et al., 2009). Some consumers may exhibit more influence over others than most. Known as opinion leaders (Chu & Kim, 2011) these individuals will be sought out based on their extensive knowledge and will intentionally divulge information as a way to persuade other consumers' preferences. Although it must be noted that other types of opinion-sharing behavior exist, such as opinion passing, which involves passing on information with no intention to influence the recipient of the message in any way (Hansen & Lee, 2013), and opinion seeking, where an individual wishes to seek out information (most likely from their network or opinion leaders) as a way to enable them to make a more informed decision (Flynn, Goldsmith, & Eastman, 1996). Online community involvement is a way of gaining the opinions, advice, and information from others, and the reasons that consumers become involved in these communities has received a lot of research attention.

A notable contribution is that of Bagozzi and Dholakia (2002) who found that consumers were motivated by both individual (positive anticipated emotions) and group (social identity) level motivations that they termed "we-intentions." Furthering this, Dholakia et al. (2004) describes five group-level motivations for consumers' participation within an OBC: purposive, self-discovery, entertainment, social enhancement, and interpersonal interactivity. However, recent research may indicate that this is not the case anymore, and the consumer has evolved into a more individualistic entity whose lack of participation is caused by the plethora of interests present in one community (Weijo et al., 2014). This lack of social identity within communities, which previously was a primary motivator (Bagozzi & Dholakia, 2002), may no longer be considered an issue because of this newfound individualistic nature. Although Dholakia et al. (2004) note that there is a distinction between small-group communities, which provide more social benefits to its members, and network-based, which provides more of an informational and instrumental value. Unlike in traditional community settings, normative influence, which is based on a system that operates around rewards and punishments, is less likely to have much influence as online reference group influence is based on norms that are communicated by the consumer or are self-reported (De Valck et al., 2009). It is clear that there is a distinction between hedonic (experiential) and utilitarian (functional) motivations for social media use identified in the literature.

Other theories that have been used to look at the underlying mechanisms of social media behavior include social exchange theory, which denotes a cost versus benefit type approach by the consumer (e.g., Wang, Yu, & Wei, 2012), and social cognitive theory (e.g., Oh & Syn, 2015), which explains a tendency for an individual to observe the outcomes of others' behavior to inform their behavior). The need to belong or sense of belongingness is also a favorite amongst researchers (e.g., Ma & Yuen, 2011), which is in line with Muniz and O'Guinn's identification of shared consciousness as the first community marker.

It is important to see how information flows in these online community environments in order to see how the mechanisms of the community work together, which leaves them open to be considered WOM networks (De Valck et al., 2009). Considering consumption communities as WOM networks also allows expansion into the motivations for contributing to the communities. Hennig-Thurau et al. (2004) found that the motivations for WOM match the motivations for contribution in communities, identifying social benefits as the strongest motivators. The information exchanged between these networks can give valuable insight to marketers by helping them to gain a better understanding of their consumers and thus be able to position their brand better or create a selling point that is distinctive and unique (De Valck et al., 2009) thus reacting to the more personalized preferences of the new media consumers.

3.8 DISCUSSION AND CONCLUDING POINTS

OBCs on social media provide a place for consumers to share their thoughts, feelings, and passions about a brand that they choose to engage with. Organizations and brands have begun to utilize this form of communication as a way of building relationships with consumers and developing insider knowledge on the needs and wants of consumers, which is crucial in the new social media environment (Naylor et al., 2012; Van Doorn et al., 2010; Verhoef et al., 2010). Sharing its grounding with traditional communities (Muniz & O'Guinn, 2001), online communities are not bound by spatial or temporal boundaries and can therefore connect millions of individuals in one place. The community provides value to the consumers who use it (Schau et al., 2009) in terms of functionality, socialization, relational, self-orientation, and emotional means (Davis et al., 2014).

Summary of Key Points

- OBCs can be a unique and insightful tool to gain insight into the opinions and experiences of consumers.
- Consumers are using OBCs in a more individualistic way, flitting between communities. This has facilitated the growth in heterogeneous communities and thus delocalization.
- Consumers create networks on social media and it is the strength of these ties that affect the transference of information from one community to another.
- Consumers are individually motivated to utilize certain social media platforms as well engage in certain social media behaviors such as sharing, which is evident within these OBCs.
- Engagement is one of the crucial ways that organizations and brands can utilize OBCs in order to facilitate relationship creation.

There needs to be a distinction between OBCs that are created by the consumer or the marketer. Using consumer-created communities can help deviate away from any negative stigma or associations with financially oriented marketer-created communities (Lee et al., 2011). This distinction should be taken into account when designing research frameworks as the participation inclination differences could affect the types of consumers present in each community. Although user-generated content is receiving quite a bit of attention, there appears to be a gap in research between the two different types of community—marketer and consumer generated—in terms of the motivators behind participation (Lee et al., 2011). Distinguishing between the balance of business and social is necessary, but more information is needed on how and when consumers prefer to be communicated with on these differing levels. A recent study by Gebauer, Fuller, & Pezzei (2013) found that sense of community mediated the relationship between co-creation, willingness to pay, and WOM. They also found that perceived fairness has a significant effect on WOM meaning, thus consumers may talk positively about a brand regardless of their purchase intent. This emphasizes the importance of the collective community aspect of consumers on their WOM behavior online.

The three community markers identified by Muniz and O'Guinn have embedded themselves firmly in the OBC literature. Yet investigating how consumers are behaving in these more fragmented groups is essential to understanding their behavior and increasing the likelihood of marketing communication effectiveness. Niche groups will have their own sense of belonging and sense of self that is distinct and unique to them, thus shared consciousness will embody different meaning for different communities. In addition, identifying distinctions between rituals and traditions to understand how they emphasize the consumers' sense of self and the meaning of the community is critical in the overall understanding of their behavior and how it is best to communicate with them through marketing messages. Brodie et al. (2013) believe that this calls for comparative research, in both online and offline communities. In addition, Pan et al. (2014) also find a gap in research regarding community diversity, which has only recently started to be filled.

Although the topic of engagement has become prevalent in the age of social media, research still needs to be done on what allows some communities to successfully engage participants (Schau et al., 2009). Future research should be used to find how the various platforms can be used as a means of engagement to develop the concept further (Sashi, 2012).

However, there is still much that needs to be done to discover the underlying dimensions of online engagement in its various contexts. Gummerus et al. (2012) and Habibi et al. (2014) also stress the need to investigate the interactions between company and community and how engagement mediates this relationship, particularly the richness these interactions can provide. Blazevic et al. (2014) believe that interactivity needs to be researched in more depth to identify the individual differences underlying consumer interaction; this is in addition to focus on intrinsic motivations to visiting an online platform. By finding out what helps facilitate consumer interaction marketers can understand their participative behaviors (Casaló, Flavián, & Guinalíu, 2008), which will contribute to the overall understanding of what makes consumers engage with specific brands (Van Doorn et al., 2010). There is also a particular need for research into engagement within consumer networks and the antecedents and consequences of these processes, in particular there is a visible gap in the literature regarding engagement within OBCs and the development of the concept as a whole (Brodie et al., 2013). In addition, Gummerus et al. (2012) highlights the lack of studies into engagement behaviors in a social media context, emphasizing a gap in the literature, which needs filling.

Key Points for Practitioners
- Practitioners need to be clear on the orientation their OBC will take. Will it be for social purposes, enabling user-generated content and discussion, or will it be for business purposes with marketer-generated content?
- Care should be taken to make sure OBCs on social media are actively managed, ensuring that they are utilized to their full potential and have a positive influence on consumer communications.
- Ensure that messages are carefully designed so that consumers can identify with the brand, if using automated responses, make sure that they do not appear automated.
- Increasing the experiential value of the community will encourage consumers to develop their identity, achievement, and competence, thus providing the necessary value that they crave.

Electronic word-of-mouth is what facilitates the continued interaction amongst OBC members, thus being able to use these models from this concept and adapt them for the sole purpose of explaining OBC engagement will be helpful at looking into interaction and engagement in this environment more closely to understand the participative behaviors. However, Gummerus et al. (2012) found that most of the consumers in OBCs were in fact passive rather than the active ones who create change and are noticed, which should also be considered in future research designs. OBCs have, in effect, their own culture which lends itself to the three community markers identified by Muniz and O'Guinn (2001), yet there exists a gap in the literature in terms of looking into the structural differences of these cultures and how consumers from "different cultures" process information and other eWOM from outside their culture (King et al., 2014). This merely adds to the need for exploration into the delocalization of online communities, as cultures are becoming blurred and the markers transcended (Weijo et al., 2014).

In addition, Thomas et al. (2013) say that there is also a gap regarding the whole notion of heterogeneous communities and their effect on communities in general. Weijo et al. (2014) suggest that future research should look at the influence of consumers who have many consumption interests and the effects this has on their brand community behavior. Habibi et al. (2014) also stress the need for research into the multiple memberships consumers can have. However, this need for looking at consumer's engagement in various communities is contradictory to Laroche et al. (2012) who are calling for more research into specific OBCs in the social media environment. Laroche et al. (2012) request compliments Gummerus et al. (2012) demand for an insight into the different types of brand communities that are in use including their dimensions and engagement behavior. Bagozzi and Dholakia (2006) claimed that both online and offline brand communities are similar because they share an identity that is well developed with joint engagement from consumers. However, this again can be challenged by Weijo et al. (2014) and Habibi et al. (2014) with their ideas of delocalization and multiple memberships.

It has been suggested that the brand personality within the social media environment is under researched and would benefit from exploration of how the personality affects the consumer self (Davis et al., 2014). In a similar stream, more research in terms of how consumer emotion affects intentions to pass on social media marketing messages and the effect these communities have on their emotions in terms of feelings and how this can be translated into knowledge for strategy advantage (Chu, 2011; Davis et al., 2014) is needed.

Laroche et al. (2012) believe that loyalty within brand communities and the process through which loyalty is gained is unclear and more research would be beneficial to understand this phenomenon, which will also impact engagement research as it is directly linked to loyalty (Brodie et al., 2013). However, Chang et al. (2013) believe that it is necessary to find out how loyalty would be affected in the face of negative events and how this negative occurrence could interact with group eWOM to influence the OBC. This is especially with regard to the differences in newly and fully established OBCs, as there exists a gap in terms of the influence of eWOM in OBCs where relationships are long established (Chang et al., 2013). Schau et al. (2009) identified four categories in which consumers help cocreate value: social networking, impressions management, community engagement, and brand use. All of these ways in which consumer's cocreate value for themselves are based on OBCs, and can create more loyal and trusting customers (Zhou et al., 2011). However it is still unclear how these practices can be used to fulfill objectives and which practices are best utilized in what circumstances thus companies would benefit on researching this to gain advantage in their strategies (Schau et al., 2009). Particularly, Laroche et al. (2012) calls for deeper insight into these value creation practices, especially in relation to the three traditional community markers (Muniz & O'Guinn, 2001), recommending a longitudinal approach.

The strength of ties between sources can also affect the persuasiveness of the communication, therefore signaling the need for more research needed in this area (Brown & Reingen, 1987; Cheung & Thadani, 2012; Duan, Gu, & Whinston, 2008; Godes & Mayzlin, 2004; Shang et al., 2006; Steffes & Burgee, 2009). Although the various methods, types of eWOM and platforms in which consumers are engaged in have led to fragmentation within the literature (King et al., 2014).

There seems to be three common elements that are present through the discussion of OBCs and their functions and characteristics; experiential, functional and self. The notion of "self" is a strong theme that emerges throughout the majority of brand community research (Veloutsou & Moutinho, 2009), and can be linked to both the functional aspects (using the functional advantages of the brand community to develop oneself and gain knowledge on how to act that affects identity) and experiential or social aspects (using the communal nature of the community to fan their need for acceptance of identity). With the continued use of OBCs as expressional and communicative outlets it is clear that consumers will use these platforms in a variety of ways to suit their needs, rather than one unifiable way amongst all. The new individualized use of these OBCs (Weijo et al., 2014), which has developed a sense of hetero-geneity (Pan et al., 2014) allowing multiple memberships and fluctuation of interests within specific communities (Habibi et al., 2014), is an area that is emergent in research at the present time. The rise in this new individualized consumer can be contributed to a change in offline culture, which has been transferred online with the advancements of new media—postmodernism. This chapter details how the change in culture has affected the social media environment, with particular focus on postmodernism.

Recommendations for Future Research

- More research needs to be done on the three community markers in the online environment. Particularly shared consciousness, as this is made more problematic with the fragmentation of niche groups of consumers as each has their own identity.
- Deeper insight into how value is created through these OBCs, with particular focus of the impact of multiple memberships.
- There should be a more in-depth look at the workings and cultures of specific communities and platforms to find out how they process information from outside their community.
- Exploration and adaptation of eWOM models should be extended to the OBC research field.
- Interactivity within OBCs and social media in general needs to be looked at in more depth, particularly the individual differences in consumer interaction on these platforms.
- Engagement within OBCs also needs to be researched further, particularly the antecedents and consequences of these processes, as well as how and why different communities are able to engage consumers better than others, especially across social media platforms.

This section has explored the phenomenon of OBCs and how they help to develop engagement and subsequently relationships with consumers. It has highlighted the notion that communities are becoming more individualized and this is therefore shifting the community focus, a behavior that organizations and brands need to be aware of. Chapter 4, Culture, explores the changing culture of consumers, which has made way for this individuation and delocalization of communities and social media use.

REFERENCES

Aaker, J. L. (1997). Dimensions of brand personality. *Journal of Marketing Research, 34,* 347–356.

Agrawal, N., & Maheswaran, D. (2005). Motivated reasoning in outcome: Bias effects. *Journal of Consumer Research, 31*(4), 798–805.

Aksoy, L., Buoye, A., Cooil, B., Keiningham, T. L., Paul, D., & Volinsky, C. (2011). Can we talk? The impact of willingness to recommend on a new-to-market service brand extension within a social network. *Journal of Services Research, 14,* 355–371.

Algesheimer, R., Dholakia, U. M., & Hermann, A. (2005). The social influence of brand community: Evidence from European Car Clubs. *Journal of Marketing, 68*(July), 19–34.

Amichai-Hamburger, Y., Wainapel, G., & Fox, S. (2002). On the internet no one knows i'm an introvert: Extroversion, neuroticism, and internet interaction. *Cyberpsychology & Behavior, 5*(2), 125–128.

Anderson, B. (1983). *Imagined communities: Reflections on the origin and spread of nationalism.* London: Verso.

Anderson, K. C., Knight, D. K., Pookulangara, S., & Josiam, B. (2014). Influence of hedonic and utilitarian motivations on retailer loyalty and purchase intention: A Facebook perspective. *Journal of Retailing and Consumer Services, 21,* 773–779.

Anderson, P. H. (2005). Relationship marketing and brand involvement of professionals through web-enhanced brand communities: The case of Coloplast. *Industrial Marketing Management, 34*(3), 285–297.

Arndt, J. (1967). Role of product-related conversations in the diffusion of a new product. *Journal of Marketing Research, 4*(August), 291–295.

Arnone, L., Colot, O., Croquet, M., Geerts, A., & Pozniak, L. (2010). Company managed virtual communities in global brand strategy. *Global Journal of Business Research, 4*(2), 97–111.

Avis, M. (2012). Brand personality factor based models: A critical review. *Australasian Marketing Journal, 20*(1), 89–96.

Bagozzi, R. P., & Dholakia, U. M. (2002). Intentional social action in virtual communities. *Journal of Interactive Marketing, 16*(2), 2–21.

Bagozzi, R. P., & Dholakia, U. M. (2006). Antecedents and purchase consequences of customer participation in small group brand communities. *International Journal of Research in Marketing, 23,* 45–61.

Baldus, B. J., Voorhees, C., & Calantone, R. (2015). Online brand community engagement: Scale development and validation. *Journal of Business Research, 68,* 978–985.

Belk, R. W. (1988). Possessions and the extended self. *Journal of Consumer Research, 15*(2), 139–168.

Belk, R. W. (2013). Extended self in a digital world. *Journal of Consumer Research, 40* (October), 477–500.

Berger, J., & Iyengar, R. (2013). Communication channels and word of mouth: How the medium shapes the message. *Journal of Consumer Research, 40,* 567–579.

Bhattacharya, C. B., & Sen, S. (2003). Consumer-company identification: a framework for understanding consumers' relationships with companies. *Journal of Marketing, 67,* 76–88.

Blazevic, V., Wiertz, C., Cotte, J., de Ruyter, K., & Keeling, D. I. (2014). GOSIP in cyberspace: Conceptualization and scale development for general online social interaction propensity. *Journal of Interactive Marketing, 28,* 87–100.

Bowden, J. L. H. (2009). The process of customer engagement: A conceptual framework. *Journal of Marketing Theory and Practice, 17*(1), 63–74.

Brodie, R. J., Hollebeek, L. D., Biljana, J., & Ilic, A. (2011). Customer engagement: Conceptual domain, fundamental propositions, and implications for research. *Journal of Service Research, 14*(3), 252–271.

Brodie, R. J., Ilic, A., Biljana, J., & Hollebeek, L. (2013). Consumer engagement in a virtual brand community: An exploratory analysis. *Journal of Business Research, 66*(1), 105–114.

Brogi, S. (2014). Online brand communities: A literature review. *Procedia: Social and Behavioural Sciences, 109*, 385–389.

Brown, J. J., & Reingen, P. H. (1987). Social ties and word-of-mouth referral behaviour. *Journal of Consumer Research, 14*(3), 350–362.

Brown, S., Kozinets, R. V., & Sherry, J. F., Jr. (2003). Teaching old brands new tricks: Retro branding and the revival of brand meaning. *Journal of Marketing, 67*, 19–33.

Bruckman, A. S., & Jensen, M. S. (2002). The mystery of the death of media MOO: Seven years of evolution of an online community in building virtual communities. In A. K. Renninger, & W. Shumar (Eds.), *Building virtual communities* (pp. 21–33). Cambridge, MA: Cambridge University Press.

Burt, R. S. (1992). *Structural holes: The social structure of competition.* Cambridge, MA: Harvard University Press.

Burt, R. S. (1997). The contingency of social capital. *Administrative Science Quarterly, 42*, 339–365.

Canniford, R. (2011). How to manage consumer tribes. *Journal of Strategic Marketing, 19* (7), 591–606.

Casaló, L. V., Flavián, C., & Guinalíu, M. (2008). Promoting consumer's participation in virtual brand communities: A new paradigm in branding strategy. *Journal of Marketing Communications, 14*(1), 19–36.

Celsi, R. L., & Olson, J. C. (1988). The role of involvement in attention and comprehension processes. *Journal of Consumer Research, 15*(2), 210–224.

Chang, A., Hsieh, S. H., & Tseng, T. H. (2013). Online brand community response to negative brand events: The role of group eWOM. *Internet Research, 23*(4), 486–506.

Chen, J., Xu, H., & Whinston, A. B. (2011). Moderated online communities and quality of user-generated content. *Journal of Management Information Systems, 28*(2), 237–268.

Cheung, C. M. K., & Thadani, D. R. (2012). The impact of electronic word-of-mouth communication: A literature analysis and integrative model. *Decision Support Systems, 54*, 461–470.

Chu, S.-C. (2011). Viral advertising in social media: Participation in Facebook groups and responses among college-aged users. *Journal of Interactive Advertising, 12*(1), 30–43.

Chu, S.-C., & Kim, Y. (2011). Determinants of consumer engagement in electronic word-of-mouth (eWOM) in social networking sites. *International Journal of Advertising, 30*(1), 47–75.

Chung, C., & Austria, K. (2010). *Social media gratification and attitude toward social media marketing messages: A study of the effect of social media marketing messages on online shopping value. Proceedings of the northeast business & economics association* (pp. 581–586). Academic Press.

Constant, D., Sproull, L., & Kiesler, S. (1996). The kindness of strangers: The usefulness of electronic weak ties for technical advice. *Organization Science, 7*, 119–135.

Cova, B., & Cova, V. (2002). Tribal marketing: The tribalisation of society and its impact on the conduct of marketing. *European Journal of Marketing, 36*(5/6), 595–620.

Davis, R., Buchanan-Oliver, M., & Brodie, R. J. (2000). Retail service branding in electronic-commerce environments. *Journal of Services Research, 3*(2), 178–186.

Davies, A., & Fitchett, J. A. (2003). Crossing culture: A multi-method enquiry into consumer behaviour and the experience of cultural transition. *Journal of Consumer Behaviour, 3*(4), 315–330.

Davis, R., Piven, I., & Breazeale, M. (2014). Conceptualising the brand in social media community: The five sources model. *Journal of Retailing and Consumer Services, 21,* 468—481.

De Valck, K., van Bruggen, G. H., & Wierenga, B. (2009). Virtual communities: A marketing perspective. *Decision Support Systems, 47,* 185—203.

De Vries, L., Gensler, S., & Leeflang, P. S. (2012). Popularity of brand posts brand fan pages an investigation effects social media marketing. *Journal of Interactive Marketing, 26*(2), 83—91.

DeLanda, M. (2006). *A new philosophy of society: Assemblage theory and social complexity.* New York, NY: Continuum.

Dellarocas, C., Gao, G., & Narayan, R. (2010). Are consumers more likely to contribute online reviews for hit or niche products? *Journal of Management Information Systems, 27*(22), 127—158.

DeMello, G., MacInnis, D. J., & Stewart, D. W. (2007). Threats to hope: Effects on reasoning about product information. *Journal of Consumer Research, 34*(August), 153—161.

Dholakia, U. M., Bagozzi, R. P., & Pearo, L. K. (2004). A social influence model of consumer participation in network- and small-group-based virtual communities. *International Journal of Research in Marketing, 21*(3), 241—263.

Di Maria, E., & Finotto, V. (2008). Communities of consumption and made in Italy. *Industry & Innovation, 15*(2), 179—197.

Dichter, E. (1966). How word-of-mouth advertising works. *Harvard Business Review,* 147—160.

Ding, Y., Phang, C. W., Lu, X., Tan, C.-H., & Sutanto, J. (2014). The role of marketer- and user-generated content in sustaining the growth of a social media brand community. In *2014 47th Hawaii international conference on system sciences (HICSS)* (pp. 1785—1792). IEEE. Available from: http://dx.doi.org/10.1109/HICSS.2014.226.

Divakaran, P. K. P. (2012). Pre-release member participation as potential predictors of post release community members' adoption behaviour: Evidence from the motion picture industry. *Behaviour & Information Technology, 32*(6), 545—559.

Divakaran, P. K. P. (2013). Does consumer or community generated ideas truly reflect market needs at all times? A different perspective on idea selection by classifying the source of new ideas and by using social identity theory. In *The 7th international days of statistics and economics* (pp. 19—21). Prague, September.

Dong, J. Q., & Wu, W. (2015). Business value of social media technologies: Evidence from online user innovation communities. *Journal of Strategic Information Systems, 24,* 113—127.

Duan, W., Gu, B., & Whinston, A. B. (2008). The dynamics of online word-of-mouth and product sales: An empirical examination of the movie industry. *Journal of Retailing, 84*(2), 233—242.

Evans, M., Jamal, A., & Foxall, G. (2009). *Consumer behaviour* (2nd ed.). West Sussex: John Wiley & Sons Ltd.

Festinger, L. (1957). *A theory of cognitive dissonance.* Stanford, CA: Stanford University Press.

Fieseler, C., & Fleck, M. (2013). The pursuit of empowerment through social media: Structural social capital dynamics in CSR-blogging. *Journal of Business Ethics, 118,* 759—775.

Firat, A. F., & Shultz, C. J. (1997). From segmentation to fragmentation: Markets and marketing strategy in the postmodern era. *European Journal of Marketing, 31*(3/4), 183—207.

Flynn, L. R., Goldsmith, R. E., & Eastman, J. K. (1996). Opinion leaders and opinion seekers: Two new measurement scales. *Journal of the Academy of Marketing Science, 24* (2), 137−147.

Fournier, S., & Avery, J. (2011). The uninvited brand. *Business Horizons, 54*(3), 193−207.

Foux, G. (2006). Consumer-generated media: Get your customers involved. *Brand Strategy, 8*(May), 38−39.

Fox, K. J. (1987). Real punks and pretenders: The social organization of a counterculture. *Journal of Contemporary Ethnography, 16*(3), 344−370.

Franke, N., & Piller, F. (2004). Value creation by toolkits for user innovation and design: The case of the watch market. *Journal of Product Innovation Management, 21,* 401−415.

Franke, N., & Shah, S. K. (2003). How communities support innovative activities: An exploration of assistance and sharing among end-users. *Research Policy, 32,* 157−178.

Frenzen, J., & Nakamoto, K. (1993). Structure, cooperation, and the flow of market information. *Journal of Consumer Research, 20*(3), 360−375.

Friedman, M., Abeele, P. V., & DeVos, K. (1992). A look at the consumption community concept through a psychological lens. In F. W. Rudmin, & M. Richins (Eds.), *SV-meaning, measure, and morality of materialism* (pp. 126−127). Provo, UT: Association for Consumer Research.

Gebauer, J., Fuller, J., & Pezzei, R. (2013). The dark and the bright side of co-creation: Triggers of member behaviour in online innovation communities. *Journal of Business Research, 66,* 1516−1527.

Godes, D., & Mayzlin, D. (2004). Using online conversations to study word-of-mouth communication. *Marketing Science, 23*(4), 545−560.

Godes, D., Mayzlin, D., Chen, Y., Das, S., Dellarocas, C., Pfeiffer, B., et al. (2005). The firm's management of social interactions. *Marketing Letters, 16*(3/4), 415−428.

Granovetter, M. S. (1973). The strength of weak ties. *American Journal of Sociology, 78,* 1360−1380.

Grensing-Pophal, L. (2009). Social media: Investing in what works. *Information Today, 26* (10), 1−2.

Gummerus, J., Liljander, V., Weman, E., & Pihlstrom, M. (2012). Customer engagement in a Facebook brand community. *Management Research Review, 35*(9), 857−877.

Gummesson, E. (2002). Relationship marketing in the new economy. *Journal of Relationship Marketing, 1*(1), 37−57.

Gummesson, E. (2006). Many-to-many marketing as grand theory. In R. F. Lusch, & S. L. Vargo (Eds.), The service-dominant logic of marketing: Dialog, debate, and directions (pp. 339−353). Armonk, NY: M.E. Sharpe.

Gwinner, K. P., Gremler, D. D., & Bitner, M. J. (1998). Relational benefits in service industries: The customer's perspective. *Journal of the Academy of Marketing Science, 26* (2), 101−114.

Habibi, M. R., Laroche, M., & Richard, M.-O. (2014). Brand communities based in social media: How unique are they? Evidence from two exemplary brand communities. *International Journal of Information Management, 34,* 123−132.

Hajli, M., & Hajli, M. (2013). Organisational development in sport: Co-creation of value through social capital. *Industrial and Commercial Training, 45*(5), 283−288.

Hansen, S. S., & Lee, J. K. (2013). What drives consumers to pass along marketer-generated eWOM in social network games? Social and game factors in play. *Journal of Theoretical and Applied Electronic Commerce Research, 8*(1), 53−68.

Hardey, M. (2011). Generation C: Content, creation, connections and choice. *International Journal of Market Research, 53*(6), 749−770.

Heider, F. (1958). *The psychology of interpersonal relations.* New York, NY: John Wiley & Sons.

Hennig-Thurau, T., Hofacker, C. F., & Bloching, B. (2013). Marketing the pinball way: Understanding how social media change the generation of value for consumers and companies. *Journal of Interactive Marketing, 27*, 237−241.

Hennig-Thurau, T., Gwinner, K. P., Walsh, G., & Gremler, D. D. (2004). Electronic word-of mouth via consumer-opinion platforms: What motivates consumers to articulate themselves on the internet? *Journal of Interactive Marketing, 18*(1), 38−52.

Hennig-Thurau, T., Malthouse, E. C., Friege, C., Gensler, S., Lobschat, L., Ranaswamy, A., et al. (2010). The impact of new media on customer relationships. *Journal of Service Research, 13*(3), 311−330.

Ho, C.-W. (2015). Identify with community or company? An investigation on the consumer behaviour in Facebook brand community. *Telematics and Informatics, 32*, 930−939.

Ho, J. Y. C., & Dempsey, M. (2010). Viral marketing: Motivations to forward online content. *Journal of Business Research, 63*, 1000−1006.

Hodis, M., Sriramachandramurthy, R., & Sashittal, H. C. (2015). Interact with me on my terms: A four segment Facebook engagement framework for marketers. *Journal of Marketing Management, 31*(11−12), 1255−1284.

Hollebeek, L. D. (2011). Demystifying customer brand engagement: Exploring the loyalty nexus. *Journal of Marketing Management, 27*(7/8), 785−807.

Hollebeek, L. D., Glynn, M. S., & Brodie, R. J. (2014). Consumer brand engagement in social media: Conceptualization, scale development and validation. *Journal of Interactive Marketing, 28*, 149−165.

Hoyer, W. D., MacInnis, D. J., & Pieters, R. (2013). *Consumer behavior* (6th ed.). International Edition. Mason, OH: Cengage Learning.

Humphrey, G. (1924). The psychology of the gestalt. *Journal of Educational Psychology, 15* (7), 401−412.

Jacobs, I. (2009). The new interaction of social media: Beyond marketing, the popular tools and techniques can also serve as a channel for support. *Customer Relationship Management, 13*(6), 12.

Jain, S., & Maheswaran, D. (2000). Motivated reasoning: A depth-of-processing perspective. *Journal of Consumer Research, 26*(4), 358−371.

Jansen, B. J., Zhang, M., Sobel, K., & Chowdury, A. (2009). Twitter power: Tweets as electronic word of mouth. *Journal of the American Society for Information Science and Technology, 60*(11), 2169−2188.

Jin, X. L., Cheung, C. M. K., Lee, M. K. O., & Chen, H. P. (2009). How to keep members using the information in a computer-supported social network. *Computers in Human Behavior, 25*, 1172−1181.

Johnson, P. R., & Yang, S. (2009). Uses and gratifications of Twitter: An examination of user motives and satisfaction of Twitter use. In *Communication Technology Division of the annual convention of the Association for Education in Journalism and Mass Communication*. Boston, MA.

Joseph, S., Lid, V., & Suthers, D. (2007). Transcendent communities. In D. Chinn, G. Erkens, & S. Puntambekar (Eds.), The computer supported collaborative learning (CSCL) conference *2007* (pp. 317−319). New Brunswick: International Society of the Learning Sciences.

Karnik, M., Oakley, I., Venkatanathan, J., Spiliotopoulos, T., & Nisi, V. (2013). Uses & gratifications of a Facebook media sharing group. *CSCW' 13 Proceedings of the 2013 conference on computer supported cooperative work* (pp. 821−826). New York, NY: ACM.

Katz, E. (1959). Mass communication research and the study of culture. *Studies in Public Communication, 2*, 1−6.

Katz, E., Gurevitch, M., & Haas, H. (1973). On the use of the mass media for important things. *American Sociological Review, 38*(April), 164−181.

Kietzmann, J. H., Hermkens, K., McCarthy, I. P., & Silvestre, B. S. (2011). Social media? Get serious! Understanding the functional building blocks of social media. *Business Horizons, 54*(3), 241−251.

King, R. A., Racherla, P., & Bush, V. D. (2014). What we know and don't know about online word-of-mouth: A review and synthesis of the literature. *Journal of Interactive Marketing, 28,* 167−183.

Koh, J., & Kim, Y. G. (2003). Sense of virtual community: A conceptual framework and empirical validation. *International Journal of Electronic Commerce, 8*(2), 75−93.

Kozinets, R. V. (1999). E-tribalized marketing? The strategic implications of virtual communities of consumption. *European Management Journal, 17*(3), 252−264.

Kozinets, R. V. (2001). Utopian enterprise: Articulating the meanings of Star Trek's culture of consumption. *Journal of Consumer Research, 28*(1), 67−88.

Kozinets, R. V., de Valck, K., Wojnicki, A. C., & Wilner, S. J. S. (2010). Networked narratives: Understanding word-of-mouth marketing in online communities. *Journal of Marketing, 74*(2), 71−89.

Kwon, E. S., Kim, E., Sung, Y., & Yoo, C. Y. (2014). Brand followers: Consumer motivation and attitude towards brand communications on Twitter. *International Journal of Advertising, 33*(4), 657−680.

Labrecque, L. I. (2014). Fostering consumer-brand relationships in social media environments: The role of parasocial interaction. *Journal of Interactive Marketing, 28,* 134−148.

Labrecque, L. I., Mathwick, C., Novak, T. P., & Hofacker, C. F. (2013). Consumer power: Evolution in the digital age. *Journal of Interactive Marketing, 27*(4), 257−269.

Laroche, M., Habibi, M. R., & Richard, M.-O. (2013). To be or not to be in social media: How brand loyalty is affected by social media? *International Journal of Information Management, 33*(1), 76−82.

Laroche, M., Habibi, M. R., Richard, M.-O., & Sankaranarayanan, R. (2012). The effects of social media based brand communities on brand community markers, value creation practices, brand trust and brand loyalty. *Computers in Human Behaviour, 28,* 1755−1767.

Latour, B. (2005). *Reassembling the social: An Introduction to actor-network theory.* New York, NY: Oxford University Press.

Law, J. (1992). Notes on the theory of the actor-network: Ordering, strategy, and heterogeneity. *Systemic Practice and Action Research, 5*(4), 379−393.

Lee, D., Kim, H. S., & Kim, J. K. (2011). The impact of online brand community type on consumer's community engagement behaviors: Consumer-created vs. marketer-created online brand community in online social-networking web sites. *Cyberpsychology, Behavior, and Social Networking, 14*(1−2), 59−63.

Lee, Y.-H., Ho, C.-H., & Chou, C. (2015). Re-visiting internet addiction among Taiwanese students: A cross-sectional comparison of students' expectations, online gaming, and online social interaction. *Journal of Abnormal Child Psychology, 43*(3), 589−599.

Levina, N., & Vaast, E. (2005). The emergence of boundary spanning competence in practice: Implications for implementation and use of information systems. *MIS Quarterly, 29*(2), 335−363.

Li, S., Clark, L., & Wheeler, C. (2013). Unlocking the marketing potential of social capital: A study to identify the dimensions of social capital considered represented within online brand communities. In *IEEE 10th international conference on e-business engineering* (pp. 138−141). Available from: http://dx.doi.org/10.1109/ICEBE.2013.21.

Liao, C., Hsu, F.-C., & To, P.-L. (2013). Exploring knowledge sharing in virtual communities. *Online Information Review, 37*(6), 891−909.

Libai, B. (2011). Comment: The perils of focusing on highly engaged customers. *Journal of Service Research, 14*(3), 275−276.

Lin, J., & Pena, J. (2011). Are you following me? A content analysis of TV networks' brand communication on Twitter. *Journal of Interactive Advertising, 12*(1), 17−29.

Liu, C., Marchewka, J. T., Lu, J., & Yu, C.-S. (2004). Beyond concern: A privacy−trust−behavioral intention model of electronic commerce. *Information Management, 42*(1), 127−142.

Liu, Y., & Shrum, L. J. (2002). What is interactivity and is it always such a good thing? Implications of definition, person, and situation for the influence of interactivity on advertising effectiveness. *Journal of Advertising, 31*(4), 53−64.

Ma, W. W. K., & Yuen, A. H. K. (2011). Understanding online knowledge sharing: An interpersonal relationship perspective. *Computers & Education, 56*, 210−219.

MacInnis, D. J., & DeMello, G. (2005). The concept of hope and its relevance to product evaluation and choice. *Journal of Marketing, 69*(1), 1−14.

Marder, B., Slade, E., Houghton, D., & Archer-Brown, C. (2016). "I like them, but won't 'like' them": an examination of impression management associated with visible political party affiliation on. *Computers in Human Behavior, 61*, 280−287.

Mathwick, C., Malhotra, N., & Rigdon, E. (2001). Experiential value: Conceptualization, measurement and application in the catalog and internet shopping environment. *Journal of Retailing, 77*(1), 9−16.

Mathwick, C., Wiertz, C., & De Ruyter, K. (2008). Social capital production in a virtual P3 community. *Journal of Consumer Research, 34*(6), 832−849.

McAlexander, J. H., Schouten, J. W., & Koenig, H. F. (2002). Building brand community. *Journal of Marketing, 66*(1), 38−54.

McCroskey, J. C., & Richmond, V. P. (1990). Willingness-to-communicate: A cognitive view. *Journal of Social Behavior and Personality, 5*, 19−37.

McKenna, K. Y. A., & Bargh, J. A. (2000). Plan 9 from cyberspace: The implications of the internet for personality and social psychology. *Personality and Social Psychology Review, 4*(1), 57−75.

Mehrabian, A. (1980). *Silent messages: Implicit communication of emotions and attitudes* (2nd ed.) Belmont, CA: Wadsworth.

Mollen, A., & Wilson, H. (2010). Engagement, telepresence and interactivity in online consumer experience: Reconciling scholastic and managerial perspectives. *Journal of Business Research, 63*, 919−925.

Moran, E., & Gossieaux, F. (2010). Marketing in a hyper-social world: The tribalization of business study and characteristics of successful online communities. *Journal of Advertising Research, 50*(3), 232−239.

Muniz, A. M., Jr., & Schau, H. J. (2005). Religiosity in the abandoned Apple Newton brand community. *Journal of Consumer Research, 31*(4), 737−747.

Muniz, A. M., & O'Guinn, T. C. (2001). Brand community. *Journal of Consumer Research, 27*(4), 412−432.

Murray, K. (1991). A test of services marketing theory: Consumer information acquisition activities. *Journal of Marketing, 55*, 10−25.

Nambisan, S., & Baron, R. A. (2010). Different roles, different strokes: Organizing virtual customer environments to promote two types of customer contributions. *Organization Science, 21*(2), 554−572.

Naylor, R. W., Lamberton, C. P., & West, P. M. (2012). Beyond the 'like' button: The impact of mere virtual presence on brand evaluations and purchase intentions in social media settings. *Journal of Marketing, 76*(6), 105−120.

Oh, S., & Syn, S. Y. (2015). Motivations for sharing information and social support in social media: A comparative analysis of Facebook, Twitter, Delicious, YouTube, and Flickr. *Journal of the Association for Information Science and Technology, 66*(10), 2045−2060.

Ouwersloot, H., & Odekerken-Schröder, G. (2008). Who's who in brand communities — and why? *European Journal of Marketing, 42*(5/6), 571–585.

Pan, Z., Lu, Y., & Gupta, S. (2014). How heterogeneous community engage newcomers? The effect of community diversity on newcomers' perception of inclusion: An empirical study in social media service. *Computers in Human Behavior, 39*, 100–111.

Park, N., Kee, K. F., & Valenzuela, S. (2009). Being immersed in social networking environment: Facebook Groups, uses and gratifications, and social outcomes. *CyberPsychology & Behavior, 12*(6), 729–733.

Patterson, P., Yu, T., & De Ruyter, K. (2006). Understanding customer engagement in services. *Paper presented at ANZMAC 2006 conference.* Brisbane.

Penaloza, L., Toulouse, N., & Visconti, L. M. (2012). *Marketing management: A cultural perspective.* Abingdon: Routledge.

Peris, R., Gimeno, M. A., Pinazo, D., Ortet, G., Carrero, V., Sanchiz, M., et al. (2002). Online chat rooms: Virtual spaces of interaction for socially oriented people. *CyberPsychology & Behavior, 5*(1), 43–51.

Phang, C. W., Zhang, C., & Sutanto, J. (2013). The influence of user interaction and participation in social media on the consumption intention of niche products. *Information & Management, 50*(8), 661–672.

Poyry, E., Parvinen, P., & Malmivaara, T. (2013). Can we get from liking to buying? Behavioral differences in hedonic and utilitarian Facebook usage. *Electronic Commerce Research and Applications, 12*, 224–235.

Putnam, R. (2000). *Bowling alone: The collapse and revival of American community.* New York, NY: Simon & Schuster.

Raacke, J., & Bonds-Raacke, J. (2008). MySpace and Facebook: Applying the uses and gratifications theory to exploring friend-networking sites. *CyberPsychology & Behavior, 11*(2), 169–174.

Raies, K., Muhlbacher, H., & Gavard-Perret, M.-L. (2015). Consumption community commitment: Newbies' and longstanding members' brand engagement and loyalty. *Journal of Business Research, 68*, 2634–2644.

Rathore, A. K., Ilavarasan, P. V., & Dwivedi, Y. (2016). Social media content and product co-creation: An emerging paradigm. *Journal of Enterprise Information Management, 29* (1), 7–18.

Reingen, P. H., & Kernan, J. B. (1986). Analysis of referral networks in marketing: Methods and illustration. *Journal of Marketing, 23*(4), 370–378.

Rosenbaum, M. S. (2008). Return on community for consumers and service establishments. *Journal of Services Research, 11*, 179–196.

Rubin, A. M. (2002). The uses-and-gratifications perspective of media effects. In J. Bryant, & D. Zillmann (Eds.), *Media effects: Advances in theory and research* (pp. 525–548). Mahwah, NJ: Lawrence Erlbaum Associates.

Ryals, L. (2008). Determining the indirect value of a customer. *Journal of Marketing Management, 24*(7/8), 847–864.

Sashi, C. M. (2012). Customer engagement, buyer-seller relationships, and social media. *Management Decision, 50*(2), 253–272.

Sawhney, M., Verona, G., & Prandelli, E. (2005). Collaborating to create: The internet as a platform for customer engagement in product innovation. *Journal of Interactive Marketing, 19*(4), 4–17.

Schau, H. J., Muñiz, A. M., & Arnould, E. J., Jr. (2009). How brand community practices create value. *Journal of Marketing, 73*(5), 30–51.

Schembri, S., Merrilees, B., & Kristiansen, S. (2010). Brand consumption and narrative of self. *Psychology and Marketing, 27*(6), 623–638.

Schouten, J. W. (1991). Selves in transition: Symbolic consumption in personal rites of passage and identity reconstruction. *Journal of Consumer Research, 17*(4), 412–425.

Schouten, J. W., & McAlexander, J. H. (1995). Subcultures of consumption: An ethnography of the new bikers. *Journal of Consumer Research, 22*(June), 43−61.

Seimiene, E. (2012). Emotional connection of consumer personality traits with brand personality traits: Theoretical considerations. *Economy Management, 17*(4), 1477−1478.

Seraj, M. (2012). We create, we connect, we respect, therefore we are: Intellectual, social, and cultural value in online communities. *Journal of Interactive Marketing, 26*(4), 209−222.

Shang, R.-A., Chen, Y.-C., & Liao, H.-J. (2006). The value of participation in virtual consumer communities on brand loyalty. *Internet Research, 16*(4), 398−418.

Shao, W., & Ross, M. (2015). Testing a conceptual model of Facebook brand page communities. *Journal of Research in Interactive Marketing, 9*(3), 239−258.

Simmons, G. (2008). Marketing to postmodern consumers: Introducing the internet chameleon. *European Journal of Marketing, 42*(3/4), 299−310.

Smith, J. L., Wagaman, J., & Handley, I. M. (2009). Keeping it dull or making it fun: Task variation as a function of promotion versus prevention focus. *Motivation and Emotion, 33*(2), 150−160.

Steffes, E. M., & Burgee, L. E. (2009). Social ties and online word of mouth. *Internet Research, 19*(1), 42−59.

Stelzner, M. (2015). Social media marketing industry report: How marketers are using social media to grow their business. *Social Media Examiner*, June 6, 2015, from http://www.socialmediaexaminer.com/social-media-marketing-industry-report-2015/.

Storbacka, K. (1997). Segmentation based on customer profitability − Retrospective analysis of retail bank customer bases. *Journal of Marketing Management, 13*(5), 479−492.

Sun, T., Youn, S., Wu, G., & Kuntaraporn, M. (2006). Online word-of-mouth (or mouse): An exploration of its antecedents and consequences. *Journal of Computer-Mediated Communication, 11*, 1104−1127.

Sung, Y., Kim, Y., Kwon, O., & Moon, J. (2010). An explorative study of Korean consumer participation in virtual brand communities in social network sites. *Journal of Global Marketing, 23*, 430−445.

Tardini, S., & Cantoni, L. A. (2005). A semiotic approach to online communities: Belonging, interest and identity in websites' and video games' communities. In *Proceedings of IADIS international conference* (pp. 371−378). Qawra, Malta.

Thomas, T., Price, L. L., & Schau, H. J. (2013). When differences unite: Resource dependence in heterogeneous consumption communities. *Journal of Consumer Research, 39*, 1010−1033.

Thomke, S., & von Hippel, E. (2002). Customer as innovators: A new way to create value. *Harvard Business Review, 80*(4), 74−81.

Turkle, S. (2011). *Alone together: Why we expect more from technology and less from each other.* New York, NY: Basic Books.

Van Doorn, J., Lemon, K. N., Mittal, V., Nass, S., Pick, D., Pirner, P., et al. (2010). Customer engagement behavior: Theoretical foundations and research directions. *Journal of Services Research, 13*, 253−266.

Van Noort, G., Voorveld, H. A. M., & Van Reijmersdal, E. A. (2012). Interactivity in brand web sites: Cognitive, affective, and behavioral responses explained by consumers' online flow experience. *Journal of Interactive Marketing, 26*, 223−234.

Vargo, S. L., & Lusch, R. F. (2004). Evolving to a new dominant logic for marketing. *Journal of Marketing, 68*(January), 1−17.

Veloutsou, C., & Moutinho, L. (2009). Brand relationships through brand reputation and brand tribalism. *Journal of Business Research, 62*, 314−322.

Verhoef, P. C., Reinartz, W. J., & Krafft, M. (2010). Customer engagement as a new perspective in customer management. *Journal of Services Research*, *13*, 247–252.

Vivek, S. D., Beatty, S. E., & Morgan, R. M. (2012). Consumer engagement: Exploring customer relationships beyond purchase. *Marketing Theory and Practice*, *20* (2), 127–145.

Von Hippel, E. (2005). *Democratizing innovation*. Cambridge, MA: The MIT Press.

Wang, X., Yu, C., & Wei, Y. (2012). Social media peer communication and impacts on purchase intentions: A consumer socialization framework. *Journal of Interactive Marketing*, *26*, 198–208.

Ward, S. (1974). Consumer socialization. *Journal of Consumer Research*, *1* (September), 1–14.

Weijo, H., Hietanen, J., & Mattila, P. (2014). New insights into online consumption communities and netnography. *Journal of Business Research*, *67*, 2072–2078.

Weinberg, B. D., & Berger, P. D. (2011). Connected customer lifetime value: The impact of social media. *Journal of Direct, Data and Digital Marketing Practice*, *12*(4), 328–344.

Weinberg, B. D., & Pehlivan, E. (2011). Social spending: Managing the social media mix. *Business Horizons*, *54*, 275–282.

Wellman, B. (2001). Physical place and cyberplace: The rise of networked individualism. *International Journal for Urban and Regional Research*, *25*(2), 227–252.

Wenger, E. (1998). *Communities of practice: Learning, meaning and identity*. Cambridge, MA: Cambridge University Press.

Whiting, A., & Williams, D. (2013). Why people use social media: A uses and gratifications approach. *Qualitative Market Research: An International Journal*, *16*(4), 362–369.

Wiertz, C., & De Ruyter, K. (2007). Beyond the call of duty: Why customers contribute to firm-hosted commercial online communities. *Organization Studies*, *28*(3), 347–376.

Wu, J.-J., Chen, Y.-H., & Chung, Y.-S. (2010). Trust factors influencing virtual community members: A study of transaction communities. *Journal of Business Research*, *63*, 1025–1032.

Yen, Y.-S. (2013). The relationship among social influence, perceived value, and usage intention in social networking sites. In *Consumer Electronics, Communications and Networks (CECNet), 2013 3rd International Conference* (pp. 699–670). IEEE, Xianning, 20–22 November.

Zabin, J. (2009). *The ROI of social media marketing: Why it pays to drive word of mouth*. San Carlos, CA: Aberdeen Group.

Zhou, Z., Zhang, Q., Su, C., & Zhou, N. (2011). How do brand communities generate brand relationships? Intermediate mechanisms. *Journal of Business Research*, *65*(7), 890–895.

CHAPTER 4

Culture

Society itself goes through incremental changes that can be observed over periods of time to highlight the differences in behavior. These cultural changes affect people in all different ways, and with the advances in Internet technology and thus social media, these cultural phenomena have moved into the online realm, visibly affecting the behavior of the individuals that utilize these platforms, therefore it is essential to note the impact of culture and the transition to postmodernism. This chapter will start by highlighting the importance of culture, in terms of its effect on consumers and the impact of social media. This will be followed by an explanation of postmodernism and why this is important to social media research. The concept of tribes and how this relates to online brand communities and social media is then discussed, finally ending in a discussion of the key points, future research directions, and recommendations for practitioners.

4.1 THE IMPORTANCE OF CULTURE

Globalization seemingly has no restrictions and has therefore been engrained into online activities, as the inclusion of online technologies becomes commonplace in our culture. Consumers that interact with the varying social media platforms and communities create cultures (Kozinets, Valck, Wojnicki, & Wilner, 2010). The connections between consumers and to the brand, means that relationships are established through this culture (Zaglia, 2013). With this integration, restructuring, and clash of values, it has become essential to understanding the impact of culture on consumers (Teerikangas, 2007), and how this has affected marketing theory and practice. Affecting the way in which we both consume and perceive things (Gibson, 1979; Nisbett & Masuda, 2003), culture will ultimately affect consumer behavior. The characteristics of consumers and the experiences they have are in a state of rapid change, in addition to the continuing developments in technology and thus social media, this means that individuals are communicating and learning through different mechanisms (Amine & Smith, 2009).

Different cultures hold different values more highly than others, as demonstrated by Hofstede's (1980) cultural dimensions theory, comprised of four, later expanded to six, dimensions which distinguishes differences in culture (Chinese Culture Connection, 1987; Hofstede, 1980; Hofstede & Bond, 1984, 1988; Hofstede & Hofstede, 2005; Hofstede, Hofstede, & Minkov, 2010). Referring to culture as "the collective programming of the mind" (Hofstede, 1980, p. 25), Hofstede was a strong believer in the unconscious aspects of culture, and believed his theory could explain the values that are placed on things which are crucial for the complete understanding of culture (Schein, 1985), which can be applied in both an online and offline context. The model explains the differing emphasis cultures place on particular values, ultimately affecting their behavior, and provides a way for understanding cross-cultural communication. Values can be influenced by consumer characteristics including their need for uniqueness (Tian and McKenzie, 2001), especially in the online context. There is perhaps a need for a reevaluation of Hofstede's (1980) cultural dimensions theory to apply it to the online domain and include online practices within the dimensions. Shared values, one of the three markers of community as identified by Muniz and O'Guinn (2001), are one of the essential drivers of culture, but as Joseph, Lid, and Suthers (2007) point out, it is quite difficult to balance and keep the identity of one community, while using various, which is what has been happening within the realm of social media environment (Pan, Lu, & Gupta, 2014; Weijo, Hietanen, & Mattila, 2014). Segmentation is becoming more and more difficult in an environment, which allows previously unrecognized similarities between consumers and surface (Amine & Smith, 2009). This is particularly visible with the heterogeneous nature of consumers becoming more prominent, thus categorizing their consumption behaviors in the online environment is problematic due to their increasing tendency to appear unique from others.

Symbolic meaning can be derived from culture, and by matching characteristics of the product or service with the culture then meaning is transferred (Hoyer, MacInnis, & Pieters, 2013). Symbolic meaning can also be derived from consumers, which can be used as a signifier of group membership or individuality. There are four functions symbolic meaning can have for consumers; emblematic (signifying membership to particular social groups), role acquisition (helping settle oneself into a new role), connectedness (signifying personal connections), and expressiveness (signifying individual uniqueness) (Hoyer et al., 2013). The role acquisition function, which signifies the transition of roles, can also mean the use of stereotypical symbols to make a consumer feel more comfortable in settling into this new role and to fit in with what is expected. Consumers in online communities who first join the community could be using stereotypical means to become part of group and then divulging into more unique ones once they have been accepted. This could explain delocalization as they have to become part of a group in order to get the most information and knowledge and then transition between groups they have joined passing on the information they acquire. Symbolic meaning and functions can combine with cultural rituals as a way of helping to craft and maintain a consumers self-concept in the online environment (Hoyer et al., 2013; Muniz & O'Guinn, 2001; Schau & Gilly, 2003), and this association of symbolism with construction of the self should be investigated further (Schembri, Merrilees, & Kristiansen, 2010). Social friendship networks, such as Facebook, which are home to various online brand communities, provide critical information on social orientations, which are essential to understanding the cultural differences in the newly networked world (Markus & Kitayama, 1991; Na et al., 2010).

4.2 POSTMODERNISM

The postmodern era has enveloped all aspects of consumers and their behavior, fragmenting commonalities, such as culture, which have often been considered unifiable (Simmons, 2008). This new environment embodies complex change in a chaotic new world full of contradictions (Addis & Podesta, 2005), where consumers are craving experiences that embody both the communal collective aspects of consumption, but to an even greater extent the renewed focus on the individual (Cova & Pace, 2006). A definition of postmodernism and effective characterization of its dimensions is problematic in the literature with terms such as "postmodernisms" (Firat & Venkatesh, 1995), to reflect the inability to summarize the concept effectively.

This postmodern era can be seen as a liberating entity whereby fragmentation and proliferation cater for the growing niche consumer interests (Goulding, 2003), facilitated by the growth in social media. This is in line with the new interpretation of the self as not being one distinct entity but a culmination of multiple versions of the self that is enabled by the new digitized world (Belk, 2013; Firat & Shultz, 1997). However, the fragmentation of consumers is just one characteristic that can be used to describe postmodernism (e.g., Firat, 1997), as many deconstruct it into a multitude of categories from a variety of disciplines (Amine & Smith, 2009). Characteristics such as hyperreality (e.g., Smith, 2001), dedifferentiation (e.g., Brown, 1995), antifoundationalism (e.g., Murphy, 1996), co-creation (e.g., Vargo & Lusch, 2004), association of opposites (e.g., Firat & Shultz, 1997), presentation (e.g., Patterson, 1998), and loss of commitment (e.g., Dawes & Brown, 2000) are just some of the characteristics associated with postmodernism. Loss of commitment is particularly important when discussing the impact of social media due to the increased heterogeneity of consumers who are not committed to one brand (Thomas, Price, & Schau, 2013), utilizing all aspects of consumption for their own individual needs of creating images for themselves as a means of distinction from others (Brown, 1995, 1997). This newly found freedom allows consumers to avoid unnecessary commitment (Dawes & Brown, 2000) encouraging multiple consumption interests and the ability to use and acquire knowledge for their own individual purposes. This has become especially prevalent in online brand communities, where consumers are flitting between communities (Weijo et al., 2014). Elliott (1993) illustrated this at the beginning of the advances in postmodernism by stating that the meanings of objects are transferable and subjective to the individual and by no means seen in a unifiable way.

However, Goulding (2003) finds this postmodern behavior as potentially alienating. Firat and Shultz (1997) term of the "touristic consumer" may be most adequate to describe the consumer of today, with consumption experiences being utilized for their immediate consequences before a new and more interesting experience can be found. This has led some to claim that this new consumer does not perhaps have the depth of involvement as previously thought (Eco, 1987; Jameson, 1990). Building on this, it can also be construed that the multiple selves that create a whole individual (Belk, 2013) are not many representations of oneself but a direct result of a confusion in identity (Kellner, 1995).

The result of this new postmodern environment is not yet evident but two very differing views have emerged. On the one hand, scholars such as Cova and Pace (2006), Cova, Kozinets, and Shankar (2007), and Dholakia, Bagozzi, and Pearo (2004) among others believe that the continued alienation caused by individualistic tendencies will cause a shift toward the more communal social interaction such as online brand communities. However, recent studies, such as those by Weijo et al. (2014), Thomas et al. (2013), Joseph et al. (2007), and Pan et al. (2014) have found evidence suggesting that individual tendencies of consumers are not diminishing but growing, facilitated by the use of online brand communities in a heterogeneous manner. This has undoubtedly caused great tension between both academics and practitioners (Simmons, 2008) as the opposing views are yet to reach an agreement. Although, as the latter views are resultant of recent research, it could point to the previous scholars, with an emphasis on reemergence of communality, as having incorrectly identified the direction of behavior at the time. This trend toward social interaction because of alienation is sometimes referred to as neotribalism (Cova & Pace, 2006; Cova et al., 2007; Dholakia et al., 2004). Simmons (2008) finds that consumers actually seek both individual and communal experiences, which is enabled by the social media environment, allowing them to use homogeneous groups to express their heterogeneous or individual tendencies.

Social media has fueled what some have called consumers "need for introspective individualism" (Simmons, 2008, p. 302). With individuals seeking the personalization now available to them, to allow the construction and development of multiple selves (Belk, 2013; Simmons, 2008). This need of individuality brings with it "narcissism, isolation, and loneliness" (Simmons, 2008, p. 306), which could explain the development of the heterogeneous community. Future research should address the discrepancies in the direction of the new postmodern consumer by finding out what engages them to behave in this way (Simmons, 2008).

4.3 CONSUMER CULTURE THEORY

Used to describe the "sociocultural, experiential, symbolic, and ideological aspects of consumption" (Arnould & Thompson, 2005, p. 868), consumer culture theory acknowledges the core theoretical assumptions within this plethora of research. Developed from the increasing recognition of the postmodern consumer, this theory highlights the growing heterogeneous nature of consumption, emphasizing the formation of a variety of contradictions such as identity and meaning. Consumer culture reflects the interconnectivity of individuals in their brand-driven production of content, used to contextualize their surroundings (Kozinets, 2001). Replicating the characteristics of postmodernism such as fragmentation, plurality, and convergence of consumption interests (Firat & Venkatesh, 1995), this theory highlights the wider influences on culture (Arnould & Thompson, 2005), recognizing the impact of multiple stakeholders that impact brand meaning (Pongsakornrungsilp & Schroeder, 2011).

There is now more of a focus on how the consumption process is a whole experience for the consumer rather than a focus on the end behavioral intention (Joy & Sherry, 2003). This is perhaps most evident in the distinction between hedonic and utilitarian motivations within the marketing literature (e.g., Anderson, Knight, Pookulangara, & Josiam, 2014), which posits that consumers engage in consumption for both experiential and functional reasons. In addition, consumer culture theory emphasizes the importance of identity in the consumption process and reignites the attention on the symbolic meaning of a brand (Kozinets, 2001). Not only this but there are now a variety of resources that are available to individuals that allow them different means to express themselves and show their individuality (e.g., Schau & Gilly, 2003) especially within the social media environment, which can be used as an expression of self (Belk, 2013).

Looking into marketplace culture, consumer culture theory reiterates the individuality of consumers in seeking out consumption interests (Kozinets, 2002), yet acknowledges the collective nature of consumers, such as with the culmination of brand communities on social media. This perhaps reignites the argument between postmodern researchers that this communal activity is caused by the feelings of alienation that accompany individualistic consumption (Cova et al., 2007; Goulding, 2003).

4.4 TRIBALISM

Communities that have developed in the postmodern era are considered somewhat unstable (Maffesoli, 1996). Sometimes referred to as tribes, these groups contain heterogeneous consumers linked by a shared consumption or brand interest (Veloutsou & Moutinho, 2009). Although the consumers within these environments do not necessarily influence each other as they have an alternative focus (Cova & Cova, 2002). The terms brand tribe and brand community are used to refer to the same consumers that culminate around one brand or interest (Cova & Pace, 2006) with distinction rarely being noted in the literature (Veloutsou & Moutinho, 2009). The postmodern construction of tribal-type brand communities is what Cova & Cova (2001) believe is the attempt at combining commerce efforts with the highly desired communal features. The role of brand communities in giving power to a group of consumers eradicates the consumer and producer functions of the consumption process (Shankar, Cherrier, & Canniford, 2006), emphasizing the importance of joint co-creation toward product development.

The notion of neotribalism, linked to consumer culture theory and postmodernism, presented by Maffesoli (1996), is perhaps a good way at outlining the culmination of today's consumers, emphasizing the individuality of consumers to distinguish themselves from others, yet responding these feelings of solidarity with group-oriented behavior. It could be argued that although they are seeking individuality, they attempt to negate this by still remaining a part of these communities, rather than leaving them completely. It could also be posited that online brand communities should be called online tribal communities, which according to Johnson and Ambrose (2006) are based on technology with an emphasis on specific protocols (which is what Muniz and O'Guinn (2001) termed shared rituals and traditions) people and purposes. However, it may be more appropriate to merely refer to them as tribes as communities emphasize subcultures, which represents a dominant influence over the consumer, rather than interspersed effects that do not have a constant impact (Goulding, Shankar, Elliott, & Canniford, 2009). In addition, the more individualistic postmodern consumer, who is adept at flitting between communities fits better with purely tribal behavior as they are not restricted by having to belong to only one group (Elliott & Davies, 2006). Utilizing resources for their own benefit (similarly to the recent findings of Weijo et al., 2014), this tribal behavior engenders no feelings of loyalty to the community, unlike that which is emphasized by Muniz and O'Guinn (2001) as one of the markers of communities. Notably difficult to manage, tribal behavior is characterized by their need for co-creation and entrepreneurial tendencies that mean they want more value from brands rather than just premade goods and services that are mass generated (Kozinets et al., 2010). Yet, Taute and Sierra (2014) argue that these characteristics of consumer tribes are wrong and rather they are characterized by allegiance and strong defence of a focal brand. The networked connections that are apparent between tribes are the main reason for consumers to engage in these entities, rather than brand communities, which focus on one brand as the means for their connections (Goulding, Shankar, & Canniford, 2011). Consumers involved in this tribal behavior rely on the social aspect of the connections they form with others (Cova, 1997), although they will exhibit passion for particular consumption behaviors (Hamilton & Hewer, 2010). Hamilton and Hewer (2010) noted that the social aspect of social media and particularly social networking sites makes it the perfect environment for the facilitation of tribal behavior. However, Greenacre, Freeman, and Donald (2013) argue that social network theory provides a better explanation and fit when dealing with behavior in communities, emphasizing the recognition in temporal order when deciphering which theory to attach to the community itself.

4.5 DISCUSSION AND CONCLUDING POINTS

The effects of culture upon consumers are something which cannot be ignored. From the very moment that Hofstede developed his individualist—collectivist scale (Hofstede, 1980), the differences within cultures have been at the forefront of many strategic alliances, defining symbolic meanings for consumers all over the world (Hoyer et al., 2013). The arrival of the postmodern era with its postmodern consumer has not evaded the effects of this cultural distinction. With individualistic tendencies becoming ever more prevalent and noticeable within consumers, and academics are quick to point out the downfalls of this behavior (Simmons, 2008). Although the individualistic consumer has indeed been subject to various lonely experiences, there seems to be no sign of this behavior stopping any time soon. Ten years ago scholars believed that this individualistic consumer would be forced into social interaction with others in a bid to rejoin the community (Cova & Pace, 2006; Cova et al., 2007; Dholakia et al., 2004)—yet this is not evidenced as being true. Sometimes referred to as brand tribes, these new individualized postmodern consumers embody neotribal nature with an emphasis on subjective, individual consumption (Cova & Pace, 2006). However, it must be noted that not every single consumer has the tendency to act in this individualistic manner, it is just becoming more prevalent and at the forefront of many academic research agendas as of present (e.g., Pan et al., 2014; Thomas et al., 2013; Weijo et al., 2014). Social media has changed the behavior of consumers, affecting marketing, where members of both communities and platforms are creators of their own culture. Thus allowing them freedom leads to a mutual and collective development and understanding (Schembri & Latimer, 2016).

Summary of Key Points
- Segmentation is becoming increasingly difficult due to the increased consumption interests of consumers, which are multiplied by the social media environment.
- Tribal consumption may be the better term to refer to the behavior that is happening on social media platforms, due to their increasing
(Continued)

Summary of Key Points—cont'd
individuality and wavering loyalty to groups and communities they are associating with.
- Consumers seek both individual and communal value from engaging with brands, especially within the online social media environment.
- Postmodernity emphasizes the heterogeneous nature of consumers, which is reflected in the social media environment between communities.

Tribalism means that consumers want to create value, through the use of communities and thus want to be active cocreators in their consumption. Offering these networks to consumers, and enabling them to link with each other is a great way to provide this value to consumers. Goulding et al. (2011) identified engagement, imagination, and alignment as three processes that facilitate the creation of a tribe, thus managers would benefit from creating an environment where they can partake in the engagement process to begin to provide the social-linking value that these tribal consumers crave. Social media is the perfect place to create these environments due to its capacity to present a variety of services and products to consumers in a networked environment that will help to deliver the social value of linking with others to consumers (Goulding et al., 2011). Due to the focus on the social value and use of tribal communities, it may be beneficial to emphasize this when engaging with these consumers rather than presenting a commercial orientation, which could result in a negative reaction (Hamilton & Hewer, 2010). In addition, Taute and Sierra (2014) emphasize examining these tribal communities in a social media context, as well as using demographics and psychographics, to gain an insight into this phenomenon. It has become evident that social media platforms develop their own culture, norms, and structure (Smith, Fischer, & Yongjian, 2012; Stadler, Brenner, & Herrmann, 2014), therefore to understand how consumers behave in these environments requires more careful in-depth analysis through more qualitative methods such as netnography (Hamilton & Hewer, 2010; Kozinets, 2006). Veloutsou and Moutinho (2009) also believe that the notion of this brand tribalism should be researched further in terms of relationship development and brand loyalty, due to the empowerment and importance of brand communities in enhancing these aspects of brand and consumer relationships.

Key Points for Practitioners

- Concentrate on platforms that facilitate linking between consumers to give them value through these networks.
- When engaging with tribal consumers, ensure that the brands role is recognized as equal to that of the consumers.
- Brands should pay careful attention to making sure they emphasize social uses of the platform they are engaging with consumers on when faced with tribal communities.
- A careful balance of communal and individual consumers needs to be catered for on social media platforms to allow the creation of value that addresses the duality of consumer needs.
- Give consumers freedom as a way of developing collective understanding, aim to facilitate a community rather than try and control it.

The multidimensionality of postmodern consumers is causing problems when addressing segmentation of the market (Amine & Smith, 2009) with many consumers displaying a variety of consumption practices. The choice consumers now have is exacerbated by social media platforms, allowing them to exercise this freedom of choice and lack of brand commitment emphasized by postmodern marketers. It may be beneficial to look into how successful organizations and brands are tackling the issue of the heterogeneous postmodern consumer to gain a deeper understanding of how to utilize these consumer characteristics to their advantage. This could be aided by conducting an analysis of additional postmodern characteristics such as intertextuality (e.g., Proctor, Papasolomou-Doukakis, & Proctor, 2002), reconstruction of self (e.g., Cova, 1996), and symbolic nature of consumption (e.g., Venkatesh, 1999). It would be beneficial to conduct this in a social media context due to the relation of the majority of postmodern characteristics as evidenced by the behavior on these platforms.

Globalization has affected consumers all over the world, yet little is known how it has affected the consumers in other countries (Arnould & Thompson, 2005). This is extremely important given the lack of geographical boundaries present in the social media environment that allows consumers to engage with others all over the world, thus influencing their purchase decisions. It would perhaps be beneficial to undertake a more in-depth look at historical influences on consumer behavior and the marketplace to understand the broader implications to today's consumers (e.g., Firat & Dholakia, 1995).

Recommendations for Future Research

- Provide an in-depth analysis of the segmentation strategies of successful brands to understand how they are addressing the fluctuating interests of the postmodern consumer.
- Exploration of additional characteristics of postmodernism, e.g., reconstruction of self, intertextuality, and symbolic nature of consumption in a social media context.
- Investigating how consumers in different cultures have been affected by globalization.
- Research interested in the culture of consumers on social media platforms should consider more qualitative approaches such as netnography to gain a deeper understanding of consumer behavior.
- Neotribalism is an area ripe for researching the postmodern consumer to understand the role of social media for marketing.

This chapter has explored the changes in culture and how this has been exacerbated and replicated within the social media environment, affecting many aspects of consumer behavior. It highlighted the importance of culture to understanding consumer behavior within this new online setting. Chapter 5, Self-Construals, explores the self-construal theory, which describes individual cultural level differences that impact on the way consumers behave in relation to others, which in a social environment is of crucial importance.

REFERENCES

Addis, M., & Podesta, S. (2005). Long life to marketing research: A postmodern view. *European Journal of Marketing*, *39*(3/4), 386−413.

Amine, L. S., & Smith, J. A. (2009). Challenges to modern consumer segmentation in a changing world: The need for a second step. *Multinational Business Review*, *17*(3), 71−99.

Anderson, K. C., Knight, D. K., Pookulangara, S., & Josiam, B. (2014). Influence of hedonic and utilitarian motivations on retailer loyalty and purchase intention: A Facebook perspective. *Journal of Retailing and Consumer Services*, *21*, 773−779.

Arnould, E. J., & Thompson, C. J. (2005). Consumer culture theory (CCT): Twenty years of research. *Journal of Consumer Research*, *31*(4), 868−882.

Belk, R. W. (2013). Extended self in a digital world. *Journal of Consumer Research*, *40*(October), 477−500.

Brown, S. (1995). *Postmodern marketing*. Oxford: Routledge.

Brown, S. (1997). *Postmodern marketing two: Telling tales*. London: International Thompson Business Press.

Chinese Culture Connection (1987). Chinese values and the search for culture-free dimensions of culture. *Journal of Cross-Cultural Psychology*, *18*(2), 143−164.

Cova, B. (1996). What postmodern means to marketing managers. *European Management Journal, 14*(5), 11−16.

Cova, B. (1997). Community and consumption: Towards a definition of the "linking value" of product or services. *European Journal of Marketing, 31*, 297−316.

Cova, B., & Cova, V. (2001). Tribal aspects of postmodern consumption research: The case of French in-line roller skates. *Journal of Consumer Behavior, 1*(1), 67−76.

Cova, B., & Cova, V. (2002). Tribal marketing: The tribalisation of society and its impact on the conduct of marketing. *European Journal of Marketing, 36*(5/6), 595−620.

Cova, B., & Pace, S. (2006). Brand community of convenience products: New forms of customer empowerment—the case 'My Nutella the Community'. *European Journal of Marketing, 40*(9/10), 1087−1105.

Cova, B., Kozinets, R. V., & Shankar, A. (2007). *Consumer tribes.* London: Butterworth Heinemann.

Dawes, J., & Brown, R. B. (2000). Postmodern marketing: Research issues for retail financial services. *Qualitative Market Research, 3*(2), 90.

Dholakia, U. M., Bagozzi, R. P., & Pearo, L. K. (2004). A social influence model of consumer participation in network- and small-group-based virtual communities. *International Journal of Research in Marketing, 21*(3), 241−263.

Eco, U. (1987). *Travels in hyper-reality.* London: Picador.

Elliott, R. (1993). Marketing and the meaning of postmodern culture. In D. Brownlie, M. Saren, R. Wensley, & R. Whittington (Eds.), *Rethinking marketing: New perspectives on the discipline and profession* (pp. 134−142). Coventry: Warwick Business School.

Elliott, R., & Davies, A. (2006). Symbolic brands and authenticity of identity performance. In J. E. Schroeder, & M. Salzer-Mörling (Eds.), *Brand culture* (pp. 155−170). London: Routledge.

Firat, A. F. (1997). Globalization of fragmentation—a framework for understanding contemporary global markets. *Journal of International Marketing, 5*(2), 77−86.

Firat, A. F., & Dholakia, N. (1995). *Consuming people: From political economy to theaters of consumption.* New York, NY: Routledge.

Firat, A. F., & Shultz, C. J. (1997). From segmentation to fragmentation: Markets and marketing strategy in the postmodern era. *European Journal of Marketing, 31*(3/4), 183−207.

Firat, A. F., & Venkatesh, A. (1995). Liberatory postmodernism and the re-enchantment of consumption. *Journal of Consumer Research, 22*(3), 239−267.

Gibson, J. J. (1979). *The ecological approach to visual perception.* Boston, MA: Houghton Mifflin.

Goulding, C. (2003). Issues in representing the postmodern consumer. *Qualitative Market Research: An International Journal, 6*(3), 152−159.

Goulding, C., Shankar, A., & Canniford, R. (2011). Learning to be tribal: Facilitating the formation of consumer tribes. *European Journal of Marketing, 47*(5/6), 813−832.

Greenacre, L., Freeman, L., & Donald, M. (2013). Contrasting social network tribal theories: An applied perspective. *Journal of Business Research, 66*, 948−954.

Hamilton, K., & Hewer, P. (2010). Tribal mattering spaces: Social-networking sites, celebrity affiliations, and tribal innovations. *Journal of Marketing Management, 26*(3−4), 271−289.

Hofstede, G. (1980). *Culture's consequences: International differences in work-related values.* Beverly Hills, CA: Sage Publications.

Hofstede, G., & Bond, M. H. (1984). Hofstede's culture dimensions: An independent validation using Rokeach's value survey. *Journal of Cross-Cultural Psychology, 15*(4), 417−433.

Hofstede, G., & Bond, M. H. (1988). The Confucian connection: From cultural roots to economic growth. *Organizational Dynamics, 16*(4), 5−21.

Hofstede, G., & Hofstede, G. J. (2005). *Cultures and organizations: Software of the mind* (2nd ed.). New York, NY: McGraw-Hill.

Hofstede, G., Hofstede, G. J., & Minkov, M. (2010). *Cultures and organizations: Software of the mind* (3rd ed.). New York, NY: McGraw-Hill.

Hoyer, W. D., MacInnis, D. J., & Pieters, R. (2013). *Consumer behavior* (6th ed.). International Edition. Mason, OH: Cengage Learning.

Jameson, F. (1990). Postmodernism and consumer society. In H. Foster (Ed.), *The anti-aesthetic essays on postmodern culture* (pp. 111–125). Port Townsend, WA: Bay Press.

Johnson, G. J., & Ambrose, P. J. (2006). Neo-tribes: The power and potential of online communities in health care. *Communications of the ACM, 49*(1), 107–113.

Joseph, S., Lid, V., & Suthers, D. (2007). Transcendent communities. In D. Chinn, G. Erkens, & S. Puntambekar (Eds.), The computer supported collaborative learning *(CSCL) conference 2007* (pp. 317–319). New Brunswick, NJ: International Society of the Learning Sciences.

Joy, A. S., & Sherry, J. F., Jr (2003). Speaking of art as embodied imagination: A multisensory approach to understanding aesthetic experience. *Journal of Consumer Research, 30*(September), 259–282.

Kellner, D. (1995). *Media culture.* London: Routledge.

Kozinets, R. V. (2001). Utopian enterprise: Articulating the meaning of Star Trek's culture of consumption. *Journal of Consumer Research, 28*(June), 67–89.

Kozinets, R. V. (2002). The field behind the screen: Using netnography for marketing research in online communities. *Journal of Marketing Research, 39*(1), 61–72.

Kozinets, R. V. (2006). Click to connect: Netnography and tribal advertising. *Journal of Advertising Research, 46*(3), 279–288.

Kozinets, R. V., Valck, K., Wojnicki, A. C., & Wilner, S. J. S. (2010). Networked narratives: Understanding word-of-mouth marketing in online communities. *Journal of Marketing, 74*(2), 71–89.

Maffesoli, M. (1996). *The time of the tribes.* London: Thousand Oaks and New Delhi: Sage.

Markus, H. R., & Kitayama, S. (1991). Culture and the self: Implications for cognition, emotion, and motivation. *Psychological Review, 98*, 224–253.

Muniz, A. M., & O'Guinn, T. C. (2001). Brand community. *Journal of Consumer Research, 27*(4), 412–432.

Murphy, N. (1996). *Beyond liberalism and fundamentalism: How modern and postmodern philosophy set the theological agenda.* Valley Forge, PA: Trinity Press International.

Na, J., Grossmann, I., Varnum, M. E. W., Kitayama, S., Gonzalez, R., & Nisbett, R. E. (2010). Cultural differences are not always reducible to individual differences. *Proceedings of the National Academy of Sciences of the United States of America, 107*, 6192–6197. Available from: http://dx.doi.org/10.1073/pnas.1001911107.

Nisbett, R. E., & Masuda, T. (2003). Culture and point of view. *Proceedings of the National Academy of Sciences of the United States of America, 100*(19), 11163–11175. Available from: http://dx.doi.org/10.1073/pnas.1934527100.

Pan, Z., Lu, Y., & Gupta, S. (2014). How heterogeneous community engage newcomers? The effect of community diversity on newcomers' perception of inclusion: An empirical study in social media service. *Computers in Human Behavior, 39*, 100–111.

Patterson, M. (1998). Direct marketing in postmodernity: Neo-tribes and direct communications. *Marketing Intelligence & Planning, 16*(1), 68–74.

Pongsakornrungsilp, S., & Schroeder, J. (2011). Understanding value co-creation in a co-consuming brand community. *Marketing Theory, 11*(3), 303–324.

Proctor, S., Papasolomou-Doukakis, I., & Proctor, T. (2002). What are television advertisements really trying to tell us? A postmodern perspective. *Journal of Consumer Behavior, 1*(3), 246–255.

Schau, H. J., & Gilly, M. C. (2003). We are what we post? Self-presentation in personal web space. *Journal of Consumer Research, 30*(3), 385–404.

Schein, E. (1985). *Organizational culture and leadership.* San Francisco, CA: Jossey-Bass.

Schembri, S., & Latimer, L. (2016). Online brand communities: Constructing and co-constructing brand culture. *Journal of Marketing Management, 32*(7–8), 628–651.

Schembri, S., Merrilees, B., & Kristiansen, S. (2010). Brand consumption and narrative of self. *Psychology and Marketing, 27*(6), 623–638.

Shankar, A., Cherrier, H., & Canniford, R. (2006). Consumer empowerment: A Foucauldian interpretation. *European Journal of Marketing, 40*, 1013–1030.

Simmons, G. (2008). Marketing to postmodern consumers: Introducing the internet chameleon. *European Journal of Marketing, 42*(3/4), 299–310.

Smith, A. N., Fischer, E., & Yongjian, C. (2012). How does brand-related user-generated content differ across YouTube, Facebook, and Twitter? *Journal of Interactive Marketing, 26*, 102–113.

Smith, M. W. (2001). *Reading simulacra: Fatal theories for postmodernity.* Albany, NY: State University of New York.

Stadler, R., Brenner, W., & Herrmann, A. (2014). *How to succeed in the digital age: Strategies from 17 top managers.* Frankfurt: Frankfurter Societats-Medien GmbH.

Taute, H. A., & Sierra, J. (2014). Brand tribalism: An anthropological perspective. *Journal of Product and Brand Management, 23*(1), 2–15.

Teerikangas, S. (2007). A comparative overview of the impact of cultural diversity on inter-organisational encounters. *Advances in Mergers and Acquisitions, 6*, 37–75.

Thomas, T., Price, L. L., & Schau, H. J. (2013). When differences unite: Resource dependence in heterogeneous consumption communities. *Journal of Consumer Research, 39*, 1010–1033.

Tian, K. T., & McKenzie, K. (2001). The long-term predictive validity of the consumers' need for uniqueness scale. *Journal of Consumer Psychology, 10*(3), 171–193.

Vargo, S. L., & Lusch, R. F. (2004). Evolving to a new dominant logic for marketing. *Journal of Marketing, 68*(1), 1–17.

Veloutsou, C., & Moutinho, L. (2009). Brand relationships through brand reputation and brand tribalism. *Journal of Business Research, 62*, 314–322.

Venkatesh, A. (1999). Postmodern perspectives for macromarketing: An inquiry into the global information and sign economy. *Journal of Macromarketing, 19*(2), 153–169.

Weijo, H., Hietanen, J., & Mattila, P. (2014). New insights into online consumption communities and netnography. *Journal of Business Research, 67*, 2072–2078.

Zaglia, M. E. (2013). Brand communities embedded in social networks. *Journal of Business Research, 66*(2), 216–223.

CHAPTER 5

Self-Construals

It is evident that there is an inherent need to understand the individual characteristics of the consumers that utilize the new social media environment, especially the culminations of consumers such as online brand communities (Moran & Gossieaux, 2010). The self-construal theory, as coined by Markus and Kitayama (1991), depicts two differing aspects of the self, which are reminiscent of Hofstede's individualism—collectivism cultural dimensions, as a way to measure individual differences. These individual differences affect motivation, cognition, emotion, and behavior have been subject to a variety of new influences in the new social media environment.

This chapter will discuss the concept of self-construals including the characteristics of both the interdependent and independent dimensions. The differences between the two self-construals, including the effect this has on marketing, messages, and consumer behavior will also be discussed. The need for uniqueness concept will be highlighted as important due to the level at which both construals crave being unique and how this has affected consumer behavior, particularly within online brand communities. This will culminate in a discussion of why the self is important in the study of online brand communities, with a final touch upon hedonic and utilitarian motivations and how these are related.

5.1 UNDERSTANDING SELF-CONSTRUALS

The self-construal theory, initially proposed by Markus and Kitayama (1991), was originally used as a way to explain the differences among cultures (Aaker & Lee, 2001; Markus & Kitayama, 1991). Expanded from the original individualist—collectivist scale by Hofstede (1980), which identified cultural level differences, the self-construal theory focused on individual level differences, which cannot be explained in depth by the original theory (Wei, Miao, Cai, & Adler, 2012).

The use of the concept has been expanded to consumer behavior (e.g., Millan & Reynolds, 2014; Polyorat & Alden, 2005), personality (e.g., Baldwin & Sinclair, 1996), and consumer psychology (e.g., Zhang & Shrum, 2009), with many studies emphasizing the importance of the self-construal in the context of the marketing discipline (e.g., Escalas & Bettman, 2005; Zhang & Shrum, 2009). Impacting emotion, motivation, behavior, and cognition, these individual dimensions have commonly been researched on an individual level (Van Baaren, Maddux, Chartrand, De Bouter, & van Knippenberg, 2003; Voyer & Franks, 2014), meaning that combining this into a comprehensive theory is difficult as knowledge is limited, forcing many to question both the theory itself and its measurement (Gudykunst & Lee, 2003; Levine et al., 2003; Voyer & Franks, 2014). Markus and Kitayama's (1991) conceptualization acknowledged individual level cultural differences (e.g., USA is more independent, whereas China is more interdependent), which have been expanded by others to explain more general individual level differences without the cultural variable.

The self-construal, which has been the subject of research in various disciplines, most notably psychology and communication for over the past two decades (Gudykunst & Lee, 2003), posits the view that the self is not just a single autonomous entity but rather, it focuses on two specific dimensions of self-concept, providing an individual level description of cultural differences in the form the independent and interdependent self-construal (Levine et al., 2003). The two aspects of the self do not lend themselves specifically to exist within one individual in isolation, they both coexist together within each individual (Aaker & Lee, 2001; Brewer & Gardner, 1996; Gudykunst et al., 1996; Singelis, 1994), although, they will differ in their strength and individuals will tend to be susceptible to the use of one or the other (Escalas & Bettman, 2005; Gudykunst & Lee, 2003). Rather they develop in relation to the surrounding environment and others around us, accruing meaning dependent upon the situation (Verplanken, Trafimow, Khusid, Holland, & Steentjes, 2009). As the self is established within the social context, the impact of others and the interdependent aspect of the self is extremely important to the creation of the self-concept (Brewer & Gardner, 1996), which has been identified as a crucial factor in association and interaction with brands and marketing (Belk, 2013). These two dimensions of the self differ on many levels such as focus of their goals (Aaker & Maheswaran, 1997; Triandis, 1990), values (Verplanken et al., 2009), interaction (Kim, Sharkey, & Singelis, 1994), product preference (Jiraporn & Desai, 2010), and network structure (Na, Kosinski, & Stillwell, 2015) among others.

Markus and Kitayama (1991, p. 229) defined the self-construals as "part of a repertoire of self-relevant schemata used to evaluate, organize, and regulate one's experience and action." They emphasized a self-construal consists of underlying traits that form part of the self-definition which "have a set of specific consequences for cognition, emotion, and motivation" (Markus & Kitayama, 1991, p. 224), which affects "what they believe about the relationship between the self and others and, especially, the degree to which they see themselves as separate from others or as connected with others" (Markus & Kitayama, 1991, p. 226). This is important to acknowledge for social media as individuals will utilize this new social environment as a way to both build relationships and self-expression. Not only this but the social media environment provides a new situation and context, which will influence an individual's self-construal and thus affect motivations, cognition, emotion, and ultimately behavior. Levine et al. (2003, p. 211) also stressed that self-construals are "an individual-level cultural orientation and is theorized to mediate and explain the effects of culture on a variety of social behaviours." The variety of platforms in the social media environment are believed to embody specific cultures (Stadler, Brenner, & Herrmann, 2014), which will thus affect the individual behaviors of those that use them. These definitions are somewhat limited as they do not acknowledge the situational and environmental effects (Gudykunst & Lee, 2003; Knowles & Gardner, 2008; White, Argo, & Sengupta, 2012). It could be argued that the variety of social environments an individual is exposed to negates that a new definition is perhaps necessary. Thus it could be argued that the self-construals are contextually and environmentally influenced independent and interdependent aspects of the self that explain how individuals perceive themselves as similar or distinct from others through differences in cognition, emotion, and motivation that can be shaped by cultural differences (citations adapted from Levine et al., 2003; Markus & Kitayama, 1991).

5.1.1 Independent Characteristics

The self-construal theory proposes two different aspects of the self: independent and interdependent. Individuals with an independent self-construal utilize their environments in a strategic way, using information as a means to express themselves (Markus & Kitayama, 1991). They are focused on themselves and seek to achieve individual goals that make them distinct so that they are not considered similar to others (Jain, Desai, & Mao, 2007; Markus & Kitayama, 1991; Singelis, 1994; Verplanken et al., 2009). Individuals that embody this self-construal pride themselves on appearing in the best possible way, distancing themselves from anything that will make them appear in a negative light (Sedikides, 1993). Individuals with this self-construal are not influenced by anyone but themselves (Song & Lee, 2013), and can be considered as "individualist, egocentric, separate, autonomous, idiocentric, and self-contained" (Markus & Kitayama, 1991, p. 226). They are also likely to bolster their identity in the face of threat (White et al., 2012). The social media environment will give an individual with an independent self-construal the opportunity to express their uniqueness, quenching their need for displaying this through self-presentational mechanisms (Lalwani & Shavitt, 2009), including crafting their identity through carefully selected privacy settings (Chen & Marcus, 2012).

5.1.2 Interdependent Characteristics

Interdependent individuals are concerned with fitting in with others, allowing them to be influenced by situation and context to pursue collective goals which guide their behavior (Gudykunst & Lee, 2003; Jain et al., 2007; Levine et al., 2003; Singelis, 1994). They ultimately wish to form relationships with others and could be considered as "sociocentric, holistic, collective, allocentric, ensemble, constitutive, contextualist, connected, and relational" (Markus & Kitayama, 1991, p. 227). They also exhibit a great need to belong, and achieving this through relationship development will boost their self-esteem (White & Lehman, 2005; White et al., 2012). Individuals with this self-construal will tend to be more flexible in their behavior to fit in with others, thus its reliance on the situation means that it is harder to comprehend without considering these influences (Markus & Kitayama, 1991). In the face of threat these individuals will change their behavior to allow them to accommodate the changing situation (White et al., 2012). Researchers believe that this self-construal has two facets: the collective interdependent self-construal (focus on the group) and the relational interdependent self-construal (focus on close relationships, e.g., family), although these were not observed in the original theory (Markus & Kitayama, 1991). The nature of the social media environment means that individuals with the interdependent self-construal readily adapt to its social platforms, achieving their need for belonging through community use and interaction with others. The variety of platforms and their unique cultures (Stadler et al., 2014) allow individuals with this self-construal to modify their behavior accordingly.

5.2 DIFFERENCES BETWEEN THE SELF-CONSTRUALS

Individuals with independent or interdependent self-construals behave, think, and react differently depending on the construal they are predisposed to, as well as contextual and environmental influences that may prime a certain self-construal to become salient, meaning an individual has a multitude of responses to a situation (Verplanken et al., 2009). The social media allows for a variety of new situations and contextual influences to alter the behavior of individuals and thus make them behave in accordance with this.

Similarly to self-construal theory, social identity theory posits that an identity consists of an individual personal identity and a social or group identity (Tajfel & Turner, 1986), both of which are context dependent. Thus an individual is likely to respond with either identity that is suited to the situation (Brewer, 1991; Tajfel & Turner, 1986). Consumers may avoid products that are negatively associated with their identity as a way to make sure their self-esteem is not hindered (White & Argo, 2009), which mimics previous thought that consumers would identify with products depending on how well they fitted in with their social identity (Kleine, Kleine, & Kernan, 1993). When under something that threatens their identity consumers will either dissociate themselves from the product, change their perception so as to accommodate the information in the threat, or accept the threat and change their behavior to reflect that (Tajfel, 1978; Tajfel & Turner, 1986). A recent study by White et al. (2012) found that independent individuals where more likely to adopt dissociation of a product under threat whereas interdependent individuals were more likely to adopt associative behavior. Replicating previous findings by Tajfel and Turner (1979) and Wright, Taylor, and Moghaddam (1990), this study demonstrated that behavior was dependent on their relationship with the group and if they could in fact dissociate themselves at all from the proposed threat. Independent individuals will be associated with an out-group, while interdependent individuals are more likely to be associated with the in-group based on their affiliation with groups and their need to belong. However, this suggestion is being threatened by findings that imply that an independent individual prefers the in-group when their self-esteem is under some sort of threat (Nakashima, Isobe, & Ura, 2008), although it must be noted that this study was conducted in a collectivist culture which have been shown to have a high consistency of interdependent individuals. Wang, Ma, and Li (2015) found that interdependent individuals were more aware of how their self was viewed by others, although this public self-consciousness was previously thought to be associated with only the independent self-construal and their concerns for ideal self-presentation (Carver & Scheier, 1987; Fenigstein, 1987). The social media environment, which consists of a variety of groups and communities on each platform, means individuals with differing self-construals may tend to use these differently. There are a variety of individuals that occupy differing social media platforms that allow individuals to come across a multitude of opinions and perspectives that may threaten their identity. It is possible that the multitude of platforms acts as a mechanism to allow those that want to dissociate from threats or negative connotations the ability to distance themselves and thus regain a higher sense of self-esteem.

Individuals have multiple selves (Belk, 2013; Suh, 2002), thus the independent and interdependent self-construal are both present within an individual, although each individual will have a chronic self-construal which is salient the majority of the time, with the other self-construal being latent. However, the self-construals can be primed through situational context, allowing the latent self-construal to be temporarily primed (Brewer & Gardner, 1996). The interdependent self-construal, which is more pliable to their environment is more affected by their context than independents and so may display more noticeable behavioral changes (Chatman & Barsade, 1995). Kumashiro, Rusbult, and Finkel (2008) also found that there may be more to the self-construals than previously thought as the saliency of one self-construal can activate the latent self-construal as a means to provide balance to the individual. The pliability of the self-construals was noted by Verplanken et al. (2009) in respect of values, where they found that each self-construal was related to different values, thus affecting their behavior. Brewer and Chen (2007) also noted the multidimensional aspects of the self, claiming that aspects of both interdependent and independent values and beliefs are present, yet some are more salient than others depending on cultural context. In the social media environment, Bechtoldt, Choi, and Nijstad (2012), who looked at creativity within online brand communities found that a community will not thrive unless individuals with both self-construal are present. Therefore it can be construed that the mix of individualistic consumers and the collectivist group members combine to make more original ideas, or perhaps the opposite construals are engaging the other self-construals as a means of producing this idea, emphasizing their salient nature. Furthermore, it could be that the mix of both types of construals is the best environment for idea generation and originality, as collectivist orientation was most original when it was combined with the more independent self-construal (Bechtoldt et al., 2012). The globalized world is more attracted to innovativeness as a basis for success and finding more information about individual consumer differences will help break down the barriers to the creative spark that fosters innovation (Bechtoldt et al., 2012). The competitive trait of the independent self-construal becomes more salient when the situational context allows them to think about themselves more (Liu & Li, 2009). Thus in the new individualized postmodern era, consumers are subject to this individualistic thought, which makes them act in a more competitive manner, utilizing online communities and the social media environment for their own gain.

Independent individuals have a more egocentric network with weak ties between others, whereas interdependent individuals have more tight knit networks that enable strong ties (Na et al., 2015). This variance in network structures and thus communication, means that attitudes may form differently which, with the access and reach of social media can be extremely damaging if the attitudes are negative. Wei et al. (2012) demonstrated that independent individuals are more likely to verbalize their complaints as well as switch brands, whereas interdependent individuals were more likely to engage in electronic word of mouth/word of mouth (eWOM/WOM) to help others avoid experiencing the same thing. The information and way in which individuals with differing self-construals will pass this information on to their networks varies, with those displaying interdependence passing on relevant yet negative content (Chen & Marcus, 2012), mimicking the choice of complaint behavior identified by Wei et al. (2012). Although both of these studies were conducted in independent cultures, which could affect the generalizability of the results. Yet, the positive influence of interdependent individuals on eWOM is also noted, with community engagement self-efficacy a result of the encounters with others within the community setting (Lee, Kim, & Kim, 2012). The effect of any WOM/eWOM communication can have a great influence on the formation of individual attitudes toward products and brands (Zhang, Moore, & Moore, 2011). Discovering who it is that consumers are communicating with and why it is essential to developing the best marketing strategies, as sharing identity with a brand and engaging on such a personal level will improve all present and future communications (Greenaway, Wright, Willingham, Reynolds, & Haslam, 2015).

Consumers can use products and brands as an extension of their selves (Belk, 1988, 2013), and a way to enhance their overall opinion of themselves, or self-esteem (Rosenberg, 1979). If an individual has a low self-esteem then they are likely to try and find ways to make this higher, such as through their use of products and brands, which will perhaps project the ideal image they want the world to see (Higgins, 1987). Independent individuals, who engage in self-presentational behavior may be considered to be trying to boost their self-esteem through these means as a bid to protect their image, unlike those who are prone to interdependence. However, high self-esteem individuals have been found to act in a more self-protective way, which would denote a relationship with independence rather than interdependence (Crocker, Thompson, McGraw, & Ingerman, 1987). This could be a result of the context-dependent nature of the self, whereby the situation primes one or other self-construal to become salient (Hannover, Birkner, & Pohlmann, 2006). The social media environment facilitates a place where projection of the ideal self is easier and thus this may boost self-esteem of those individuals who utilize the online environment for this purpose. However, it is thought that the online and social media environment allow the perfect place for individuals to present their actual selves (Gilmore & Pine, 2007).

Self-congruity allows an individual to use brands and products as a way to embody what they stand for as a means of self-presentation (Sirgy, 1982). This self-congruence will affect their response to the brand (Malar, Krohmer, Hoyer, & Nyffenegger, 2011), the relationship an individual has with the brand, and how involved they become (Celsi & Olson, 1988). Hence the personality of the brand is incredibly important to this perception (Aaker, 1999; Belk, 1988). Not only will self-congruency affect individual identity, it will also affect communications within or outside their group (Escalas & Bettman, 2005), thus considering group or community differences is important (Graupmann, Jonas, Meier, Hawelka, & Aichhorn, 2012). The social media environment allows individuals to come into contact with many brands and products, which must be able to reflect self-congruity, for individuals to engage with them on such an identity defining medium. The self-construals, which reflect different values, may not consider products and brands to reflect their selves in the same way. In fact independent individuals prefer less differentiated products whereas interdependent individuals prefer more innovative products (Jiraporn & Desai, 2010). This is perhaps contradictory to the standard assumption that only independent self-construals utilize their consumption experiences as a means of differentiating themselves from others, which would presume a preference for the more unique product. Although, it has also been found that interdependent consumers prefer safer products (rather than risky, which independent individuals prefer) (Hamilton & Biehal, 2005), as they wish to fit in with the group and use the same brands and products which will be reflected in their behavior (Mandel, 2003). Although these findings are conflicting, the evidence that both self-construals exist within each individual, with one or other becoming salient to provide balance and depending on situation context could explain these findings (Brewer & Chen, 2007; Brewer & Gardner, 1996; Kumashiro et al., 2008).

5.2.1 Need for Uniqueness

Need for uniqueness theory asserts that people are implored by their desire to appear distinct from others (Simonson & Nowlis, 2000; Snyder & Fromkin, 1977), using the consumption experience as a way of delineating from others in a bid to express their uniqueness (Cheema & Kaikati, 2010; Ruvio, 2008). Although some consumers seek this uniqueness more than others, individuals may only assert this uniqueness to a certain degree so as not to upset social norms, as they also need to be considered to some extent similar to others (Brewer, 1991; Snyder & Fromkin, 1977). As the self-construals proposed by Markus and Kitayama (1991) are seen as distinct in their motivations, they have often been used as a predictive tool for this uniqueness seeking behavior (e.g., Chang, 2015). The battle between belonging and uniqueness replicates the relationship between the two self-construals as they also coexist within each individual (Song & Lee, 2013). This is the tenet of optimal distinctiveness theory (Brewer, 1991; Shore et al., 2010), which asserts that individuals have to balance the need to belong within a group with the need to appear unique (Song & Lee, 2013), which has also been demonstrated by Timmor and Katz-Navon (2008).

It is well noted in the literature that consumers use their consumption choices to distinguish themselves from others (Ruvio, Shoham, & Brenčič, 2008; Tian, Bearden, & Hunter, 2001), although recent studies have shown that this is exercised in different ways. Song and Lee (2013) found that consumers with an independent self-construal are motivated by their need for uniqueness, whereas consumers with an interdependent self-construal are motivated by their need for distinctiveness, therefore confirming that all individuals crave uniqueness in some way. Millan and Reynolds (2014) also found that interdependent consumers seek uniqueness to some extent through their consumption of hedonic/symbolic products as a means of fitting in with the group, also confirming the status symbolic consumption of independent consumers. Although both of these studies measured uniqueness in an offline purchasing behavior capacity DeAndrea, Shaw, and Levine (2010) found that culture, which is synonymous with the differing self-construals, has an impact on the way an individual communicates, especially in relation to their self and anything which enables them to appear distinct from others. A study by Lynn and Harris (1997) found that it was indeed the individual motivations that inspire some individuals to assert their uniqueness through consumption behaviors, making the self-construal one of the more appropriate concepts to apply to examining these differences. The need for uniqueness model has been adapted to the consumer need for uniqueness model which is described as "the trait of pursuing differentness relative to others through the acquisition, utilization, and disposition of consumer goods for the purpose of developing and enhancing one's self-image and social image" (Tian & McKenzie, 2001, p. 172). Although the reasons behind uniqueness seeking and influences regarding this behavior appear to be subject to a gap in the literature (Song & Lee, 2013).

This behavior can be readily observed through the postmodern consumer, whereby the freedom of consumers reduces their commitment needs (Dawes & Brown, 2000), allowing them to utilize many consumption experiences to craft their multiple selves (Belk, 2013) enabling distinction from others (Brown, 1995, 1997). This postmodern consumer may exhibit their self through community use by using the consumption interests and brands for reasons of expression (Cova & Pace, 2006; Dholakia, Bagozzi, & Pearo, 2004). This could reiterate Song and Lee's (2013) finding that both the independent and interdependent self-construal craves uniqueness to some degree, with the postmodern consumer integrating this need for uniqueness in their overt behavior as a means of combating the increased alienation from their individualistic tendencies (Goulding, 2003). This behavior of utilizing consumption interests as a way of establishing a degree of uniqueness is enabled by the use of social media and its ability to facilitate the development and creation of online brand communities.

5.2.2 Communities and the "Self"

One of the things that the social media environment has drastically affected is the concept of "self" or more specifically the "extended self" as proposed by Belk (1988). The plethora of new technological advancements, most notably social media has led to dematerialization, reembodiment, sharing, coconstruction of the self and distributed memory that has destroyed the original illusion that individuals embody one core self-concept, facilitating the notion that we are multifaceted beings with multiple selves (Belk, 2013). These selves can manifest and express themselves online, which are enabled by the many platforms available on social media. The multiple platforms are beneficial for fulfilling different objectives, many to do with enhancing ones self-concept, or more specifically their multiple selves (Belk, 2013). Due to the communal nature and self-expressive purposes of social media and online brand communities this can be through things such as self-expression, presentation of self, or bolstering self-esteem (Back et al., 2010; Wilcox & Stephen, 2013; Yeo, 2012). Consumers can use these online brand communities to identify on the level of both the group and individual (Chang, Hsieh, & Tseng, 2013), although, Bodner and Prelec (2003), and Loewenstein (1999) believed that consumers expression of identity was for their own benefit rather than that of others. Consumers place great importance on anything that coincides with their self—thus communication via mechanisms such as eWOM will be more likely if it is considered relevant to this self (Berthon, Pitt, & Campbell, 2008; Hennig-Thurau, Gwinner, Walsh, & Gremler, 2004).

Social identity theory is of great relevance to online brand communities as when forming a social identity people will tend to affiliate themselves with particular groups, which will allow them to identify with all things related to that group and thus build on their social identity (Grayson & Martinec, 2004; Tajfel & Turner, 1986). It could therefore be argued that the self is directly related to engagement. Bagozzi and Dholakia, (2002, p. 4) believe that "a person achieves a social identity [in a community] through self-awareness of one's membership in a group and the emotional and evaluative significance of this membership." However, Schau, Muñiz, and Arnould (2009) believe that this identity is created through the development of value creating practices that allow for resources that are mutually delineated within the community to be exchanged. The things that we consume are reflections of our identity (Belk, 1988; Holbrook, 1992; Kernan & Sommers, 1967; Kleine, Kleine, & Kernan, 1992; Solomon, 1983), and depending on the identity contributes to the consumers self (Kleine et al., 1993). Enacting in an online brand community can therefore be seen as a way of showcasing a certain identity, with the use of the group and subsequent behavior within that environment subject to the same ridicule and judgement as actual possessions (Kleine et al., 1993). However, social identity is subject to contextual influence and depending on the environment this will enable certain identities to be portrayed. A recent study by Champniss, Wilson, and Macdonald (2015) found that social identities can be constructed in a relatively short space of time, with an impact that is strong enough that particular behaviors appear regardless of previous attitudes held.

The narrative strategies that are used in social media communications show how consumers will deliberately alter their communication strategies to be in line with what they are trying to project and communicate— and thus be in line with their self (Kozinets, de Valck, Wojnicki, & Wilner, 2010). This transformation of WOM has moved from consumers communicating with other consumers on the basis of wanting to help and without any direct influence, to a model where companies are actively trying to influence influential consumers or opinion leaders (Arndt, 1967; Brooks, 1957; Engel, Kegerreis, & Blackwell, 1969; Gatignon & Robertson, 1986; Katz & Lazarsfeld, 1955). It is now in the stage of coproduction where companies are targeting consumers individually moving to a relationship based model, where deliberate tactics are being used as influential strategies (Kozinets et al., 2010; Vargo & Lusch, 2004). The communication that happens within online brand communities can also be referred to as social WOM or sWOM and refers to WOM that is communicated when it is suitable for the consumer at a convenient time and place that is shared from one consumer to many others (Sun, Youn, Wu, & Kuntaraporn, 2006). The discrepancy in terms needs to be addressed as at the present time eWOM is the preferred term used for all communication online.

As the interactions with other consumers help consumers to receive their identity it is unsurprising that many consumers will turn to this type of environment for support (Hajli & Hajli, 2013). The community that consumers engage in will help consumers to create their identity and transform it and they will therefore feel closer to this community as well as closer to the brand that hosts the community, ultimately leading to feelings of trust and loyalty and in turn economic value, which can be in the form of current or future purchases (Davis, Piven, & Breazeale, 2014; Park, Lee, & Han, 2007). Interdependent individuals are more trusting than independent individuals (Liu, Rau, & Wendler, 2015), interestingly this is highly evident when incentives are individually focused (Guo & Main, 2011). Therefore it is essential that the social value of these communities is not overlooked and the experience that consumers get while in these communities is positive as a negative experience could transform into negative reactions to the brand.

It can also be said that the relationship that consumers have with a brand mimics that of the social relationships they have (Aggarwal, 2004). This is similar to Divakaran (2012) who noted that what happens in the online world is a reflection of what is happening offline. Greenaway et al. (2015) found that in-group member communications (i.e., those between members of a group or community) are more effective than communications with out-group members (i.e., those communications that are from members outside the group or community). If in-group communication are more effective, then it could be construed that the more independent consumers who migrate between communities are not integrating themselves enough and therefore communication from them toward the group are disregarded in some way. Escalas and Bettman (2005) also previously found brands with symbolic images that align with the in-group are more successful in enhancing self-brand connections among consumers. Their study also found that independent consumers are more affected by out-group associations than interdependent consumers as they strive to create a unique identity and differentiate themselves (Escalas & Bettman, 2005). Symbolic consumption and self has long been associated with identity construction (Elliott, 1997), therefore identifying the brand meaning on the level of individual differences, such as self-construal, can help integrate this into something of symbolic value for consumers (Schembri, Merrilees, & Kristiansen, 2010). Graupmann et al. (2012) found that a threat from the in-group that provided a restriction gained more reactance from the independent than interdependent self-construal, again reiterating their need for uniqueness. Na et al. (2015) also found that in-groups (interdependent individuals) are less likely to accept structural holes within their networks, meaning that individualists (independent individuals) are more likely to make up the out-group. The conflict that arises with out-group members and the different formations of out-groups also deserves further research (Escalas & Bettman, 2005).

Consumption of brands through communities is something that is individual to each consumer and can help an individual through the constant change of their self-identity (Brodie, Hollebeek, Biljana, & Ilic, 2011). In this way brands can help track the changes in collective identity and what their advocates and consumers are turning into. They are then able to change their strategies and tactics to accommodate the changing characteristics and quirks of their consumers (Aaker, 1997; Avis, 2012; Seimiene, 2012). By being able to adapt, organizations and brands are able to form close relationships with consumers which transposes into loyalty and trust, meaning even if they do alter their self-identity they will be more inclined to remain close to the brand based on their acceptance and tracking of these changes. If consumers identify with the brand and it is replicative of their own identities, then they are more likely to become involved with the brand (Johnson & Eagly, 1989). The relationships formed in brand communities, although help an individual with their constant changing self-identity, can also help to guide the choices made while in the process of changing this self-identity. This is because they can provide information toward the choices the consumer is making and this will therefore provide informational value and a way for the consumer to address other options (Davis et al., 2014). The bond formed with other consumers in this process will likely strengthen the bond that the consumer has with the brand as the relationships within the brand community will provide value on an emotional and supportive social level which they will be grateful for, thus creating value. This will ultimately help in strengthening the relationship with the brand as a whole (Davis, Buchanan-Oliver, & Brodie, 2000). The use of online brand communities make it easier for others to help in the coconstruction of others identities, which is aided by the disinhibition effect that allows multiple identities to be tested online (Belk, 2013). However, it must be noted that the need for self-expression can be satisfied with exposure to other self-expressive brands that are available, which do not have to be in the same category as the original self-expressive brand (Chernev, Hamilton, & Gal,

2011). Exposure to a self-expressive brand can mean that a consumer is less susceptible to influence from other self-expressive brands, though only for a short duration (Chernev et al., 2011). The social media environment allows consumers to be exposed to a multitude of brands on a regular basis.

Self-orientation is one of the most important dimensions of the five sources model as it refers to how the self aligns with a brand (Davis et al., 2014). Consuming the brand through communities allows their identities to be created and enhanced or changed with the help of others. The social dimension of the five sources model is also important as the social interaction that a consumer engages in online will give them the opportunity to build a representation of the self-identity, which will add value to the consumer's lives based on the social interactions (Davis et al., 2014). In addition, the emotional dimension is also important as it increases hedonic experience—resulting in a positive brand reaction (Rosenbaum, 2008).

5.2.3 Hedonic and Utilitarian Motivations

According to Holbrook and Hirschman (1982) consumption has two aspects: instrumental aka utilitarian and emotional satisfaction aka hedonic. In other words, people will engage in consumption based on the benefit or pleasure they receive from the process. Utilitarian motivations are based on the benefits they will get from engaging in consumption, e.g., reputation, reward, such as that sought by the independent self-construal (Markus & Kitayama, 1991). Whereas hedonic-motivated consumers are more focused on the experience the consumption process will provide them (Holbrook & Hirschman, 1982)—such as that gained from relations with others that are sought by the interdependent self-construal (Markus & Kitayama, 1991). Although it could be assumed that the utilitarian-motivated consumer is driven by the individualistic tendencies of status-seeking (looking for information) research by Millan and Reynolds (2014) found contradictory evidence that it is actually the interdependent consumer that can be associated with this utilitarian motivation. Both personality traits and the context of which consumers are consuming affect their motivations (Babin, Darden, & Griffin, 1994; Hartman, Shim, Barber, & O'Brien, 2006) with attitudes toward knowledge sharing being affected by sharing culture and self-efficacy (Liao, Hsu, & To, 2013). These motivations have been associated with independent and interdependent self-construal due to the attributes that each motivations has. The majority of models that have tried to outline hedonic and utilitarian motivations have been based on perceived usefulness—not only does this limit generalizability to other reasons behind their motivations but it also presumes that all consumers have an underlying utilitarian motivation (Poyry, Parvinen, & Malmivaara, 2013).

Liao et al. (2013) found that hedonic motivations are more important in knowledge sharing than utilitarian motivations, thus it could be construed that consumers embodying the interdependent self-construal have a higher predisposition to provide knowledge as they are more active members of the community and engage with others. However, as recent studies have suggested, consumers are becoming more individualistic and therefore this could indicate that utilitarian motivations are becoming more relevant (Weijo, Hietanen, & Mattila, 2014). Hedonic motivation, which has a direct impact on intention to search (To, Liao, & Lin, 2007), is related to the relationship between information access and loyalty as outlined by Anderson, Knight, Pookulangara, and Josiam (2014)—they are compelled to search for information and on finding this information will increase their loyalty to the organization or brand and therefore have an indirect effect on purchase intent. If more hedonic values were applied to online platforms then this would stimulate enjoyment which would generate search intention and ultimately purchase intention. By neglecting this aspect of motivation it is possible that many consumers are being left out as the utilitarian consumers are being catered for. Discovering the experiential meaning of brands, such as that of the online brand community for consumers, is essential for marketers (Schembri et al., 2010), and this can be better realized through careful examination and consideration of consumers individual differences. Online communities can cater for hedonic values, where they can provide entertainment and enjoyment value by communicating with like-minded individuals and sharing knowledge and experiences (Liao et al., 2013). The enjoyment that consumers perceive as being able to receive from different online actions can influence their intentions to use different aspects of the online environment (Van der Heijden, 2004). Thus, hedonic users, who seek experiences and enjoyment from their consumption experiences, may be more likely to engage in online brand communities as a way of gaining value from the experience.

Utilitarian behavior is strictly goal-directed with consumers looking for efficiency and information they can use to inform their purchases, whereas hedonic behavior is looking for the fun experience and entertainment value (Cotte, Chowdhury, Ratneshwar, & Ricci, 2006). Online consumer behavior has been found to be explained by both utilitarian and hedonic dimensions (Cotte et al., 2006; Hartman et al., 2006; Mäenpää, Kanto, Kuusela, & Paul, 2006), which determine different usage behaviors. Online communities, which normally have an interest- or utility-based function, must pay attention to which group of consumers they are trying to attract as value dissimilarity between consumers will have an effect of their engagement intention (Pan, Lu, & Gupta, 2014). With social media stressing the importance of personalization in everything, utilitarian-motivated consumers will be more inclined to use social media platforms for searching purposes due to the central focus on personal preferences making it more efficient (Mikalef, Pateli, & Giannakos, 2013). Utilitarian-motivated consumers tend to engage in more "lurking" behavior, only engaging in communication with other consumers when it is of direct benefit to them, preferring to browse to build up their store of information (Bateman, Gray, & Butler, 2010; Bloch, Sherrell, & Ridgway, 1986). However, De Valck, van Bruggen, and Wierenga (2009) believes that this distinction may be far too simple, distinguishing six types of online community members ranging from the core members who are in the simplified version the "posters" to the opportunists which are the "lurkers" as well as the conversationalists, informationalists, hobbyists, and functionalists which fall in between. They note that the functionalists and opportunists make up 50% of the members of the community; therefore it can be posited that it is these types of "lurker" consumers which form the weak ties that bridge the communities and strengthen networks (Granovetter, 1973). This links in with what has been described as the membership life cycle by Alon, Brunel, and Siegal (2005) and Kim (2000) who both describe a progressive process in which consumers initially start in informational and instrumental activities, eventually developing a relationship and thus commitment, followed by an end phase which allows members to again refocus on their informational and instrumental needs. This cyclic relationship could have an association with the lifespan of the Internet and social media, as consumers who joined and utilized the Internet and social media during its initial introduction would theoretically be the consumers who are reaching the end of their membership life cycle, and therefore this would go some way to explaining the newly visible individualistic tendencies of consumers. It would also parallel with generation C (Hardey, 2011), who have grown up with the social media environment and are perhaps more individualistic in their tendencies. Thus social media behavior could be resultant of new and old consumers utilizing the various platforms and online communities for their own unique needs.

Behavior can be context dependent and influenced by others—social influence (Elek, Miller-Day, & Hecht, 2006; Salancik & Pfeffer, 1978; Salganik, Dodds, & Watts, 2006), which is a notable characteristic of the interdependent self-construal (Markus & Kitayama, 1991). If consumers can be influenced by others, and are engaged in communications via online brand communities then network externality effect can occur, whereby the perceived value of a product or service is increased due to others adopting or using it (Brynjolfsson & Kemerer, 1996; Katz & Shapiro, 1985). Perceived value has three dimensions: utilitarian, hedonic, and social values (Yen, 2013). Utilitarian value is concerned with functionality—convenience, time saved, utility, and monetary savings (Teo, 2001), whereas hedonic value is about the experience and feelings (Overby & Lee, 2006), social value to relationships and support as well as the expression of self and image (Kim, Gupta, & Koh, 2011). A study by De Valck et al. (2009) found that the more consumers are engaged with the social aspects of the community, e.g., engaging in chatting, the less influence the community will have on their information retrieval. This experiential focus is clearly motivated by hedonic preferences and could suggest that the independent self-construal, is not so suited to knowledge seeking behavior, although this would need to be researched further.

5.3 SELF-CONSTRUALS IN THE NEW MARKETING ENVIRONMENT

The technological developments that have enabled social media to thrive have fueled consumer's desire for personalization and value, which have developed in direct relation to the interactive online environment. Just like the self-construal, which develops in relation to its surrounding environment (Verplanken et al., 2009), social media has grown based on the expanding demands of consumers. The self, which develops in relation to its social context (Brewer & Gardner, 1996), has thus had to adapt to the changing environment which now incorporates an online factor. People now interact both online and offline and this has contributed to the new postmodern culture. This newfound interaction online, which highly concerns the interdependent aspect of the self-construal, is critical to associations with brands and marketing (Belk, 2013).

Social media is developing quickly and adapting to the growing independent consumer, who seeks this personalization and unique value for themselves. Consequently the independent aspect of the self (or self-construal) has to become pliable to the new online environment. With its aspects of strategic manipulation (Markus & Kitayama, 1991), independent individuals will benefit from the multitude of online platforms as each can be used to fulfill a different objective. This creation of egocentric networks (Na et al., 2015) by the independent individual will act as a fountain of knowledge and provide them with valuable information to craft their self.

The social media environment has transformed the illusion that the self is one core being and instead contributed to the notion that it is multifaceted (Belk, 2013). With the self-construals two distinct aspects coexisting within each individual (Aaker & Lee, 2001; Brewer & Gardner, 1996; Gudykunst et al., 1996; Singelis, 1994), the aspect of a multifaceted self can be looked at through this lens, contributing to understanding the self as a whole. The differing self-construals become more salient depending on the situation and context of their environment (Escalas & Bettman, 2005; Gudykunst & Lee, 2003), meaning it is possible for the social media environment to allow one individual to express their chronic and primed self. The notion of multiple memberships provided by Habibi, Laroche, and Richard (2014) is the perfect example of the self-construal being context dependent as they can develop within this changing environment (Verplanken et al., 2009), allowing both dimensions to become activated at separate points. These multiple memberships have been aided by the proliferation and fragmentation that have created niche groups of consumers (Goulding, 2003), facilitating the context-dependent self-construal changes. The freedom of the Internet means that consumers do not have to commit (Dawes & Brown, 2000), allowing them the freedom to move between communities and activate the self-construal that is more suited to the online environment they are in at the time. This disinhibition effect (Belk, 2013) where multiple identities can be tested online, is more feasible in this social media setting. Although, the geographical dispersion and lack of spatial proximity within these online communities and social media platforms can lead them to be considered imagined communities (Anderson, 1983), highlighting the unreliable nature of the changing environment in which individuals find themselves in.

Consumers will use these online settings to supplement their multiple selves and will thus derive meaning and associations that are congruent with their selves (Schembri et al., 2010) from their networks and interactions. Independent consumers, who are more concerned with self-presentation and identity creation (Veloutsou, 2009), will be highly concerned with anything that is associated with them as the meanings can be transferrable, thus they would not want to be associated with an organization or a brand that made them look unfavorable to others as they wish to be seen as unique and separated from them (Markus & Kitayama, 1991). These individuals will be highly concerned with how they first appear to others (Markus & Kitayama, 1991). Thus, the surface level dissimilarity, identified by Pan et al. (2014) as more important than deep-level dissimilarity, will play a more important role for these consumers online. Although it can be posited that consumers wish to use these online environments as a way to express their actual self (how the individual actually sees themselves), and they therefore seek ways to do this (Gilmore & Pine, 2007).

The social media environment has become part of everyday life and is now integrated into a great deal of day-to-day activities. The social aspect of this environment means that the self, which is established within its social context, is greatly influenced by this new media and the other individuals which utilize it. The interdependent aspect of the self, which is based on relationships with others (Markus & Kitayama, 1991), could be greatly affected by this new social setting. The social aspect of social media means that the interdependent aspect of the self-construal is more visible within these environments, culminating in groups such as online brand communities. Shared consciousness, which is often considered to be the most important community marker (Brogi, 2014), is congruent with the aspects of the interdependent self-construal, in terms of seeing oneself in relation to others. Although, the independent self, which is also responsive to their social environment (though in a more strategic manner) (Markus & Kitayama, 1991), is evidently becoming susceptible to these new social changes.

The interdependent self-construal, which emphasizes collective goals and relationships with others can be considered to contribute more to online communities as those who contribute frequently are driven by group dedication rather than brand loyalty (Wiertz & De Ruyter, 2007). Therefore their interaction propensity, or how much they wish to interact is subject to how committed they are to the community

(Blazevic, Wiertz, Cotte, de Ruyter, & Keeling, 2014; Wiertz & De Ruyter, 2007). Interdependent individuals who are more committed to the community and their goals will be more inclined to interact with other consumers within online brand community environments. It has been found that socially active and extraverted individuals positively predict online social platform use (Correa, Hinsley, & de Zuniga, 2010; Wilson, Fornasier, & White, 2010). However, this active behavior within this online environment is present only within the minority of online brand community members, as the majority are passive (Gummerus, Liljander, Weman, & Pihlstrom, 2012). Although the different self-construals can be seen to be more effective at differing aspects of the online environment, Bechtoldt et al. (2012) has found that both individual and collective elements are essential for originality within the online brand community. Thus it can be construed that the self-construals, are both needed for an online brand community to thrive. Interdependent consumers are also a positive influence on eWOM as their relationship with other consumers allows them to affect the behavioral intentions of these others (Lee et al., 2012).

Weak ties are effective at linking individuals across groups (Brown & Reingen, 1987; Frenzen & Nakamoto, 1993; Reingen & Kernan, 1986), and independent individuals who seek information as a way of reemphasizing themselves (Markus & Kitayama, 1991), can be seen to form these weak ties across the networks as their network structure is more egocentric (Na et al., 2015). This is opposed to the interdependent individual who has a more close-knit network (Na et al., 2015) and will therefore form stronger ties within their relationships with others. These weaker ties can be considered to bring individuals together on a deeper level (Constant, Sproull, & Kiesler, 1996; Granovetter, 1973; Tardini & Cantoni, 2005; Wellman, 2001). This structure can be seen in the observation by Dholakia et al. (2004) of the distinction between both small-group communities (close-knit) and network-based (egocentric) communities.

5.4 DISCUSSION AND CONCLUDING POINTS

The self-construals that were originally proposed by Markus and Kitayama (1991) have been utilized throughout marketing as a way of studying the individual differences within consumers to advance knowledge of consumer behavior. Expanding on the individualist—collectivist scales that were developed by Hofstede (1980) the self-construals have provided an in-depth way to distinguish between the behavior, emotions, cognitions, and motivations of people. However, the differences between these different consumers have been largely neglected in the literature, leaving much room for exploration into individual differences that motivate community use (Chang et al., 2013). The expression of self in the public domain (such as the social media environment) requires further investigation to expand the literature regarding what the perceived function of this is (Chernev et al., 2011). The notion that consumers use brands as a way of constructing their "self" is not new (Belk, 1988; Schembri et al., 2010), yet, the neglect of this by marketing literature in terms of individual differences cannot be ignored. Finding the various ways that consumers use brands can help strategy development in order to best align with the selves of the consumers, thus fulfilling crucial psychological as well as social value and needs (Elliott & Wattanasuwan, 1998; Keller, 2003).

Summary of Key Points

- Individual's selves are multifaceted, incorporating two aspects of independence and interdependence that have implications for motivation, cognition, emotion, and behavior.
- Social media allows the different self-construals to complete their goals of self-presentation (independent) and belonging (interdependent).
- The exposure to a variety of brands and products on social media forces independent and interdependent individuals to selectively choose who they engage with as a means of reflecting an extension of their selves.
- Both self-construals display a need for uniqueness to some degree, which could explain the growing tendency toward individual social media and thus online brand community use.

Defining two aspects of the self-concept, the independent and interdependent self-construal, have become synonymous with either uniqueness, status-seeking motivations (independent) or group oriented, relationship-seeking motivation (interdependent). Several studies have utilized these concepts as a way of trying to help strategically leverage these individual differences in areas such as actual purchase behavior (Millan & Reynolds, 2014), in-group versus out-group (Graupmann et al., 2012) and communal strength (Mattingly, Oswald, & Clark, 2011). This merely highlights the importance of communities and the extent to which they are involved in the self, allowing self-expressive and relationship developing behaviors (Chang et al., 2013) that are consistent with the two differing aspects of the self-construal. Not only this but the motivations underlying the use of online brand communities, normally referred to as hedonic and utilitarian (Holbrook & Hirschman, 1982) are also synonymous with the self-construal and their ability to help distinguish between individual differences as well as observed online behavior. The concept of online brand communities has been studied in quite great detail, exploring the values and benefits of the uses of such environments for both consumers and marketers (e.g., Schau et al., 2009), yet, there has been little focus on self within these environments, which lends itself to a gap within the literature (Belk, 2013). It is important to consider the self-construal within the online brand community context because of the effects that they have on cognition, motivation, and emotion (Markus & Kitayama, 1991), which will ultimately affect how they behave within this environment.

The variety of identities that can be created are replicas of the multiple selves that exist within consumers (Ahuvia, 2005), and can thus be seen as expressions of the many aspects of the self-concept. Further research should be conducted on looking at how to strengthen the link between the self-concept of consumers and the brands they engage with (Berthon et al., 2008), to help find another communicative tool with which to engage consumers (Schembri et al., 2010). Greenaway et al. (2015) believe that the communication techniques and production of communication within the in-group and out-group should be investigated further. Investigation of the self-construal in any context will help in developing both training programmes and strategies to respond to anything from a threat to a compliment (Wei et al., 2012). The commercial nature of online brand communities means that the motivations that drive users toward these communication mediums should also be looked at within this commercialized environment (Poyry et al., 2013; To et al., 2007). A better understanding of hedonic and utilitarian motivations within both different community settings and contexts should be the focus of future research (Liao et al., 2013), especially regarding hedonic or experiential value of online brand communities (Flint, 2006; Poyry et al., 2013). As hedonic value is so personal to consumers there may be ethical considerations that need addressing and this should also be considered within future research scopes (Kemp, Bui, & Chapa, 2012).

Key Points for Practitioners

- Marketers should focus on projecting more individualized branding that consumers can relate to in terms of consistency with self and self-congruity.
- The marketing messages for products or brands that are considered either highly independent or interdependent could utilize priming techniques to make one or other self-construal salient. Identifying the product preferences of individuals companies will be able to effectively promote the right product to the right audience, again providing cost savings and time.
- Managers should create online communities that allow both independent and interdependent individuals the capacity to participate to enable idea creation and originality.
- Create an emotional link with the brand by utilizing the traits of the differing self-construals to engage in communication via these new mechanisms of communication (e.g., social media). Provide both individual and interdependent expressive outlets to recognize both types of individual consumers.

Forming close relationships with consumers allows for the development of loyalty and trust. If marketers can distinguish between trust issues and align their messages with the correct salient self then individuals will be more inclined to view marketing communications in a positive light, whether online or offline. Self-expressive tendencies like expression of WOM/eWOM also present a gap in the literature with regards to contextual factors affecting these behaviors linking to their willingness to engage (Eisingerich, Chun, Liu, Jia, & Bell, 2015; Shin, Song, & Biswas, 2014).

With use of the Internet becoming more individualized (Weijo et al., 2014), consumers are becoming more independent, seeking the personalization that is available in a bid for unique consumption experiences to help them develop their self (Belk, 2013; Simmons, 2008). Examining the uniqueness seeking tendencies of the interdependent consumer (Millan & Reynolds, 2014), would help provide some context to the increasingly individualized consumer. Focus on individual branding, which is a demand of the new media consumers, can help solve self-congruity problems identified by Malar et al. (2011). Marketers can utilize priming techniques to allow the congruent self-construal to become salient in order for them to identify with the brand (White et al., 2012), although, this has ethical considerations which should be acknowledged. In addition to this Lee et al. (2012) believes that priming an interdependent or in-group identity to facilitate eWOM could allow marketers to start conversations with consumers and allow communities to form. Jain et al. (2007) asks that the individualist and collectivist aspects be looked at in relation to the extent they exhibit pliability of the self. There appears to be a gap in knowledge regarding what it is that makes a consumer favor a certain self-construal over the other (Voyer & Franks, 2014) rather than solely just cultural influences. However, the idea of only knowing who contributes and who does not does not allow managers and marketers to identify the key targets of their messages. The crucial area to explore are the drivers of this behavior and the effects that this behavior has on the consumer that will provide the most important information to both practitioners and theorists (De Valck et al., 2009).

Recommendations for Future Research

- There is a need to examine the ways in which individuals seek uniqueness which has only received relatively limited attention within the literature.
- It would be beneficial to understand how the different self-construals utilize brands as a means of constructing their identity, especially in the social media environment facilitation of identity construction is enabled.
- The self-expressive mechanism of consumers such as eWOM need to be looked at in terms of the individual differences such as self-construal.
- Further work should focus on the individual differences in motivations for utilizing online platforms such as that of brand communities.
- Researchers should investigate the context or particular environmental influences that make on or other self-construal become salient, particularly in the social media environment where access and exposure to products and brands is high.

Examining the product preferences of the different self-construals will help in developing categories of products and distinguishing between the more suitable products for each self-construal (Jain et al., 2007). Not only this but marketers can also use this information to develop advertising strategies as a way of emphasizing these different aspects (Song & Lee, 2013), as well as distinguishing between different products, including those consumed privately and publicly (Ratner & Kahn, 2002). The differences in feedback mechanisms on products and services are also crucial to marketers so that they know which channels to utilize for what type of feedback (Wei et al., 2012). Not only this, but it may help develop online social media environments as well.

The social media environment is the perfect place to examine the social interdependent self-construal (Voyer & Franks, 2014), as well as the environmental and social influences that impact the sharing behavior of each self-construal online (Chen & Marcus, 2012). Not only has self-construal theory been adept at explaining theoretical behavior, it can also be used to develop the physical environment to help facilitate a more relatable purchasing setting (e.g., vibrant for independents) (Millan & Reynolds, 2014). Brodie, Ilic, Biljana, and Hollebeek (2013) claim that future research should combine consumer behavior theories as a way to address individual identities, including their social nature. Although the self-construal identifies individual differences in behavior, motivation, emotion, and cognition it must be acknowledged that there are other individual differences that can help marketers and managers to understand their consumers e.g., learning (Sauce & Matzel, 2013), achievement (e.g., Daniels et al., 2008), and personality (e.g., Westenburg & Block, 1993).

This chapter has explored the self-construal theory and its relation to the social media environment in helping individuals to craft their identity online. It highlights the need for marketers to focus on the individual differences in consumer behavior, especially within the online environment where their identity is projected to a multitude of individuals, thus their brand choices and engagement may be more strategic than previously thought. Chapter 6, Synthesis and Discussion of Research, culminates the research covered in Chapter 2, The New Marketing Environment; Chapter 3, Online Brand Communities; Chapter 4, Culture; and this chapter, detailing sampling and methodology techniques as well as summarizing current, developing, and future research in the areas of social media.

REFERENCES

Aaker, J. L. (1997). Dimensions of brand personality. *Journal of Marketing Research, 34*, 347—356.

Aaker, J. L. (1999). The malleable self: The role of self-expression in persuasion. *Journal of Marketing Research, 36*(February), 45—57.

Aaker, J. L., & Lee, A. Y. (2001). 'I' seek pleasures and 'We' avoid pains: The role of self-regulatory goals in information processing and persuasion. *Journal of Consumer Research, 28*(June), 33—49.

Aaker, J. L., & Maheswaran, D. (1997). The effect of cultural orientation on persuasion. *Journal of Consumer Research, 24*(October), 315—328.

Aggarwal, P. (2004). The effects of brand relationship norms on consumer attitudes and behaviour. *Journal of Consumer Research, 31*(1), 87–101.

Ahuvia, A. (2005). Beyond the extended self: Loved objects and consumers' identity narratives. *Journal of Consumer Research, 32*(June), 171–184.

Alon, A., Brunel, F., & Siegal, W. S. (2005). Ritual behavior and community life-cycle: Exploring the social psychological roles of net rituals in the development of online consumption communities. In C. Haugvedt, K. Machleit, & R. Yalch (Eds.), *Online consumer psychology: Understanding how to interact with consumers in the virtual world.* Hillsdale, NJ: Albaum.

Anderson, B. (1983). *Imagined communities: Reflections on the origin and spread of nationalism.* London: Verso.

Anderson, K. C., Knight, D. K., Pookulangara, S., & Josiam, B. (2014). Influence of hedonic and utilitarian motivations on retailer loyalty and purchase intention: A Facebook perspective. *Journal of Retailing and Consumer Services, 21*, 773–779.

Arndt, J. (1967). Role of product-related conversations in the diffusion of a new product. *Journal of Marketing Research, 4*(August), 291–295.

Avis, M. (2012). Brand personality factor based models: A critical review. *Australasian Marketing Journal, 20*(1), 89–96.

Babin, B. J., Darden, W. R., & Griffin, M. (1994). Work and/or fun: Measuring hedonic and utilitarian shopping value. *Journal of Consumer Research, 20*(4), 644–656.

Back, M. D., Stopfer, J. M., Vazire, S., Gaddis, S., Schmukle, S. C., Egloff, B., et al. (2010). Facebook profiles reflect actual personality, not self-idealization. *Psychological Science, 21*(3), 372–374.

Bagozzi, R. P., & Dholakia, U. M. (2002). Intentional social action in virtual communities. *Journal of Interactive Marketing, 16*(2), 2–21.

Baldwin, M. W., & Sinclair, L. (1996). Self-esteem and 'if . . . then' contingencies of interpersonal acceptance. *Journal of Personality and Social Psychology, 71*, 1130–1141.

Bateman, P. J., Gray, P. H., & Butler, B. S. (2010). The impact of community commitment on participation in online communities. *Information Systems Research, 22*(4), 841–854.

Bechtoldt, M. N., Choi, H.-S., & Nijstad, B. A. (2012). Individuals in mind, mates by heart: Individualistic self-construal and collective value orientation as predictors of group creativity. *Journal of Experimental Social Psychology, 48*, 838–844.

Belk, R. W. (1988). Possessions and the extended self. *Journal of Consumer Research, 15*, 139–168.

Belk, R. W. (2013). Extended self in a digital world. *Journal of Consumer Research, 40* (October), 477–500.

Berthon, P., Pitt, L., & Campbell, C. (2008). Ad lib: When customers create the ad. *California Management Review, 50*(4), 6–30.

Blazevic, V., Wiertz, C., Cotte, J., de Ruyter, K., & Keeling, D. I. (2014). GOSIP in cyberspace: Conceptualization and scale development for general online social interaction propensity. *Journal of Interactive Marketing, 28*, 87–100.

Bloch, P. H., Sherrell, D. L., & Ridgway, N. M. (1986). Consumer search: An extended framework. *Journal of Consumer Research, 13*(1), 119–126.

Bodner, R., & Prelec, D. (2003). Self-signaling and diagnostic utility in everyday decision making. In I. Brocas, & J. D. Carrillo (Eds.), *The psychology of economic decisions* (pp. 89–104). Oxford: Oxford University Press.

Brewer, M. B. (1991). The social self: On being the same and different at the same time. *Personality and Social Psychology Bulletin, 17*(5), 475–482.

Brewer, M. B., & Chen, Y. R. (2007). Where (who) are collectives in collectivism? Toward conceptual clarification of individualism and collectivism. *Psychological Review, 114*, 133–151.

Brewer, M. B., & Gardner, W. (1996). Who is this "We"? Levels of collective identity and self representations. *Journal of Personality and Social Psychology, 71*(1), 83–93.

Brodie, R. J., Hollebeek, L. D., Biljana, J., & Ilic, A. (2011). Customer engagement: Conceptual domain, fundamental propositions, and implications for research. *Journal of Service Research, 14*(3), 252–271.

Brodie, R. J., Ilic, A., Biljana, J., & Hollebeek, L. (2013). Consumer engagement in a virtual brand community: An exploratory analysis. *Journal of Business Research, 66*(1), 105–114.

Brogi, S. (2014). Online brand communities: A literature review. *Procedia: Social and Behavioural Sciences, 109*, 385–389.

Brooks, R. C., Jr. (1957). 'Word of Mouth' advertising in selling new products. *Journal of Marketing, 22*(October), 154–161.

Brown, J. J., & Reingen, P. H. (1987). Social ties and word-of-mouth referral behaviour. *Journal of Consumer Research, 14*(3), 350–362.

Brown, S. (1995). *Postmodern marketing*. London: Routledge.

Brown, S. (1997). *Postmodern marketing two: Telling tales*. London: International Thompson Business Press.

Brynjolfsson, E., & Kemerer, C. F. (1996). Network externalities in microcomputer software: An economic analysis of the spreadsheet market. *Management Science, 42*(12), 1627–1647.

Carver, C. S., & Scheier, M. F. (1987). The blind men and the elephant: Selective examination of the public-private literature gives rise to a faulty perception. *Journal of Personality, 55*(3), 525–541.

Celsi, R. L., & Olson, J. C. (1988). The role of involvement in attention and comprehension processes. *Journal of Consumer Research, 15*(2), 210–224.

Champniss, G., Wilson, H. N., & Macdonald, E. K. (2015). Why your customers social identities matter. *Harvard Business Review, 93*, 88–96, January–February.

Chang, A., Hsieh, S. H., & Tseng, T. H. (2013). Online brand community response to negative brand events: The role of group eWOM. *Internet Research, 23*(4), 486–506.

Chang, C. (2015). Self-construal and Facebook activities: Exploring differences in social interaction orientation. *Computers in Human Behavior, 53*, 91–101.

Chatman, J. A., & Barsade, S. G. (1995). Personality, organizational culture, and cooperation: Evidence from a business simulation. *Administrative Science Quarterly, 40*, 423–443.

Cheema, A., & Kaikati, A. M. (2010). The effect of need for uniqueness on word of mouth. *Journal of Marketing Research, 47*(3), 553–563.

Chen, B., & Marcus, J. (2012). Students' self-presentation on Facebook: An examination of personality and self-construal factors. *Computers in Human Behavior, 28*, 2091–2099.

Chernev, A., Hamilton, R., & Gal, D. (2011). Competing for consumer identity: Limits to self-expression and the perils of lifestyle branding. *Journal of Marketing, 75*(May), 66–82.

Constant, D., Sproull, L., & Kiesler, S. (1996). The kindness of strangers: The usefulness of electronic weak ties for technical advice. *Organization Science, 7*, 119–135.

Correa, T., Hinsley, A. W., & de Zuniga, H. G. (2010). Who interacts on the Web? The intersection of users' personality and social media use. *Computers in Human Behavior, 26*, 247–253.

Cotte, J., Chowdhury, T. G., Ratneshwar, S., & Ricci, L. M. (2006). Pleasure or utility? Time planning style and Web usage behaviors. *Journal of Interactive Marketing, 20*(1), 45–57.

Cova, B., & Pace, S. (2006). Brand community of convenience products: New forms of customer empowerment—the case 'My Nutella the Community'. *European Journal of Marketing, 40*(9/10), 1087–1105.

Crocker, J., Thompson, L. L., McGraw, K. M., & Ingerman, C. (1987). Downward comparison, prejudice, and evaluations of others: Effects of self-esteem and threat. *Journal of Personality and Social Psychology, 52*, 907–916.

Daniels, L. M., Haynes, T. L., Stupinsky, R. H., Perry, R. P., Newall, N. E., & Pekrun, R. (2008). Individual differences in achievement goals: A longitudinal study of cognitive, emotional, and achievement outcomes. *Contemporary Educational Psychology, 33*(4), 584–608.

Davis, R., Buchanan-Oliver, M., & Brodie, R. J. (2000). Retail service branding in electronic-commerce environments. *Journal of Services Research, 3*(2), 178–186.

Davis, R., Piven, I., & Breazeale, M. (2014). Conceptualising the brand in social media community: The five sources model. *Journal of Retailing and Consumer Services, 21*, 468–481.

Dawes, J., & Brown, R. B. (2000). Postmodern marketing: Research issues for retail financial services. *Qualitative Market Research, 3*(2), 90.

De Valck, K., van Bruggen, G. H., & Wierenga, B. (2009). Virtual communities: A marketing perspective. *Decision Support Systems, 47*, 185–203.

DeAndrea, D. C., Shaw, A. S., & Levine, T. R. (2010). Online language: The role of culture in self-expression and self-construal on Facebook. *Journal of Language and Social Psychology, 29*(4), 425–442.

Dholakia, U. M., Bagozzi, R. P., & Pearo, L. K. (2004). A social influence model of consumer participation in network- and small-group-based virtual communities. *International Journal of Research in Marketing, 21*(3), 241–263.

Divakaran, P. K. P. (2012). Pre-release member participation as potential predictors of post release community members' adoption behaviour: Evidence from the motion picture industry. *Behaviour & Information Technology, 32*(6), 545–559.

Eisingerich, A. B., Chun, H. H., Liu, Y., Jia, H., & Bell, S. J. (2015). Why recommend a brand face-to-face but not on Facebook? How word-of-mouth on online social sites differs from traditional word-of-mouth. *Journal of Consumer Psychology, 21*(1), 120–128.

Elek, E., Miller-Day, M., & Hecht, M. L. (2006). Influences of Personal, Injunctive, and Descriptive Norms on Early Adolescent Substance use. *Journal of Drug Issues, 36*(1), 147–172.

Elliott, R., & Wattanasuwan, K. (1998). Brands as Symbolic resources for the construction of identity. *International Journal of Advertising, 17*, 131–144.

Elliott, R. (1997). Existential consumption and irrational desire. *European Journal of Marketing, 31*(3/4), 285–296.

Engel, J. F., Kegerreis, R. J., & Blackwell, R. D. (1969). Word-of-Mouth Communication by the Innovator. *Journal of Marketing, 33*(July), 15–19.

Escalas, J. E., & Bettman, J. R. (2005). Self-Construal, Reference Groups and Brand Meaning. *Consumer Research, 32*(December), 378–389.

Fenigstein, A. (1987). On the Nature of Public and Private Self-Consciousness. *Journal of Personality, 55*(3), 543–554.

Flint, D. J. (2006). Innovation, symbolic interaction and customer valuing: Thoughts stemming from a service-dominant logic of marketing. *Marketing Theory, 6*(3), 349–362.

Frenzen, J., & Nakamoto, K. (1993). Structure, Cooperation, and the Flow of Market Information. *Journal of Consumer Research, 20*(3), 360–375.

Gatignon, H., & Robertson, T. S. (1986). An Exchange Theory Model of Interpersonal Communication. In R. J. Lutz (Ed.), *Advances in Consumer Research* (Vol. 13, pp. 534–538). Provo, UT: Association for Consumer Research.

Gilmore, J. H., & Pine, J. B., II (2007). *Authenticity: What Consumers Really Want*. Boston: Harvard Business School Press.

Goulding, C. (2003). Issues in representing the postmodern consumer. *Qualitative Market Research: An International Journal, 6*(3), 152−159.

Granovetter, M. S. (1973). The strength of weak ties. *American Journal of Sociology, 78*, 1360−1380.

Graupmann, V., Jonas, E., Meier, E., Hawelka, S., & Aichhorn, M. (2012). Reactance, the self, and its group: When threats to freedom come from the ingroup versus the outgroup. *European Journal of Social Psychology, 42*, 164−173.

Grayson, K., & Martinec, R. (2004). Consumer perceptions of iconicity and indexical-ity and their influence on assessments of authentic market offerings. *Journal of Consumer Research, 31*(2), 296−312.

Greenaway, K. H., Wright, R. G., Willingham, J., Reynolds, K. J., & Haslam, S. A. (2015). Shared Identity is Key to effective communication. *Personality and Social Psychology Bulletin, 41*(2), 171−182.

Gudykunst, W. B., & Lee, C. M. (2003). Assessing the Validity of Self-Construal Scales. *Human Communication Research, 29*(2), 253−274.

Gudykunst, W. B., Matsumoto, Y., Ting- Toomey, S., Nishida, T., Kim, K., & Heyman, S. (1996). The influence of Cultural Individualism-collectivism, Self-construals, and Individual Values on Communication Styles across Cultures. *Human Communication Research, 22*(4), 510−543.

Gummerus, J., Liljander, V., Weman, E., & Pihlstrom, M. (2012). Customer Engagement in a Facebook Brand Community. *Management Research Review, 35*(9), 857−877.

Guo, W., & Main, K. (2011). Trust Or Not: The Role of Self-Construal in Interacting With Salespeople. In D. W. Dahl, G. V. Johar, & S. M. J. van Osselaer (Eds.), *Advances in Consumer Research* (38MN: Association for Consumer Research.

Habibi, M. R., Laroche, M., & Richard, M.-O. (2014). Brand Communities based in social media: How unique are they? Evidence from two exemplary brand communities. *International Journal of Information Management, 34*, 123−132.

Hajli, M., & Hajli, M. (2013). Organisational development in sport: Co-creation of value through social capital. *Industrial and Commercial Training, 45*(5), 283−288.

Hamilton, R. W., & Biehal, G. J. (2005). Achieving your goals or protecting their future? The effects of self-view on goals and choices. *Journal of Consumer Research, 32*, 277−283.

Hannover, B., Birkner, N., & Pohlmann, C. (2006). Ideal selves and self-esteem in people with independent or interdependent self-construal. *European Journal of Social Psychology, 36*, 119−133.

Hardey, M. (2011). Generation C: Content, creation, connections and choice. *International Journal of Market Research, 53*(6), 749−770.

Hartman, J. B., Shim, S., Barber, B., & O'Brien, M. (2006). Adolescents' utilitarian and hedonic web-consumption behavior: Hierarchical influence of personal values and innovativeness. *Psychology and Marketing, 23*(10), 813−839.

Hennig-Thurau, T., Gwinner, K. P., Walsh, G., & Gremler, D. D. (2004). Electronic word-of mouth via consumer-opinion platforms: What motivates consumers to articulate themselves on the internet? *Journal of Interactive Marketing, 18*(1), 38−52.

Higgins, T. E. (1987). Self-Discrepancy: A Theory Relating Self and Affect. *Psychological Review, 94*(3), 319−340.

Hofstede, G. (1980). *Culture's Consequences: International Differences in Work-Related Values*. California: Sage Publications.

Holbrook, M. B. (1992). Patterns, personalities, and complex relationships in the effects of self on mundane everyday consumption: These are 495 of my most and least favorite things. In J. F. Sherry, & B. Sternthal (Eds.), *Advances in Consumer Research* (Vol. 19, pp. 417–423). Provo, UT: Association for Consumer Research.

Holbrook, M. B., & Hirschman, E. C. (1982). The experiential aspects of consumption: Consumer fantasies, feelings, and fun. *Journal of Consumer Research, 9*(2), 132–140.

Jain, S. P., Desai, K. K., & Mao, H. (2007). The influence of chronic and situational self-construal on categorization. *Journal of Consumer Research, 34*(June), 66–76.

Jiraporn, N., & Desai, K. K. (2010). Adoption of Network Externality Products: The Interactive Influence of Self-Construal, Branding Strategy, and Source of Information. *Advances in Consumer Research, 37*, 471–472.

Johnson, B. T., & Eagly, A. (1989). Effects of involvement on persuasion: A meta-analysis. *Psychological Bulletin, 106*(2), 290–314.

Katz, E., & Lazarsfeld, P. F. (1955). *Personal Influence.* New York: The Free Press.

Katz, M. L., & Shapiro, C. (1985). Network externalities competition, and comparability. *American Economic Review, 75*(3), 424–440.

Keller, K. L. (2003). *Strategic brand management: Building, measuring, and managing brand equity* (2nd EditionEnglewood Cliffs, NJ: Pearson Education International.

Kemp, E., Bui, M., & Chapa, S. (2012). The Role of Advertising in Consumer Emotion Management. *International Journal of Advertising, 31*(2), 339–353.

Kernan, J. B., & Sommers, M. S. (1967). Meaning, value and theory of promotion. *Journal of Communication, 17*, 109–135.

Kim, A. J. (2000). *Community Building on the Web: Secret Strategies for Successful Online Communities.* Berkeley, CA: Peachpit.

Kim, H.-W., Gupta, S., & Koh, J. (2011). Investigating the intention to purchase digital items in social networking communities: A customer value perspective. *Information & Management, 48*, 228–234.

Kim, M. S., Sharkey, W. F., & Singelis, T. M. (1994). The Relationship between Individuals' Self-Concepts and Perceived Importance of Interactive Constraints. *International Journal of Intercultural Relations, 18*(1), 117–140.

Kleine, R. E. I. I. I., Kleine, S. S., & Kernan, J. B. (1992). Mundance Consumption and the self: A conceptual orientation and prospects for consumer research. In J. F. Sherry, & B. Sternthal (Eds.), *Advances in Consumer Research* (Vol. 19, pp. 417–423). Provo, UT: Association for Consumer Research.

Kleine, R. E. I. I. I., Kleine, S. S., & Kernan, J. B. (1993). Mundane Consumption and the Self: A Social-Identity Perspective. *Journal of Consumer Psychology, 2*(3), 209–235.

Knowles, M. L., & Gardner, W. L. (2008). Benefits of Membership: The Activation and Amplification of Group Identities in Response to Social Rejection. *Personality and Social Psychology Bulletin, 34*(9), 1200–1213.

Kozinets, R. V., de Valck, K., Wojnicki, A. C., & Wilner, S. J. S. (2010). Networked Narratives: Understanding Word-of-Mouth Marketing in Online Communities. *Journal of Marketing, 74*(2), 71–89.

Kumashiro, M., Rusbult, C. E., & Finkel, E. J. (2008). Navigating personal and relational concerns: The quest for equilibrium. *Journal of Personality and Social Psychology, 95*, 94–110.

Lalwani, A. K., & Shavitt, S. (2009). The "Me" I claim to be: Cultural self-construal elicits self-presentational goal pursuit. *Journal of Personality and Social Psychology, 97*, 88–102.

Lee, D., Kim, H. S., & Kim, J. K. (2012). The role of self-construal in consumers' electronic word of mouth (eWOM) in social networking sites: A social cognitive approach. *Computers in Human Behavior, 28*, 1054−1062.

Levine, T. R., Bresnahan, M. J., Park, H. S., Lapinski, M. K., Wittenbaum, G. M., Shearman, S. M., et al. (2003). Self-Construal Scales Lack Validity. *Human Communication Research, 29*(2), 210−252.

Liao, C., Hsu, F.-C., & To, P.-L. (2013). Exploring Knowledge Sharing in Virtual Communities. *Online Information Review, 37*(6), 891−909.

Liu, C.-J., & Li, S. (2009). Contextualized self: When the self runs into social dilemmas. *International Journal of Psychology, 44*(6), 451−458.

Liu, J., Rau, P.-L. P., & Wendler, N. (2015). Trust and online information-sharing in close relationships: A cross-cultural perspective. *Behaviour & Information Technology, 34*(4), 363−374.

Loewenstein, G. (1999). Because it is there: The challenge of mountaineering ... for utility theory. *Kyklos, 52*(3), 315−343.

Lynn, M., & Harris, J. (1997). Individual differences in the pursuit of self uniqueness through consumption. *Journal of Applied Social Psychology, 27*(21), 1861−1883.

Mäenpää, K., Kanto, A., Kuusela, H., & Paul, P. (2006). More hedonic versus less hedonic consumption behaviour in advanced Internet bank services. *Journal of Financial Services Marketing, 11*(1), 4−16.

Malar, L., Krohmer, H., Hoyer, W. D., & Nyffenegger, B. (2011). Emotional brand attachment and brand personality: The relative importance of the actual and ideal self. *Journal of Marketing, 75*(July), 35−52.

Mandel, N. (2003). Shifting selves and decision making: The effects of self-construal priming on consumer risk-taking. *Journal of Consumer Research, 30*, 30−40.

Markus, H. R., & Kitayama, S. (1991). Culture and the self: Implications for cognition, emotion, and motivation. *Psychological Review, 98*, 224−253.

Mattingly, B. A., Oswald, D. L., & Clark, E. M. (2011). An examination of relational-interdependent self-construal, communal strength, and pro-relationship behaviours in friendships. *Personality and Individual Differences, 50*, 1243−1248.

Mikalef, P., Pateli, A., & Giannakos, M. (2013). Why are users of social media inclined to word-of-mouth? In C. Douligeris, N. Polemi, A. Karantjias, & W. Lamersdorf (Eds.), *Collaborative, trusted and privacy-aware e/m-services* (Vol. 399, pp. 112−123). Greece: Springer Berlin Heidelberg.

Millan, E., & Reynolds, J. (2014). Self-construals, symbolic and hedonic preferences, and actual purchase behavior. *Journal of Retailing and Consumer Services, 21*, 550−560.

Moran, E., & Gossieaux, F. (2010). Marketing in a hyper-social world: The tribalization of business study and characteristics of successful online communities. *Journal of Advertising Research, 50*(3), 232−239.

Na, J., Kosinski, M., & Stillwell, D. J. (2015). When a tool is introduced in different cultural contexts: Individualism-collectivism and social network on Facebook. *Journal of Cross-Cultural Psychology, 46*(3), 355−370.

Nakashima, K., Isobe, C., & Ura, M. (2008). Effect of self-construal and threat to self-esteem on ingroup favouritism: Moderating effect of independent/interdependent self-construal on use of ingroup favouritism for maintaining and enhancing self-evaluation. *Asian Journal of Social Psychology, 11*, 286−292.

Overby, J. W., & Lee, E. J. (2006). The effects of utilitarian and hedonic online shopping value on consumer preference and intentions. *Journal of Business Research, 59*(10/11), 1160−1166.

Pan, Z., Lu, Y., & Gupta, S. (2014). How heterogeneous community engage newcomers? The effect of community diversity on newcomers' perception of inclusion: An empirical study in social media service. *Computers in Human Behavior, 39*, 100−111.

Park, D., Lee, J., & Han, I. (2007). The effect of online consumer reviews on consumer purchasing intention: The moderating role of involvement. *International Journal of Electronic Commerce, 11*(4), 125−148.

Polyorat, K., & Alden, D. L. (2005). Self-construal and need-for-cognition effects on brand attitudes and purchase intentions in response to comparative advertising in Thailand and the United States. *Journal of Advertising, 34*(1), 37−48.

Poyry, E., Parvinen, P., & Malmivaara, T. (2013). Can we get from liking to buying? Behavioral differences in hedonic and Utilitarian Facebook usage. *Electronic Commerce Research and Applications, 12*, 224−235.

Ratner, R. K., & Kahn, B. E. (2002). The impact of private versus public consumption on variety-seeking behavior. *Journal of Consumer Research, 29*, 246−257.

Reingen, P. H., & Kernan, J. B. (1986). Analysis of referral networks in marketing: Methods and illustration. *Journal of Marketing, 23*(4), 370−378.

Rosenbaum, M. S. (2008). Return on community for consumers and service establishments. *Journal of Services Research, 11*, 179−196.

Rosenberg, M. (1979). *Conceiving the Self*. New York, NY: Basic Books.

Ruvio, A. (2008). Unique like everybody else? The dual role of consumers' need for uniqueness. *Psychology and Marketing, 25*(5), 444−464.

Ruvio, A., Shoham, A., & Brenčič, M. M. (2008). Consumers' need for uniqueness: Short-form scale development and cross-cultural validation. *International Marketing Review, 25*(1), 33−53.

Salancik, G. R., & Pfeffer, J. (1978). A social information processing approach to job attitudes and task design. *Administrative Science Quarterly, 23*(2), 224−253.

Salganik, M. J., Dodds, P. S., & Watts, D. J. (2006). Experimental study of inequality and unpredictability in an artificial cultural market. *Science, 311*(5762), 854−856.

Sauce, B., & Matzel, L. D. (2013). The causes of variation in learning and behavior: Why individual differences matter. *Frontiers in Psychology, 4*(395), 1−8.

Schau, H. J., Muñiz, A. M., & Arnould, E. J., Jr. (2009). How brand community practices create value. *Journal of Marketing, 73*(5), 30−51.

Schembri, S., Merrilees, B., & Kristiansen, S. (2010). Brand consumption and narrative of self. *Psychology and Marketing, 27*(6), 623−638.

Sedikides, C. (1993). Assessment, enhancement, and verification determinants on the self-evaluation process. *Journal of Personality and Social Psychology, 65*(2), 317−338.

Seimiene, E. (2012). Emotional connection of consumer personality traits with brand personality traits: Theoretical considerations. *Economy Management, 17*(4), 1477−1478.

Shin, D., Song, J. H., & Biswas, A. (2014). Electronic word-of-mouth (eWOM) generation in new media platforms: The role of regulatory focus and collective dissonance. *Marketing Letters, 25*, 153−165.

Shore, L. M., Randel, A. E., Chung, B. G., Dean, M. A., Ehrhart, K. H., & Singh, G. (2010). Inclusion and diversity in work groups: A review and model for future research. *Journal of Management, 37*(4), 1262−1289.

Simmons, G. (2008). Marketing to postmodern consumers: Introducing the internet chameleon. *European Journal of Marketing, 42*(3/4), 299−310.

Simonson, I., & Nowlis, S. M. (2000). The role of explanations and need for uniqueness in consumer decision making: Unconventional choices based on reasons. *Journal of Consumer Research, 27*, 49−68.

Singelis, T. M. (1994). The measurement of independent and interdependent self-construals. *Personality and Social Psychological Bulletin, 20*, 580−591.

Sirgy, M. J. (1982). Self-concept in consumer behavior: A critical review. *Journal of Consumer Research, 9*(3), 287−300.

Snyder, C. R., & Fromkin, H. L. (1977). Abnormality as a positive characteristic: The development and validation of a scale measuring need for uniqueness. *Journal of Abnormal Psychology, 86*(5), 518–527.

Solomon, M. R. (1983). The role of products as social stimuli: A symbolic interactionism perspective. *Journal of Consumer Research, 10*, 319–329.

Song, D., & Lee, J. (2013). Balancing "We" and "I": Self-construal and an alternative approach to seeking uniqueness. *Journal of Consumer Behaviour, 12*, 506–516.

Stadler, R., Brenner, W., & Herrmann, A. (2014). *How to succeed in the digital age: Strategies from 17 top managers*. Frankfurt: Frankfurter Societats-Medien GmbH.

Suh, E. M. (2002). Culture, identity consistency, and subjective well-being. *Journal of Personality and Social Psychology, 83*(6), 1378–1391.

Sun, T., Youn, S., Wu, G., & Kuntaraporn, M. (2006). Online word-of-mouth (or mouse): An exploration of its antecedents and consequences. *Journal of Computer-Mediated Communication, 11*, 1104–1127.

Tajfel, H. (1978). *Differentiation between social groups*. London: Academic Press.

Tajfel, H. H., & Turner, J. C. (1979). An Integrative Theory of Intergroup Conflict. In W. G. W. G. Austin, & S. S. Worchel (Eds.), *The Social Psychology of Intergroup Relations*. Monterey, CA: Brooks-Cole.

Tajfel, H. H., & Turner, J. C. (1985). The Social Identity Theory of Intergroup Behavior. In S. S. Worchel, & W. G. Austin (Eds.), *Psychology of Intergroup Relations* (pp. 6–24). Chicago: Nelson-Hall.

Tajfel, H., & Turner, J. C. (1986). The social identity theory of intergroup behavior. In S. Worchel, & W. G. Austin (Eds.), *Psychology of intergroup relations* (pp. 7–24). Chicago, IL: Nelson Hall.

Tardini, S., & Cantoni, L. A. (2005). A semiotic approach to online communities: Belonging, interest and identity in websites' and video games' communities. *Proceedings of IADIS international conference* (pp. 371–378). Qawra, Malta.

Teo, T. (2001). Demographic and motivation variables associated with Internet usage activities. *Internet Research, 11*(2), 125–137.

Tian, K. T., Bearden, W. O., & Hunter, G. L. (2001). Consumers' need for uniqueness: Scale development and validation. *Journal of Consumer Research, 28*, 50–66.

Tian, K. T., & McKenzie, K. (2001). The long-term predictive validity of the consumers' need for uniqueness scale. *Journal of Consumer Psychology, 10*(3), 171–193.

Timmor, Y., & Katz-Navon, T. (2008). Being the same and different: A model explaining new product adoption. *Journal of Consumer Behaviour, 7*, 249–262.

To, P.-L., Liao, C., & Lin, T.-H. (2007). Shopping motivations on internet: A study based on utilitarian and hedonic value. *Technovation, 27*, 77–787.

Triandis, H. C. (1990). Cross-cultural studies of individualism and collectivism. *Journal of Cross-Cultural Psychology, 21*(2), 139–157.

Van Baaren, R. B., Maddux, W. W., Chartrand, T. L., De Bouter, C., & van Knippenberg, A. (2003). It takes two to mimic: Behavioral consequences of self-construals. *Journal of Personality and Social Psychology, 84*, 1093–1102.

Van der Heijden, H. (2004). User acceptance of hedonic information systems. *MIS Quarterly, 28*(4), 695–704.

Vargo, S. L., & Lusch, R. F. (2004). Evolving to a new dominant logic for marketing. *Journal of Marketing, 68*(January), 1–17.

Veloutsou, C. (2009). Brands as relationship facilitators in consumer markets. *Marketing Theory, 9*(1), 127–130.

Verplanken, B., Trafimow, D., Khusid, I. K., Holland, R. W., & Steentjes, G. M. (2009). Different selves, different values: Effects of self-construals on value activation and use. *European Journal of Social Psychology, 39*, 909–919.

Voyer, B. G., & Franks, B. (2014). Toward a better understanding of self-construal theory: An agency view of the processes of self-construal. *Review of General Psychology, 18*(2), 101–114.

Wang, Y., Ma, S., & Li, D. (2015). Customer participation in virtual brand communities: The self-construal perspective. *Information & Management, 52*(5), 577–587.

Wei, W., Miao, L., Cai, L. A., & Adler, H. (2012). The influence of self-construal and co-consumption others on consumer complaining behaviour. *International Journal of Hospitality Management, 31*, 764–771.

Weijo, H., Hietanen, J., & Mattila, P. (2014). New insights into online consumption communities and netnography. *Journal of Business Research, 67*, 2072–2078.

Wellman, B. (2001). Physical place and CyberPlace: The rise of networked individualism. *International Journal for Urban and Regional Research, 25*(2), 227–252.

Westenburg, M. P., & Block, J. (1993). Ego development and individual differences in personality. *Journal of Personality and Social Psychology, 65*(4), 792–800.

White, K., & Argo, J. J. (2009). Social identity threat and consumer preferences. *Journal of Consumer Psychology, 19*(3), 313–325.

White, K., & Lehman, D. R. (2005). Looking on the bright side: Downward counterfactual thinking in response to negative life events. *Personality and Social Psychology Bulletin, 31*(10), 1413–1424.

White, K., Argo, J. J., & Sengupta, J. (2012). Dissociative versus associative responses to social identity threat: The role of consumer self-construal. *Journal of Consumer Research, 39*(December), 704–719.

Wiertz, C., & De Ruyter, K. (2007). Beyond the call of duty: Why customers contribute to firm-hosted commercial online communities. *Organization Studies, 28*(3), 347–376.

Wilcox, K., & Stephen, A. (2013). Are close friends the enemy? Online social networks, self-esteem, and self-control. *Journal of Consumer Research, 40*(1), 90–103.

Wilson, K., Fornasier, S., & White, K. M. (2010). Psychological predictors of young adults' use of social networking sites. *Cyberpsychology, Behavior, and Social Networking, 13*, 173–177.

Wright, S. C., Taylor, D. M., & Moghaddam, F. M. (1990). The relationship of perceptions and emotions to behavior in the face of collective inequality. *Social Justice Research, 4*(3), 229–250.

Yen, Y.-S. (2013). The relationship among social influence, perceived value, and usage intention in social networking sites. *Consumer Electronics, Communications and Networks (CECNet), 2013 3rd International Conference, IEEE* (pp. 699–670). Xianning, 20–22 November.

Yeo, T. E. D. (2012). Social-media early adopters don't count: How to seed participation in interactive campaigns by psychological profiling of digital consumers. *Journal of Advertising Research, 52*(3), 297–308.

Zhang, L., Moore, M., & Moore, R. (2011). The effect of self-construal's on the effectiveness of comparative advertising. *Marketing Management Journal, 21*(1), 195–206.

Zhang, Y., & Shrum, L. J. (2009). The influence of self-construal on impulsive consumption. *Journal of Consumer Research, 35*, 838–850.

CHAPTER 6

Synthesis and Discussion of Research

Social media presents a new environment that is ripe for investigation, to provide new insight into how this platform can be used for both social and organizational use. Not only is this new form of communication allowing individuals to communicate with each other, but it is allowing organizations and brands to create relationships based on its interactive capacity. The result of a postmodern shift, consumers on social media are utilizing online brand communities, strategically gathering and utilizing information as a way to enhance and inform their self. This chapter is a synthesis of the current research which is taking place in social media, with a focus on online brand community and self-construal contexts in relation to this new environment.

This section will start by summarizing current research within the social media environment, linking in with online brand communities and self-construals. This is followed by an examination of the developing research within the same areas. Next the methodology and sample preferences of these studies are discussed, with a focus on future suggestions and limitations. Finally, the sections end with a summary of future research areas and gaps, with a summary of the key points.

6.1 CURRENT RESEARCH

The current research within social media as a whole is focusing on specific platforms, most notably Facebook (e.g., Anderson, Knight, Pookulangara, & Josiam, 2014; Blachnio, Przepiorka, & Rudnicka, 2016; Blight, Jageillo, & Ruppel, 2015; Chu, 2011; Grieve, Indian, Witteveen, Tolan, & Marrington, 2013; Hollenbaugh & Ferris, 2014; Hong, Huang, Lin, & Chiu, 2014; Lee, Ahn, & Kim, 2014; Lee-Won, Shim, Joo, & Park, 2014; Lonnqvist & Deters, 2016; Malik, Dhir, & Nieminen, 2016; Shao & Ross, 2015; Toma & Hancock, 2013; Yaakop, 2013), and Twitter (e.g., Chen, 2011; Jansen, Zhang, Sobel, & Chowdury, 2009;

Lee & Kim, 2014; Naaman, Boase, & Lai, 2010; Yoo, Choi, Choi, & Rho, 2014), examining them mostly in the context of that specific platform which has limited application possibilities. Although some research has focused on multiple platforms (e.g., Canhoto & Clark, 2013; Hughes, Rowe, Batey, & Lee, 2012; Karapanos, Teixeira, & Gouveia, 2016; Smith, Fischer, & Yongjian, 2012; Zafarani & Liu, 2016), research of this nature seems to be scarce. However, the studies that have utilized a cross-platform design are focusing on the user characteristics such as personality (e.g., Hughes et al., 2012), and behaviors (e.g., Buccafurri, Lax, Nicolazzo, & Nocera, 2015), which recognizes the need to identify the individual differences of the people that utilize these social media platforms (such as self-construals). Focusing on one specific platform is beneficial but does not recognize the need for integration and consistency across communication channels (Navarro-Bailon, 2012). By expanding research to include multiple platforms, marketers can learn how to integrate their marketing communications across these platforms. Marketers are still looking into how they can integrate social media and traditional media into one communication (Hanna, Rohm, & Crittenden, 2011), which is becoming even more prevalent due to the popularity of certain social media sites used to accompany TV such as Twitter. By incorporating this new media with traditional media marketers will be able to not only more fully integrate their communications but will also have a wider range of tools they can use rather than just discarding the old means. Thus they will have many more channels in which to communicate with their consumers and attract new ones to their offerings.

Brand and organizational use of social media seems to be concentrated on developing frameworks for either social media categorization (e.g., Killian & McManus, 2015; Shankar & Hollinger, 2007; Winer, 2009), engagement (e.g., Baldus, Voorhees, & Calantone, 2015; Hodis, Sriramachandramurthy, & Sashittal, 2015; Hollebeek, Glynn, & Brodie, 2014), analysis (e.g., Effing & Spil, 2016; Kietzmann, Hermkens, McCarthy, & Silvestre, 2011), measurement approaches and metrics (e.g., Barger & Labrecque, 2013; Peters, Chen, Kaplan, Ognibeni, & Pauwels, 2013), and integration (Navarro-Bailon, 2012). There is also a focus on trying to create the perfect social media mix (e.g., Weinberg & Pehlivan, 2011), which again could be aided by cross-platform research. Constantinides (2014) stresses the importance of verifying social media strategies so that these platforms can be utilized effectively.

The core function social media for consumers of value creation, is also proving popular in current research (e.g., Hennig-Thurau, Hofacker, & Bloching, 2013), with many organizations seeking the best ways that they can utilize these platforms to achieve the best value for their consumers in addition to giving them a competitive advantage. Building relationships is one of the ways in which organizations are giving value to their consumers, allowing some research streams to focus on how data can be gathered and understood from these relationships (e.g., Hansen, 2011). Engagement is the crucial element of relationship building, and as such, a variety of studies have tried to understand this concept (e.g., Brodie, Ilic, Biljana, & Hollebeek, 2013), revealing its multidimensionality and complexity. Linked to engagement, interactivity has also been a strong focus of researchers (e.g., Blazevic, Wiertz, Cotte, de Ruyter, & Keeling, 2014; Labrecque, 2014), looking at how technology can enhance the engagement process along with its measurement. Similarly to general social media research, studies that are focusing on online brand communities are also focused on how value is created on social media platforms, including the practices and behaviors that lead to value creation and a strong focus on social capital creation (Li, Clark, & Wheeler, 2013; Schau, Muñiz, & Arnould, 2009).

A lot of online brand community studies are also focusing on engagement within brand communities and the ways in which this can be utilized as a means of expanding existing social media strategies (e.g., Gummerus, Liljander, Weman, & Pihlstrom, 2012), as engagement creates value for both organizations and consumers. Linked in with the concept of engagement is the consumption activities, which happen in online brand communities within social media (Davis, Piven, & Breazeale, 2014). Although the phenomenon of online brand communities is not a new concept, the dimensions of brand communities, the types of brand community, and the different behavioral practices that happen in each of these platforms are the focus of much current research (Gummerus et al., 2012; Habibi, Laroche, & Richard, 2014). In addition, the types of content that are created in online brand communities are also at the forefront of investigations at the present time (e.g., Ding, Phang, Lu, Tan, & Sutanto, 2014). Self-construal theory has incorporated online brand communities including behavior of in-groups and out-groups (e.g., Graupmann, Jonas, Meier, Hawelka, & Aichhorn, 2012), creative tendencies (e.g., Bechtoldt, Choi, & Nijstad, 2012), participation within communities (e.g., Wang, Ma, & Li, 2015), and strength of the community (e.g., Mattingly, Oswald, & Clark, 2011).

Yet, research focused on the social media environment as a whole has some-what neglected the self-construal theory as a means to explain the individual differences in behavior, which Moran and Gossieaux (2010) believe is crucial. The few that have looked at the self-construals within social media (e.g., Bechtoldt et al., 2012; Chang, 2015; DeAndrea, Shaw, & Levine, 2010; Lee, Kim, & Kim, 2012; Na, Kosinski, & Stillwell, 2015; Wang et al., 2015) typically do not conceptualize their argument in solid theoretical foundations, or focus on one platform. Other research has been focused on the effect of self-construals on consumer behavior such as complaining tendencies (Wei, Miao, Cai, & Adler, 2012), actual purchase behavior (Millan & Reynolds, 2014), the role of self-construal in electronic word of mouth (eWOM) behavior (Lee et al., 2012), and responses to threat (White, Argo, & Sengupta, 2012); all of which have noted differences between the behaviors of the two self-construals. Pure marketing research involving the self-construal includes a focus on the effect of construals on comparative advertising (Zhang, Moore, & Moore, 2011) and product categories (Hamilton & Biehal, 2005; Jiraporn & Desai, 2010), which is useful in helping identify marketing communications strategies. There is also a tendency to add other concepts and theories to better explain the self-construal differences, e.g., need for uniqueness theory (Song & Lee, 2013).

The power that consumers possess has meant that research has focused on addressing the sources and impacts of this power such as through eWOM (Cheung & Thadani, 2012). A variety of aspects of this form of communication have been researched such as its relation to purchase inten-tion (e.g., Doh & Hwang, 2009; Lee & Youn, 2009), valence of message (e.g., Park & Lee, 2009; Sen & Lerman, 2007), message source (e.g., Baber et al., 2016; See-To & Ho, 2014), volume (e.g., Gupta & Harris, 2005; Park, Lee, & Han, 2007), attitude (e.g., Lee, Park, & Han, 2008), its role in co-creation and personalization (e.g., Franke, Keinz, & Steger, 2009; Li, 2016), and buzz and traffic creation (e.g., Luo & Zhang, 2013). The empowerment of consumers and growth in personalization has made researchers focus their attention on consumer-generated content (Berthon, Pitt, & Campbell, 2008), which is becoming more prevalent as consumers are creating media which can be spread around quickly. Opinion leaders and seekers are also becoming the focus of much research as brands realize their potential power in being able to influence a multitude of consumers (e.g., Chu & Kim, 2011; Hansen & Lee, 2013). The structure of consumer networks is also receiving a lot of attention in the literature (e.g., Na et al., 2015) as well as audience composition (e.g., Lampe, Ellison, & Steinfield,

2008; Wolf, Gao, Berendt, & Pierson, 2015), effects of network structure on consumer behavior (e.g., Hill, Provost, & Volinsky, 2006), and the influence of networks (e.g., Sohn, 2014). Identifying the structure of a consumer's network will help marketers to learn the route of eWOM and information sharing. In addition, many brands are interested in how social media can give them an effective return on their investment, and how the environment can be monetized. This has led to an increase in focus on the area of social commerce (e.g., Yadav, de Valck, Hennig-Thurau, Hoffman, & Spann, 2013), although the concept is in clear need for development as many attempts at monetizing the various platforms have been unsuccessful (Hennig-Thurau et al., 2013).

In summary, research within the social media sphere is concentrating on utilizing the various platforms to develop their marketing strategies and help deliver the best value to consumers, yet due to the rapid developments within Internet technology, social media, and platforms, outlining a definitive strategy is problematic. Scholars are trying to find out more about the consumers who use social media for things like shopping or merely information sources as a way of trying to determine how value is created as this can be transferred across. Online brand community research is heavily focusing on value creation within this environment as communities can facilitate such a nurturing atmosphere that can help create value in terms of information and relationships, etc. Scholars are looking at how they are able to engage consumers more on these platforms as a means of developing their strategies in order to create a better experience for the consumers that use this environment. Current research within self-construal theory is heavily focused on group and community relations between the two self-construals—this environment is one of the most highly used within the social media platforms. Self-construals are prevalent in marketing research and scholars are using them to explain variations in consumer behavior, e.g., actual purchase behavior, which could help to develop marketing strategies.

6.2 DEVELOPING RESEARCH

Developing research that has not fully come into fruition yet seems to be focused on developing generalized terms and typologies so that confusion is stopped, collaboration can be aided, and better research conducted (Campbell, Cohen, & Ma, 2014). Terms such as "social media based brand communities" (Laroche, Habibi, Richard, & Sankaranarayanan,

2012), "new media" (Hennig-Thurau et al., 2013), and even "social media" provide ambiguity in terms of a succinct definition, which is causing some confusion within the research community. Scholars need to agree on definitions or create distinct characteristics that embody alternative terms, as a means to create fluency within the literature.

Social commerce, although a topic of great focus now, has not been fully researched and so further research into how to use social media for selling and transactions is the focus of much emerging work (Yadav et al., 2013). Little empirical evidence has been given in terms of using social media platforms for selling purposes, which has caused some to doubt the applicability of the media for these purposes (Hennig-Thurau et al., 2013). Although, there is little evidence that has proven that it is beneficial to use for selling, more research could be conducted in other areas with a means of trying to get more people to use it for selling or buying purposes. Perhaps Peters et al. (2013) outlined metrics in user-generated content, engagement motivations, network structure, and social roles and interaction would be helpful. For instance, getting more consumers engaged within a specific platform will make them more likely to use these platforms and develop trust and loyalty, ultimately increasing the chances that they will purchase using the platform. However, engagement is not easily understood and more research into communication strategies to encourage engagement and interaction is necessary (Brodie et al., 2013).

Although social media has been around for a while, marketers are still looking into how they can integrate social media and traditional media into one integrated communication (Hanna et al., 2011). By incorporating the new media with traditional media, marketers will be able to not only more fully integrate their communications but will be able to have a wider range of tools they can use rather than just discarding the old ways they can reembrace them and update how they are used. Marketing researchers within the social media environment are also interested in eWOM and the creation of buzz and traffic through the various social media platforms (Luo & Zhang, 2013). Some scholars have used the characteristics of eWOM/WOM to distinguish other types of behaviors, e.g., engagement within communities (Dellocras, Gao, & Narayan, 2010). The focus on the communication between consumers and brands can be attributed to the problems that it can cause them if a consumer is unhappy or has had a negative experience with the brand (Tuten & Solomon, 2013). There is a new interest in the differences between consumer- and marketer-created communities and content which is fueling the debate on what is best to encourage engagement (Ding et al., 2014; Lee, Kim, & Kim, 2011). Engagement as a whole and the ensuing interaction is also developing at the present time (Brodie et al., 2013), with much left to discover. Looking into how consumers engage and interact within these different communities and deciphering what makes them contribute or observe will be a step toward helping to explain engagement within these environments.

Online brand community research has seen a renewed focus on individuality and heterogeneous consumption (Pan, Lu, & Gupta, 2014; Thomas, Price, & Schau, 2013; Weijo, Hietanen, & Mattila, 2014), which is in need of more in-depth research. The structure of the online brand community has changed and allowed multiple memberships among the individual consumer, however, research on this as well as the individuals that are utilizing the online brand communities in this way is few and far between. By exploring the individual consumer uses of online brand communities within the social media environment, researchers can assess how best to use these platforms to communicate and engage consumers as a means of strengthening their marketing strategies.

Developing research in this area also has a strong focus on branding and how these communities can be used as a means of developing brand personality (Davis et al., 2014). The link between brands and the self within these online brand communities could be a great way of exploring brand personality as it holds such a personal connection with consumers and an outlet for self-expression (Back et al., 2010; Wilcox & Stephen, 2013; Yeo, 2012). By finding out how consumers view the brand and the different ways they use the online brand community, brands can develop their personality in accordance with what the individuals that support the brand have. To do this brands must look at individual behavior within these platforms to gain insight into the differences between consumers and acknowledge both active and passive members of the community (De Valck, van Bruggen, & Wierenga, 2009), to gain a complete picture of their brand through the eyes of consumers.

Self-construal research, which centers on the individual differences, seems to be focused on applying new theories to the original concept (e.g., Voyer & Franks, 2014). By extending the self-construal theory to include other theories from other perspectives the whole concept can be extended and applied in more depth to areas such as marketing to help develop their strategies. The need for uniqueness is one such theory

(Song & Lee, 2013) and also seems to be holding promise for developing research, with current scholars calling for more in-depth information regarding the differences in uniqueness of the self-construals (Millan & Reynolds, 2014). Other promising areas within this domain that are relevant to social media and marketing are threat reactions (e.g., White et al., 2012) as examining these in more detail will provide evidence as to how each individual will react when under some sort of threat to their identity. The social media environment provides the perfect place for threats to appear, meaning more research of this aspect of self-construal would be beneficial. In addition, Chen and Marcus (2012) suggest that contextual influences on self-construals, such as that of the social media environment can be developed further to understand its impact. These contextual influences will also have an effect on how far the individual is willing to engage with a brand on these social media platforms through mechanisms such as eWOM (Eisingerich, Chun, Liu, Jia, & Bell, 2015), therefore this aspect of self-construals could also be developed further. Investigating the online environment to establish how individuals are interacting and reacting to things is important in crafting the right strategy to target them.

6.3 METHODS AND SAMPLES

Analysis of the literature has found that in terms of methodology, many studies utilized qualitative approaches such as in-depth interviews (e.g., Killian & McManus, 2015; Schau et al., 2009), discussion groups (e.g., Winer, 2009), focus groups, and qualitative surveys (e.g., Hodis et al., 2015). Online brand community research has also used quantitative approaches such as likert-type scaled online surveys (e.g., Anderson et al., 2014; Gummerus et al., 2012), which has allowed a variety of inferences to be made and strengthened research within the area. Some studies have also utilized a longitudinal netnographical approach (e.g., Kozinets, de Valck, Wojnicki, & Wilner, 2010; Schau et al., 2009), which allows for a study over a longer period of time to validate findings (Kozinets et al., 2010). The majority of self-construal research uses scales, which attempt to measure the individual difference variables between the two self-construal scales (Cross, Hardin, & Gercek-Swing, 2011). Likert style scales such as the self-construal scale by Singelis (1994), Gudykunst et al. (1996), and Leung and Kim (1997) are common. The 20 statements test is also a particularly common form of assessing the two self-construals whereby participants have to complete sentences beginning with "I am" which are then analyzed by the researcher. However, this method is quite difficult to compare across studies as the definition of interdependent and independent self-construal must be the same for a comparison to be made (Cross et al., 2011). Psychological methods are also used such as that by Kitayama, Park, Sevincer, Karasawa, and Uskul (2009), which uses implicit measures. Finally self-report measures are also common based on the increasing notion that the self-construal is a multidimensional construct (Cross et al., 2011). Many scholars such as Levine et al. (2003) and Gudykunst and Lee (2003) debate the validity of the self-construal scales used saying that they do not address the multidimensionality of the concept. The heavy focus on qualitative techniques limits generalizability, which could be overcome by the use of more quantitative methods (Effing & Spil, 2016). The recent studies that have been carried out centering on brand communities and the processes within these, such as eWOM, have been more than forthcoming in suggesting future methodological approaches to answering the plethora of research questions that presents itself. These suggestions include in-depth interviews (Kim, Sung, & Kang, 2014; Weijo et al., 2014), textual content analysis (King, Racherla, & Bush, 2014), pluralistic approaches—combining both quantitative and qualitative methods with larger sample sizes (Brodie et al., 2013), and experimental approaches (Cross et al., 2011; Kim et al., 2014), which are favored over others in self-construal research (e.g., Bechtoldt et al., 2012; Champniss, Wilson, & Macdonald, 2015; White et al., 2012). Researchers have also suggested that future research in social media should incorporate longitudinal approaches more heavily, perhaps based on a case study methodology (Canhoto & Clark, 2013; Davis et al., 2014). Others have suggested using experimental techniques (e.g., Luo & Zhang, 2013; Winer, 2009) and observational methods (e.g., Lee et al., 2011), suggesting behavior needs to be tracked while it is happening in a more naturalistic setting (Lee et al., 2011; Poyry, Parvinen, & Malmivaara, 2013), although, external validity and the impact these environments have on participants should be considered (Sohn, 2014). The study by De Valck et al. (2009), which utilized a multimethod approach could provide the basis for other similar studies. The netnographical approach used in their study as well as by Habibi et al. (2014) would also answer the calls for a more naturalistic, observational approach (Lee et al., 2011; Poyry et al., 2013).

Much of the current research within social media as a whole is seen to be focusing on specific platforms and examining them only in the context of that specific platform which has limited application possibilities. Research within brand communities also tends to be focused on one specific platform due to their nature, this can provide a very in-depth insight into the workings of brand communities as studies are typically undertaken over a longer period of time and therefore provide more valid findings (e.g., Habibi et al., 2014). The most common platforms to be analyzed are Facebook (e.g., Anderson et al., 2014; Hodis et al., 2015), which emphasizes the results of a recent report by Stelzner (2015) that Facebook is the platform marketers want to know more about, and Twitter (e.g., Chen, 2011; Lee & Kim, 2014), with little focus being paid to other popular media sharing social media such as Instagram. With the majority of the small amount of research that has been done on Instagram utilizing a form of content analysis (e.g., Bakhshi, Shamma, & Gilbert, 2014; Hu, Manikonda, & Kambhampati, 2014) or data crawling (e.g., Ferrara, Interdonato, & Tagarelli, 2014). The majority of Twitter research has been based in single countries such as the United States (Li & Li, 2014), and Asian countries such as Korea (e.g., Lee & Kim, 2014; Yoo et al., 2014) with most using online survey approaches (e.g., Chen, 2011; Lee & Kim, 2014; Yoo et al., 2014), and only a few using methods such as experimental approaches (e.g., Li & Li, 2014). Most of the Facebook studies use single countries for their analysis (e.g., Lonnqvist & Itkonen, 2016; Ryan & Xenos, 2011; Seidman, 2013), with only very few using two countries for comparison (e.g., Brailovskaia & Bierhoff, 2016; Lee-Won et al., 2014; Lonnqvist & Deters, 2016). Nearly all Facebook research has utilized a survey methodology for data collection (e.g., Blachnio et al., 2016; Blight et al., 2015; Grieve et al., 2013; Hollenbaugh & Ferris, 2014; Hong et al., 2014; Lee-Won et al., 2014; Malik et al., 2016; Shao & Ross, 2015), with the exception of studies such as Tobina, Vanmana, Verreynnea, and Saeria (2015) who utilized an experimental approach. Students are the most popular sample choice of social media research as they are the most active users of social media sites (e.g., Choi & Ahluwalia, 2013; Clark & Evans, 2014; Toma & Hancock, 2013; Yaakop, 2013; Yen, 2013), especially within Facebook research (e.g., Blachnio et al., 2016; Blight et al., 2015; Hong et al., 2014; Lee et al., 2014; Lonnqvist & Deters, 2016), and within brand community research many studies have utilized self-selection samples (Liao, Hsu, & To, 2013; Poyry et al., 2013). This presents a bias in the research as there are a growing number of other generations utilizing this medium of communication. The student sample is also heavily utilized.

Suggestions to expand current social media research into other areas is common (e.g., Hodis et al., 2015; Killian & McManus, 2015), which would aide validity and verifying findings. Utilizing single platforms also means generalizability issues are common (Anderson et al., 2014; Davis et al., 2014; Effing & Spil, 2016; Gummerus et al., 2012), for instance that which is limited to single-country samples, such as Lee, Ho, and Chou (2015) who used Taiwan, Sohn (2014) whose sample was from the United States and Baber et al. (2016) who based is study in Pakistan. This presents generalizability issues as the findings may not be applicable to other cultures and again highlights the importance of expanding research to incorporate a cross-platform design. In addition, studies tend to focus on only one firm or industry (e.g., Galeotti & Goyal, 2009; Luo, 2009), which also limits generalizability. By developing research to incorporate multiple platforms in this way, marketers can learn how to integrate their marketing communications across these platforms as well as how to allocate their resources to better inform strategic decisions (Smith et al., 2012). Cross-platform research that has been conducted has used a variety of methods to analyze the varying platforms, including multiple methods such as survey and experience narration (e.g., Karapanos et al., 2016), questionnaires (e.g., Hughes et al., 2012), observational cross-site analysis of elements such as content (e.g., Smith et al., 2012) and network structure analysis (e.g., Zafarani & Liu, 2016). Prior work in online community research has been particularly good at focusing on various communities, not just one (e.g., Schau et al., 2009) which is in line with the emerging concept of consumers engaging in multiple communities and having multiple memberships (Habibi et al., 2014; Weijo et al., 2014). Some authors, such as Davis et al. (2014), have used a triangulation approach by combining online data gathering with offline interviews to develop grounded theory.

Studies that have focused on developing frameworks have tended to use managers as their samples (e.g., Killian and McManus, 2015; Winer, 2009). Although this is essential when trying to determine organizational strategic frameworks, it has to be asked whether having a more varied sample would provide a deeper insight into the strategies organizations should be developing. Future research should therefore consider utilizing larger sample sizes (Lee et al., 2011). Much of the research concerning the self-construals has taken place in the distinctive highly independent cultures such as the United States (e.g., Jain, Desai, & Mao, 2007; Jiraporn & Desai, 2010; Lee et al., 2012; White et al., 2012; Zhang et al., 2011) or the highly collectivist cultures such as Asia (e.g., Bechtoldt et al., 2012; Graupmann et al., 2012; Liu & Li, 2009), with only few utilizing European Samples (e.g., Millan & Reynolds, 2014; Verplanken, Trafimow, Khusid, Holland, & Steentjes, 2009). In addition, few have utilized samples from multiple cultures with the exception of those such as Verplanken et al. (2009) and Graupmann et al. (2012). It must also be noted that previous work on online brand communities on social media has focused on collective or individual rather than incorporating both types of engagement and the reasons for this (e.g., Kozinets et al., 2010; Schau et al., 2009). Furthermore, there have been problems with model development as it is difficult to separate antecedents, moderators, and consequences. Limitations of methodology and samples are highlighted below in Table 6.1.

6.4 GAPS AND AREAS FOR FUTURE RESEARCH

Many aspects of marketing practices have been influenced by the rise in social media, and Chung and Austria (2010) call for research in how aspects of lifestyle, technology, and perspective now affect these marketing practices, and ask for a focus on not only content and information but its currency and how this can be delivered, which could pose a challenge to researchers. Perhaps there should be more studies such as that by Buccafurri, Lax, Nicolazzo, and Nocera (2016) who look at developing multiple-social-networking applications, to address this issue. Delivering the best value to consumers is critical to helping both consumers and brands stay satisfied and develop, yet, delivering this value in a society that is constantly changing and increasing in demands of personalization and rapid technology development is hard, especially when trying to develop a marketing strategy that can communicate the brand properly. Cross-platform research is problematic and researchers question the applicability across multiple platforms, which means a new approach to studying these consumers within these social media platforms must be developed. Researchers need to find a way to engage consumers across social media, which is difficult when consumers are demanding so much more individual attention and personalization. Many researchers have called for individual elements of this problem to be addressed such as Chang, Hsieh, and

Table 6.1 Limitations of methodology and samples used in previous research

Limitations	Future suggestions	Citations
Self-selection bias/snowball sampling	Longitudinal approaches over a longer period to give less active users a chance to contribute. Netnography is one example	Canhoto and Clark (2013), Chiu, Wang, Fang, and Huang (2014), De Valck et al. (2009), Gummerus et al. (2012), Laroche et al. (2012), Liao et al. (2013)
Small sample/more active users as sample (e.g., students)	Use bigger, more representative sample	Choi and Ahluwalia (2013), Clark and Evans (2014), Lee et al. (2011); Schembri, Merrilees, and Kristiansen (2010), Toma and Hancock (2013), Yaakop (2013), Yen (2013)
Generalizability—including single-country studies	Use bigger, more representative sample	Anderson et al. (2014), Campbell, Piercy, and Heinrich (2012), Chu (2011), Davis et al. (2014), Gummerus et al. (2012), Lee and Kim (2014), Li and Li (2014), Luo and Zhang (2013), Schembri et al. (2010), Yaakop (2013), Yoo et al. (2014)
Experimental approaches isolating variables	Experiments must be adapted and improved to track behavior in real time	Lee et al. (2011), Navarro-Bailon (2012), Poyry et al. (2013)
Scope-limited to one product, brand, industry, or platform	Utilizing other platforms and more under researched product categories/industries. Cross-platform research. Possible triangulation	Anderson et al. (2014), Blachnio et al. (2016), Blight et al. (2015), Brodie et al. (2013), Chu (2011), Davis et al. (2014), Grieve et al. (2013), Gummerus et al. (2012), Navarro-Bailon (2012), Yaakop and Hemsley-Brown (2014)
Lock of longitudinal research	Gather data over a longer period of time to validate findings	Canhoto and Clark (2013), Davis et al. (2014)

Tseng (2013) who called for more research into individual differences in interaction, Pan et al. (2014) and Thomas et al. (2013) that want a more in-depth look at heterogeneous communities as well as Weijo et al. (2014) who highlighted their individualized use and the research gap concerning these individualized consumers. Therefore looking at how individual consumers are using these communities and finding out how they are engaging will help further knowledge and develop strategies, which will target individual engagement rather than specific platforms.

Summary of Key Points

- Cross-platform research is lacking and should therefore be utilized more with study designs.
- The most commonly researched platforms are Facebook and Twitter, leaving other platforms such as Snapchat, Instagram, WhatsApp, etc. lacking the same depth of understanding.
- Students are a heavily utilized sample because of their high tendency to utilize and be active within the social media environment.
- Generalizability issues are common due to much focus on single platforms, products, and brands.
- There is a huge focus on trying to find out more about the individuals that utilize the varying social media platforms, which should be considered within future research.

Much research has focused on traditional online brand communities such as those that are on Facebook, where relationships can form and develop, yet, less attention has been paid to microblogging sites such as Twitter, which have drastically grown in popularity. Kim et al. (2014) is one such exception to the rule, looking at the role of eWOM on Twitter. They found that in order for consumers to pass on the brands message they had to first identify with the brand, linking the self to the brand. Brand communities are harder to define on Twitter and may be more accurately described as imagined communities as the symbolic brand meaning and the level of identification is what joins consumers together through a sense of commitment (Gruzd, Wellman, & Takhteyev, 2011). The consumers on this platform cannot be categorized as the same as regular online brand community members due to their limited motivation to engage with others via this platform (Kim et al., 2014). The Twitter platform is still relatively undiscovered and much research can still be undertaken on this unique platform such as consumer engagement in mentioning a brand, valence of eWOM messages, and opinion passing behaviors (Kim et al., 2014). Other platforms such as Instagram, Pinterest, WhatsApp, and Snapchat have also received limited attention within the literature, suggesting these need to be researched further to gather a more in-depth understanding of each platform. Online brand community research has also focused on specific communities and indicated that future research should be adapted for other platforms (e.g., Anderson et al., 2014; Chu, 2011; Gummerus et al., 2012). The focus on specific contexts allows for insight into the notion that not all approaches are beneficial for all types of industry (Fieseler & Fleck, 2013; Hajli & Hajli, 2013).

Future Research concerning self-construals on social media should be directed at the differences between the interaction behaviors of the two (Millan & Reynolds, 2014), as well as the responses to things such as identity threat (White et al., 2012), which can play a major part in how a consumer associates or dissociates with a brand. Actual purchase behavior and relations to the self-construals is still an area that could be fruitful for research (Millan & Reynolds, 2014), as well as the importance of emotions in the reactions of the different self-construals (Cross et al., 2011). Consumer behavior theories should be incorporated as a means of understanding the various identities consumers have (Brodie et al., 2013). Addressing these issues within a social media context would allow for a more in-depth understanding of how the self is conceptualized within the online environment, with the possibility of cross-platform research providing even more insight. It is perhaps the social-level of the self-construal concept, which needs to be researched further (Voyer & Franks, 2014) due to its reliance on situational influence, something which is suited to be examined in the social environment of social media. Identifying how the different self-construals share information online will again provide a more in-depth look at conceptualization of the self within this new environment (Chen & Marcus, 2012). There is a possibility to incorporate new theories into the self-construal concept as a means of explaining their differences and similarities in behavior, particularly form social and psychological disciplines. It has also been suggested that the self-construal theory itself can also be applied to other research as a means of expanding it, e.g., Prieler and Choi (2014) who suggested utilizing the theory to extend research on body image on social media.

Key Points for Practitioners
- Ensure that feedback mechanisms are in place when utilizing social media to enable negative brand experiences or comments to be picked up and handled quickly.
- Treat all consumers as individuals and avoid mass marketing to them on a large scale as this reduces their feelings of individuality.
- Integrate marketing communication where possible to allow consistent messaging across platforms.
- Instead of trying to follow developed frameworks and measurement approaches, delve deeper into what it is that the individual organization needs.
- Make sure that the value of the consumer is the focus for all within the organization.

Consumers are subject to a variety of information in the social media environment that influences their decisions, either confirming what they previously thought or providing conflicting information that causes them to question their choices. This highlights the need to look at where this information comes from (Yadav et al., 2013), including message valence. Communication between consumers is more trustworthy than that which is received from an organization or brand (Chung & Austria, 2010; Foux, 2006), thus signaling an area for more research to determine whether this affects their loyalty (Hennig-Thurau et al., 2010). The power of eWOM communication within the social media environment can influence other types of information, which also needs to be addressed (Chung & Austria, 2010; Mangold & Faulds, 2009; Yadav et al., 2013). The control of consumers and how the co-creation process affects consumer decisions also needs to be further addressed (Chung & Austria, 2010; Constantinides, 2014).

Recommendations for Future Research

- The development of a new approach to cross-platform research is needed.
- An in-depth look at how individuals are utilizing online brand communities is needed to highlight the new issues of the heterogeneous consumer.
- Other platforms such as microblogs like Twitter and photo-sharing platforms like Snapchat, Instagram, and Pinterest need a lot more focus. Perhaps first establishing the unique behaviors and motivations on these platforms will provide a basis for getting this stream of research started.
- Establishing individual differences between consumers will provide more focus for understanding what different consumers want from their social media experiences.
- There is a need to focus on information sources, particularly in the form of secondary word of mouth, and sharing behaviors. This also links in to viral aspects of social media which are also in need of attention.
- Using samples other than students would be beneficial, especially as more of the older generation are using social media at present.
- Cross-country research is also a promising opportunity for researchers, enabling more than just a two-way comparison.

This chapter has presented a synthesis of the current, developing, and future research directions within the social media environment, including focus on online brand communities and integrating self-construal theory to understand these platforms. It highlights the various methodological and sampling techniques utilized in this area currently along with suggestions for how it can be developed in the future. There is a continuing need to develop and understand the multitude of social media platforms, specifically the power of groups of consumers and how individuals utilize the environment for the development of their self.

REFERENCES

Anderson, K. C., Knight, D. K., Pookulangara, S., & Josiam, B. (2014). Influence of hedonic and utilitarian motivations on retailer loyalty and purchase intention: A Facebook perspective. *Journal of Retailing and Consumer Services, 21*, 773–779.

Baber, A., Thurasamy, R., Malik, M. I., Sadiq, B., Islam, S., & Sajjad, M. (2016). Online word-of-mouth antecedents, attitude and intention-to-purchase electronic products in Pakistan. *Telematics and Informatics, 33*, 388–400.

Back, M. D., Stopfer, J. M., Vazire, S., Gaddis, S., Schmukle, S. C., Egloff, B., et al. (2010). Facebook profiles reflect actual personality, not self-idealization. *Psychological Science, 21*(3), 372–374.

Bakhshi, S., Shamma, D. A., & Gilbert, E. (2014). Faces engage us: Photos with faces attract more likes and comments on Instagram. In *CHI '14 proceedings of the SIGCHI conference on human factors in computing systems* (pp. 965–974). Available from: http://dx.doi.org/10.1145/2556288.2557403.

Baldus, B. J., Voorhees, C., & Calantone, R. (2015). Online brand community engagement: Scale development and validation. *Journal of Business Research, 68,* 978–985.

Barger, V. A., & Labrecque, L. I. (2013). An integrated marketing communications perspective on social media metrics. *International Journal of Integrated Marketing Communications, 5*(1), 64–76.

Bechtoldt, M. N., Choi, H.-S., & Nijstad, B. A. (2012). Individuals in mind, mates by heart: Individualistic self-construal and collective value orientation as predictors of group creativity. *Journal of Experimental Social Psychology, 48,* 838–844.

Berthon, P., Pitt, L., & Campbell, C. (2008). Ad lib: When customers create the ad. *California Management Review, 50*(4), 6–30.

Blachnio, A., Przepiorka, A., & Rudnicka, P. (2016). Narcissism and self-esteem as predictors of dimensions of Facebook use. *Personality and Individual Differences, 90,* 296–301.

Blazevic, V., Wiertz, C., Cotte, J., de Ruyter, K., & Keeling, D. I. (2014). GOSIP in cyberspace: Conceptualization and scale development for general online social interaction propensity. *Journal of Interactive Marketing, 28,* 87–100.

Blight, M. G., Jageillo, K., & Ruppel, E. K. (2015). "Same stuff different day": A mixed method study of support seeking on Facebook. *Computers in Human Behavior, 53,* 366–373.

Brailovskaia, J., & Bierhoff, H.-W. (2016). Cross-cultural narcissism on Facebook: Relationship between self-presentation, social interaction and the open and covert narcissism on a social networking site in Germany and Russia. *Computers in Human Behavior, 55,* 25–57.

Brodie, R. J., Ilic, A., Biljana, J., & Hollebeek, L. (2013). Consumer engagement in a virtual brand community: An exploratory analysis. *Journal of Business Research, 66*(1), 105–114.

Buccafurri, F., Lax, G., Nicolazzo, S., & Nocera, A. (2015). Comparing Twitter and Facebook user behaviour: Privacy and other aspects. *Computers in Human Behavior, 52,* 87–95.

Buccafurri, F., Lax, G., Nicolazzo, S., & Nocera, A. (2016). A model to support design and development of multiple-social-network applications. *Information Sciences, 331,* 99–119.

Campbell, C., Piercy, N., & Heinrich, D. (2012). When companies get caught: The effect of consumers discovering undesirable firm engagement online. *Journal of Public Affairs, 12*(2), 120–126.

Campbell, C., Cohen, J., & Ma, J. (2014). Advertisements just aren't advertisements anymore: A new typology for evolving forms of online 'advertising'. *Journal of Advertising Research, 54*(1), 7–10.

Canhoto, I. A., & Clark, M. (2013). Customer service 140 characters at a time: The user's perspective. *Journal of Marketing Management, 29*(5–6), 522–544.

Champniss, G., Wilson, H. N., & Macdonald, E. K. (2015). Why your customers social identities matter. *Harvard Business Review, 93*(January–February), 88–96.

Chang, A., Hsieh, S. H., & Tseng, T. H. (2013). Online brand community response to negative brand events: The role of group eWOM. *Internet Research, 23*(4), 486–506.

Chang, C. (2015). Self-construal and Facebook activities: Exploring differences in social interaction orientation. *Computers in Human Behavior, 53,* 91–101.

Chen, B., & Marcus, J. (2012). Students' self-presentation on Facebook: An examination of personality and self-construal factors. *Computers in Human Behavior, 28,* 2091–2099.

Chen, G. M. (2011). Tweet this: A uses and gratifications perspective on how active Twitter use gratifies a need to connect with others. *Computers in Human Behavior, 27,* 755—762.

Cheung, C. M. K., & Thadani, D. R. (2012). The impact of electronic word-of-mouth communication: A literature analysis and integrative model. *Decision Support Systems, 54,* 461—470.

Chiu, C.-M., Wang, E. T. G., Fang, Y.-H., & Huang, H.-Y. (2014). Understanding customers' repeat purchase intentions in B2C e-commerce: the roles of utilitarian value, hedonic value and perceived risk. *Information Systems Journal, 24,* 85—114.

Choi, B., & Ahluwalia, R. (2013). Determinants of brand switching: The role of consumer inferences, brand commitment, and perceived risk. *Journal of Applied Social Psychology, 43,* 981—991.

Chu, S., & Kim, Y. (2011). Determinants of consumer engagement in electronic word-of-mouth (eWOM) in social networking sites. *International Journal of Advertising, 30* (1), 47—75.

Chu, S.-C. (2011). Viral advertising in social media: Participation in Facebook groups and responses among college-aged users. *Journal of Interactive Advertising, 12*(1), 30—43.

Chung, C., & Austria, K. (2010). *Social media gratification and attitude toward social media marketing messages: A study of the effect of social media marketing messages on online shopping value. Proceedings of the Northeast Business & Economics Association* (pp. 581—586). Academic Press.

Clark, J. K., & Evans, A. T. (2014). Source credibility and persuasion: The role of message position in self-validation. *Personality and Social Psychology Bulletin, 40*(8), 1024—1036.

Constantinides, E. (2014). Foundations of social media marketing. *Procedia-Social and Behavioral Sciences, 148,* 40—57.

Cross, S. E., Hardin, E. E., & Gercek-Swing, B. (2011). The what, how, why and where of self-construal. *Personality and Social Psychology Review, 15*(2), 142—179.

Davis, R., Piven, I., & Breazeale, M. (2014). Conceptualising the brand in social media community: The five sources model. *Journal of Retailing and Consumer Services, 21,* 468—481.

De Valck, K., van Bruggen, G. H., & Wierenga, B. (2009). Virtual communities: A marketing perspective. *Decision Support Systems, 47,* 185—203.

DeAndrea, D. C., Shaw, A. S., & Levine, T. R. (2010). Online language: The role of culture in self-expression and self-construal on Facebook. *Journal of Language and Social Psychology, 29*(4), 425—442.

Dellocras, C., Gao, G., & Narayan, R. (2010). Are consumers more likely to contribute online reviews for hit or niche products? *Journal of Management Information Systems, 27* (22), 127—158.

Ding, Y., Phang, C. W., Lu, X., Tan, C.-H., & Sutanto, J. (2014). The role of marketer- and user-generated content in sustaining the growth of a social media brand community. In *2014 47th Hawaii International Conference on System Sciences (HICSS)* (pp. 1785—1792). IEEE.

Doh, J., & Hwang, J. S. (2009). How consumers evaluate eWOM (electronic word-of-mouth) messages. *Cyberpsychology & Behavior, 12*(2), 193—197.

Effing, R., & Spil, T. A. M. (2016). The social strategy cone: Towards a framework for evaluating social media strategies. *International Journal of Information Management, 36,* 1—8.

Eisingerich, A. B., Chun, H. H., Liu, Y., Jia, H., & Bell, S. J. (2015). Why recommend a brand face-to-face but not on Facebook? How word-of-mouth on online social sites differs from traditional word-of-mouth. *Journal of Consumer Psychology, 21*(1), 120—128.

Ferrara, E., Interdonato, R., & Tagarelli, A. (2014). Online popularity and topical interests through the lens of Instagram. In *HT '14 Proceedings of the 25th ACM conference on hypertext and social media* (pp. 24−34).

Fieseler, C., & Fleck, M. (2013). The pursuit of empowerment through social media: Structural social capital dynamics in CSR-blogging. *Journal of Business Ethics, 118,* 759−775.

Foux, G. (2006). Consumer-generated media: Get your customers involved. *Brand Strategy, 202*(May), 38−39.

Franke, N., Keinz, P., & Steger, C. J. (2009). Testing the value of customization: When do customers really prefer products tailored to their preferences? *Journal of Marketing, 73*(5), 103−121.

Galeotti, A., & Goyal, S. (2009). Influencing the influencers: A theory of strategic diffusion. *Journal of Economics, 40*(3), 509−532.

Graupmann, V., Jonas, E., Meier, E., Hawelka, S., & Aichhorn, M. (2012). Reactance, the self, and its group: When threats to freedom come from the ingroup versus the outgroup. *European Journal of Social Psychology, 42,* 164−173.

Grieve, R., Indian, M., Witteveen, K., Tolan, G. A., & Marrington, J. (2013). Face-to-face or Facebook: Can social connectedness be derived online? *Computers in Human Behavior, 29,* 604−609.

Gruzd, A., Wellman, B., & Takhteyev, Y. (2011). Imagining Twitter as an imagined community. *American Behavioral Scientist, 55*(10), 1294−1318.

Gudykunst, W. B., & Lee, C. M. (2003). Assessing the validity of self-construal scales. *Human Communication Research, 29*(2), 253−274.

Gudykunst, W. B., Matsumoto, Y., Ting-Toomey, S., Nishida, T., Kim, K., & Heyman, S. (1996). The influence of cultural individualism-collectivism, self-construals, and individual values on communication styles across cultures. *Human Communication Research, 22*(4), 510−543.

Gummerus, J., Liljander, V., Weman, E., & Pihlstrom, M. (2012). Customer engagement in a Facebook brand community. *Management Research Review, 35*(9), 857−877.

Gupta, P., & Harris, J. (2005). How e-WOM recommendations influence product consideration and quality of choice: A motivation to process information perspective. *Journal of Business Research, 63*(9−10), 1041−1049.

Habibi, M. R., Laroche, M., & Richard, M.-O. (2014). Brand communities based in social media: How unique are they? Evidence from two exemplary brand communities. *International Journal of Information Management, 34,* 123−132.

Hajli, M., & Hajli, M. (2013). Organisational development in sport: Co-creation of value through social capital. *Industrial and Commercial Training, 45*(5), 283−288.

Hamilton, R. W., & Biehal, G. J. (2005). Achieving your goals or protecting their future? The effects of self-view on goals and choices. *Journal of Consumer Research, 32,* 277−283.

Hanna, R., Rohm, A., & Crittenden, V. L. (2011). We're all connected: The power of the social media ecosystem. *Business Horizons, 54*(3), 265−273.

Hansen, D. L. (2011). Exploring social media relationships. *On the Horizon, 19*(1), 43−51.

Hansen, S. S., & Lee, J. K. (2013). What drives consumers to pass along marketer-generated eWOM in social network games? Social and game factors in play. *Journal of Theoretical and Applied Electronic Commerce Research, 8*(1), 53−68.

Hennig-Thurau, T., Hofacker, C. F., & Bloching, B. (2013). Marketing the pinball way: Understanding how social media change the generation of value for consumers and companies. *Journal of Interactive Marketing, 27,* 237−241.

Hennig-Thurau, T., Malthouse, E. C., Friege, C., Gensler, S., Lobschat, L., Ranaswamy, A., et al. (2010). The impact of new media on customer relationships. *Journal of Service Research, 13*(3), 311−330.

Hill, S., Provost, F., & Volinsky, C. (2006). Network-based marketing: Identifying likely adopters in consumer networks. *Statistical Science, 21*(2), 256−276.

Hodis, M., Sriramachandramurthy, R., & Sashittal, H. C. (2015). Interact with me on my terms: A four segment Facebook engagement framework for marketers. *Journal of Marketing Management, 31*(11−12), 1255−1284.

Hollebeek, L. D., Glynn, M. S., & Brodie, R. J. (2014). Consumer brand engagement in social media: Conceptualization, scale development and validation. *Journal of Interactive Marketing, 28*, 149−165.

Hollenbaugh, E. E., & Ferris, A. L. (2014). Facebook self-disclosure: Examining the role of traits, social cohesion, and motives. *Computers in Human Behavior, 30*, 50−58.

Hong, F.-Y., Huang, D.-H., Lin, H.-Y., & Chiu, S.-L. (2014). Analysis of the psychological traits, Facebook usage, and Facebook addiction model of Taiwanese university students. *Telematics and Informatics, 31*, 591−606.

Hu, Y., Manikonda, L., & Kambhampati, S. (2014). *What we Instagram: A first analysis of Instagram photo content and user types. Eighth international AAAI conference on weblogs and social media* (pp. 595−598). *Palo Alto, CA: The AAAI Press.*

Hughes, D. J., Rowe, M., Batey, M., & Lee, A. (2012). A tale of two sites: Twitter vs. Facebook and the personality predictors of social media usage. *Computers in Human Behavior, 28*, 561−569.

Jain, S. P., Desai, K. K., & Mao, H. (2007). The influence of chronic and situational self-construal on categorization. *Journal of Consumer Research, 34*(June), 66−76.

Jansen, B. J., Zhang, M., Sobel, K., & Chowdury, A. (2009). Twitter power: Tweets as electronic word of mouth. *Journal of the American Society for Information Science and Technology, 60*(11), 2169−2188.

Jiraporn, N., & Desai, K. K. (2010). Adoption of network externality products: The interactive influence of self-construal, branding strategy, and source of information. *Advances in Consumer Research, 37*, 471−472.

Karapanos, E., Teixeira, P., & Gouveia, R. (2016). Need fulfillment and experiences on social media: A case on Facebook and WhatsApp. *Computers in Human Behavior, 55*, 888−897.

Kietzmann, J. H., Hermkens, K., McCarthy, I. P., & Silvestre, B. S. (2011). Social media? Get serious! Understanding the functional building blocks of social media. *Business Horizons, 54*(3), 241−251.

Killian, G., & McManus, K. (2015). A marketing communications approach for the digital era: Managerial guidelines for social media integration. *Business Horizons, 58*, 539−549.

Kim, E., Sung, Y., & Kang, H. (2014). Brand followers' retweeting behaviour on Twitter: How brand relationships influence brand electronic word-of-mouth. *Computers in Human Behavior, 37*, 8−25.

King, R. A., Racherla, P., & Bush, V. D. (2014). What we know and don't know about online word-of-mouth: A review and synthesis of the literature. *Journal of Interactive Marketing, 28*, 167−183.

Kitayama, S., Park, H., Sevincer, A. T., Karasawa, M., & Uskul, A. K. (2009). A cultural task analysis of implicit independence: Comparing North America, Western Europe, and East Asia. *Journal of Personality and Social Psychology, 97*, 236−255.

Kozinets, R. V., de Valck, K., Wojnicki, A. C., & Wilner, S. J. S. (2010). Networked narratives: Understanding word-of-mouth marketing in online communities. *Journal of Marketing, 74*(2), 71−89.

Labrecque, L. I. (2014). Fostering consumer-brand relationships in social media environments: The role of parasocial interaction. *Journal of Interactive Marketing, 28,* 134−148.

Lampe, C., Ellison, N. B., & Steinfield, C. (2008). *Changes in use and perception on Facebook. Proceedings of the 2008 ACM conference on computer supported cooperative work* (pp. 721−730). New York, NY: ACM.

Laroche, M., Habibi, M. R., Richard, M.-O., & Sankaranarayanan, R. (2012). The effects of social media based brand communities on brand community markers, value creation practices, brand trust and brand loyalty. *Computers in Human Behaviour, 28,* 1755−1767.

Lee, D., Kim, H. S., & Kim, J. K. (2011). The impact of online brand community type on consumer's community engagement behaviors: Consumer-created vs. marketer-created online brand community in online social-networking web sites. *Cyberpsychology, Behavior, and Social Networking, 14*(1−2), 59−63.

Lee, D., Kim, H. S., & Kim, J. K. (2012). The role of self-construal in consumers' electronic word of mouth (eWOM) in social networking sites: A social cognitive approach. *Computers in Human Behavior, 28,* 1054−1062.

Lee, E., Ahn, J., & Kim, Y. J. (2014). Personality traits and self-presentation at Facebook. *Personality and Individual Differences, 69,* 162−167.

Lee, E.-J., & Kim, Y. W. (2014). How social is Twitter use? Affiliative tendency and communication competence as predictors. *Computers in Human Behavior, 39,* 296−305.

Lee, J., Park, D. H., & Han, I. (2008). The effect of negative online consumer reviews on product attitude: An information processing view. *Electronic Commerce Research and Applications, 7*(3), 341−352.

Lee, M., & Youn, S. (2009). Electronic word of mouth (eWOM): how eWOM platforms influence consumer product judgement. *International Journal of Advertising: The Quarterly Review of Marketing Communications, 28*(3), 473−499.

Lee, Y.-H., Ho, C.-H., & Chou, C. (2015). Re-visiting internet addiction among Taiwanese students: A cross-sectional comparison of students' expectations, online gaming, and online social interaction. *Journal of Abnormal Child Psychology, 43*(3), 589−599.

Lee-Won, R., Shim, M., Joo, Y. K., & Park, S. G. (2014). Who puts the best "face" forward on Facebook? Positive self-presentation in online social networking and the role of self-consciousness, actual-to-total Friends ration, and culture. *Computers in Human Behavior, 39,* 413−423.

Leung, T., & Kim, M. S. (1997). *A revised self-construal scale.* Honolulu: University of Hawaii at Manoa.

Levine, T. R., Bresnahan, M. J., Park, H. S., Lapinski, M. K., Wittenbaum, G. M., Shearman, S. M., et al. (2003). Self-Construal Scales Lack Validity. *Human Communication Research, 29*(2), 210−252.

Li, C. (2016). When does web-based personalization really work? The distinction between actual personalization and perceived personalization. *Computers in Human Behavior, 54,* 25−33.

Li, S., Clark, L., & Wheeler, C. (2013). Unlocking the marketing potential of social capital: A study to identify the dimensions of social capital considered represented within online brand communities. In *IEEE 10th international conference on e-business engineering* (pp. 138−141). Available from: http://dx.doi.org/10.1109/ICEBE.2013.21.

Li, Z., & Li, C. (2014). Twitter as a social actor: How consumers evaluate brands differently on Twitter based on relationship norms. *Computers in Human Behavior, 39,* 187−196.

Liao, C., Hsu, F.-C., & To, P.-L. (2013). Exploring knowledge sharing in virtual communities. *Online Information Review, 37*(6), 891−909.

Liu, C.-J., & Li, S. (2009). Contextualized self: When the self runs into social dilemmas. *International Journal of Psychology, 44*(6), 451–458.

Lonnqvist, J.-E., & Deters, F.-G. (2016). Facebook friends, subjective well-being, social support, and personality. *Computers in Human Behavior, 55*, 113–120.

Lonnqvist, J.-E., & Itkonen, J. V. A. (2016). Homogeneity of personal values and personality traits in Facebook social networks. *Journal of Research in Personality, 60*, 24–35.

Luo, X. (2009). Quantifying the long-term impact of negative word of mouth on cash flows and stock prices. *Marketing Science, 28*(1), 148–165.

Luo, X., & Zhang, J. (2013). How do consumer buzz and traffic in social media marketing predict the value of the firm? *Journal of Management and Information Systems, 30*(2), 213–238.

Malik, A., Dhir, A., & Nieminen, M. (2016). Uses and gratifications of digital photo sharing on Facebook. *Telematics and Informatics, 33*, 129–138.

Mangold, W. G., & Faulds, D. J. (2009). Social media: The new hybrid element of the promotion mix. *Business Horizons, 52*(4), 357–365.

Mattingly, B. A., Oswald, D. L., & Clark, E. M. (2011). An examination of relational-interdependent self-construal, communal strength, and pro-relationship behaviours in friendships. *Personality and Individual Differences, 50*, 1243–1248.

Millan, E., & Reynolds, J. (2014). Self-construals, symbolic and hedonic preferences, and actual purchase behavior. *Journal of Retailing and Consumer Services, 21*, 550–560.

Moran, E., & Gossieaux, F. (2010). Marketing in a hyper-social world: The tribalization of business study and characteristics of successful online communities. *Journal of Advertising Research, 50*(3), 232–239.

Na, J., Kosinski, M., & Stillwell, D. J. (2015). When a tool is introduced in different cultural contexts: Individualism-collectivism and social network on Facebook. *Journal of Cross-Cultural Psychology, 46*(3), 355–370.

Naaman, M., Boase, J., & Lai, C.-H. (2010). Is it really about me? Message content in social awareness streams. In *Proceedings of the 2010 ACM conference on computer supported cooperative work.* (pp. 189 – 192). (February 6–10). Savannah, GA: Association for Computing Machinery.

Navarro-Bailon, M. A. (2012). Strategic consistent messages in cross-tool campaigns: Effects in brand image and brand attitude. *Journal of Marketing Communications, 18*(3), 189–202.

Pan, Z., Lu, Y., & Gupta, S. (2014). How heterogeneous community engage newcomers? The effect of community diversity on newcomers' perception of inclusion: An empirical study in social media service. *Computers in Human Behavior, 39*, 100–111.

Park, C., & Lee, T. (2009). Information direction, website reputation and eWOM effect: A moderating role of product type. *Journal of Business Research, 62*(1), 61–67.

Park, D. H., Lee, J., & Han, I. (2007). The effect of on-line consumer reviews on consumer purchasing intention: The moderating role of involvement. *International Journal of Electronic Commerce, 11*(4), 125–148.

Peters, K., Chen, Y., Kaplan, A. M., Ognibeni, B., & Pauwels, K. (2013). Social media metrics—a framework and guidelines for managing social media. *Journal of Interactive Marketing, 27*(4), 281–298.

Poyry, E., Parvinen, P., & Malmivaara, T. (2013). Can we get from liking to buying? Behavioral differences in hedonic and Utilitarian Facebook usage. *Electronic Commerce Research and Applications, 12*, 224–235.

Prieler, M., & Choi, J. (2014). Broadening the scope of social media effect research on body image concerns. *Sex Roles, 71*(11), 378–388.

Ryan, T., & Xenos, S. (2011). Who uses Facebook? An investigation into the relationship between the Big Five, shyness, narcissism, loneliness, and Facebook usage. *Computers in Human Behavior, 27*, 1658–1664.

Schau, H. J., Muñiz, A. M., & Arnould, E. J., Jr. (2009). How brand community practices create value. *Journal of Marketing*, *73*(5), 30−51.

Schembri, S., Merrilees, B., & Kristiansen, S. (2010). Brand Consumption and Narrative of Self. *Psychology and Marketing*, *27*(6), 623−638.

See-To, E. W. K., & Ho, K. K. W. (2014). Value co-creation and purchase intention in social network sites: The role of electronic Word-of-mouth and trust-a theoretical analysis. *Computers in Human Behavior*, *31*, 182−189.

Seidman, G. (2013). Self-presentation and belonging on Facebook: How personality influences social media use and motivations. *Personality and Individual Differences*, *54*, 402−407.

Sen, S., & Lerman, D. (2007). Why are you telling me this? An examination into negative consumer reviews on the Web. *Journal of Interactive Marketing*, *21*(4), 76−94.

Shankar, V., & Hollinger, M. (2007). Online advertising: Current scenario and emerging trends. *Marketing Science Institute Report*, 07−206.

Shao, W., & Ross, M. (2015). Testing a conceptual model of Facebook brand page communities. *Journal of Research in Interactive Marketing*, *9*(3), 239−258.

Singelis, T. M. (1994). The measurement of independent and interdependent self-constr-uals. *Personality and Social Psychological Bulletin*, *20*, 580−591.

Smith, A. N., Fischer, E., & Yongjian, C. (2012). How does brand-related user-generated content differ across YouTube, Facebook, and Twitter? *Journal of Interactive Marketing*, *26*, 102−113.

Sohn, D. (2014). Coping with information in social media: The effects of network structure and knowledge on perception of information value. *Computers in Human Behavior*, *32*, 145−151.

Song, D., & Lee, J. (2013). Balancing "We" and "I": Self-construal and an alternative approach to seeking uniqueness. *Journal of Consumer Behaviour*, *12*, 506−516.

Stelzner, M. (2015). Social media marketing industry report: How marketers are using social media to grow their business. *Social Media Examiner*. 6, June 2015 from: <http://www.socialmediaexaminer.com/SocialMediaMarketingIndustryReport2015.pdf>.

Thomas, T., Price, L. L., & Schau, H. J. (2013). When differences unite: Resource dependence in heterogeneous consumption communities. *Journal of Consumer Research*, *39*, 1010−1033.

Tobina, S. J., Vanmana, E. J., Verreynnea, M., & Saeria, A. K. (2015). Threats to belonging on Facebook: Lurking and ostracism. *Social Influence*, *10*(1), 31−42.

Toma, C. L., & Hancock, J. T. (2013). Self-affirmation underlies Facebook use. *Personality and Social Psychology Bulletin*, *39*, 321−330.

Tuten, T. L., & Solomon (2013). *Social media marketing* (International Edition New Jersey: Pearson Education.

Verplanken, B., Trafimow, D., Khusid, I. K., Holland, R. W., & Steentjes, G. M. (2009). Different selves, different values: Effects of self-construals on value activation and use. *European Journal of Social Psychology*, *39*, 909−919.

Voyer, B. G., & Franks, B. (2014). Toward a better understanding of self-construal theory: An agency view of the processes of self-construal. *Review of General Psychology*, *18*(2), 101−114.

Wang, Y., Ma, S., & Li, D. (2015). Customer participation in virtual brand communities: The self-construal perspective. *Information & Management*, *52*(5), 577−587.

Wei, W., Miao, L., Cai, L. A., & Adler, H. (2012). The influence of self-construal and co-consumption others on consumer complaining behaviour. *International Journal of Hospitality Management*, *31*, 764−771.

Weijo, H., Hietanen, J., & Mattila, P. (2014). New insights into online consumption communities and netnography. *Journal of Business Research*, *67*, 2072−2078.

Weinberg, B. D., & Pehlivan, E. (2011). Social spending: Managing the social media mix. *Business Horizons, 54*, 275–282.

White, K., Argo, J. J., & Sengupta, J. (2012). Dissociative versus associative responses to social identity threat: The role of consumer self-construal. *Journal of Consumer Research, 39*(December), 704–719.

Wilcox, K., & Stephen, A. (2013). Are close friends the enemy? Online social networks, self-esteem, and self-control. *Journal of Consumer Research, 40*(1), 90–103.

Winer, R. S. (2009). New communications approaches in marketing: Issues and research directions. *Journal of Interactive Marketing, 23*, 108–117.

Wolf, R. D., Gao, B., Berendt, B., & Pierson, J. (2015). The promise of audience transparency. Exploring users' perceptions and behaviors towards visualizations of networked audiences on Facebook. *Telematics and Informatics, 32*, 890–908.

Yaakop, A. (2013). Like it or not: Issue of credibility in Facebook advertising. *Asian Social Science, 9*(3), 154–163.

Yadav, M. S., de Valck, K., Hennig-Thurau, T., Hoffman, D. L., & Spann, M. (2013). Social commerce: A contingency framework assessing marketing potential. *Journal of Interactive Marketing, 27*, 311–323.

Yaakop, A., & Hemsley-Brown, J. (2014). Attitudes toward Specific Advertising Media (AM): Informative or Manipulative? *Asian Social Science, 10*(7), 200–212.

Yen, Y.-S. (2013). The Relationship among Social Influence, Perceived Value, and Usage Intention in Social Networking Sites. Consumer Electronics, Communications and Networks (CECNet), 2013 3rd International Conference, IEEE, Xianning, 20–22 Nov, 699–70.

Yeo, T. E. D. (2012). Social-media early adopters don't count: How to seed participation in interactive campaigns by psychological profiling of digital consumers. *Journal of Advertising Research, 52*(3), 297–308.

Yoo, J., Choi, S., Choi, M., & Rho, J. (2014). Why people use Twitter: Social conformity and social value perspectives. *Online Information Review, 38*(2), 265–283.

Zafarani, R., & Liu, H. (2016). Users joining multiple sites: Friendship and popularity variations across sites. *Information Fusion, 28*, 83–89.

Zhang, L., Moore, M., & Moore, R. (2011). The effect of self-construal's on the effectiveness of comparative advertising. *Marketing Management Journal, 21*(1), 195–206.

CHAPTER 7

Conclusion

This book was written to provide a comprehensive overview on the subject of social media from a marketing perspective. The key areas of literature were examined, including emphasis on the importance of the individual differences between consumers and how this affects their social media use. There are a variety of studies that look at social media, many of which emphasize its practical applicability within the marketing function. However, attempts at outlining a suitable strategy or framework based on these have been unsuccessful, leading to confusion for practitioners regarding how to effectively utilize the medium. Many have accepted the benefits that social media can provide in terms of relationship building and providing value to consumers, yet effectively integrating it into the preexisting marketing mix seems to be problematic for many. The question of whether social media can be seen as an additional marketing mix element or a new marketing environment in itself needs to be considered, as there are many aspects of the seven Ps that find new meaning within this online social context. Examining this social media environment in terms of its marketing potential holds endless possibilities to enable connections with consumers, aiding understanding for both manager and marketers.

The power that consumers now have means that they are influencers of the final brand offering, aiding in the development of products and services by engaging in co-creation opportunities. Electronic word of mouth (eWOM) is just one such opportunity that consumers can utilize within the social media environment to help cocreate the brand offering, providing information on preferences, functionality and suitability that enable better product and service development. In addition, eWOM functions as a crucial part of communication between consumers, which is aided by tie strength. These networked connections between individuals facilitate the transfer of information between consumers, influencing their decision making process and as a result their purchase intent. Many marketers are focused on how they can get a return on their investment from utilizing social media in their marketing campaigns, which has led to a focus on social commerce. The problem is that there are so many social media platforms, it is hard to recognize which one will be the most cost effective and beneficial, again contributing to the confusion of how to best use social media for marketing purposes. One of the key areas practitioners need to concentrate on is monitoring these social media platforms to find out how their consumers are using the platforms and what types of information they are more receptive to, engaging on a more personal level, which should echo throughout the entire organization. However, the key metrics that marketers need to effectively analyze this environment are lacking, and much of the research on social media within the marketing discipline lacks a cross-platform design, leaving a gap within the literature that is in dire need of being filled. It is clear that many marketers want to utilize the variety of social media platforms that are available to them, yet do not know how to balance their use or even integrate one platform into their marketing plans, let alone more.

The relationship focus that has developed in the marketing discipline means that communal orientations are now at the forefront of many strategies. Online brand communities, which can culminate around a particular interest, brand, or even platform on social media share the three markers of traditional communities. These communities help to develop increased engagement and interaction, which is enabled by the interactive social environment that allows consumers to communicate among each other. However, consumers are becoming more individualized in their usage of these communities, with many flitting between them and utilizing this information for their own individual gain. Commonly motivated by self-expression and identity creation, these communities allow like-minded individuals the opportunity to express their brand preferences. They provide marketers the opportunity to gain an insightful look into consumers and their behavior, with many studies addressing online brand communities as a key function of social media for marketing purposes. However, this is merely one culmination of consumers within the social media environment, leaving individual behavior under researched.

The development of social media comes alongside the surge in postmodernism, seeing the individual consumer reignited, aided by this new environment. The recognition of the growing heterogeneous nature of consumers that utilize online brand communities and the variety of social media platforms strategically for their own gain, highlights the need to focus on individual behaviors rather than a concentration on groups and culminations of consumers. The understanding of individuals' utilization of these platforms is key to understanding how best to use them for marketing purposes, with the two self-construal dimensions being just one way of doing this. Highlighting two distinct aspects of the self, these two dimensions reflect the dual need of consumers to have both communal and individual experiences. Identifying very different behavior and motivations, the independent and interdependent self-construal provides a distinct way to approach the individual differences of consumers from a marketing perspective.

Although this book provided a comprehensive overview of social media from a marketing perspective it is not without its limitations. Firstly, social media is looked at solely from a marketing perspective and therefore several elements of literature have not been considered within this review. Secondly, the purpose of this book was to provide an overview of the topic, thus further publications could look at specific areas of social media for marketing purposes to address the area in more detail. There is a visible lack of theoretical work around social media that can be used for academic development and research around the topic. This book aimed to fill this gap by providing a theoretical viewpoint on social media from a marketing perspective that can be used by academics who are interested in both marketing and/or social media.

INDEX